POSTHISTORIC MAN

Posthistoric
MAN

An Inquiry

RODERICK SEIDENBERG

BEACON PRESS   *Beacon Hill*   Boston

To
C. H. S.

CONTENTS

POSTHISTORIC MAN

I

THE AXIOM OF ORGANIZATION

The collectivizing trend of society under machine production, whether that society calls itself democratic, Fascist, or socialist, is irrevocable.
—WALDO FRANK in *Chart for Rough Water*

I

MODERN MAN HAS learned to accommodate himself to a world increasingly organized. The trend toward ever more explicit and consciously drawn relationships is profound and sweeping; it is marked by depth no less than by extension. Affecting virtually every aspect and condition of man's affairs, it is everywhere apparent: in our systems of production, distribution, and consumption; in the operations of labor, capital, and finance; in the spheres of communication and transportation; in art, in sport, in education; in the fields of commerce, industry, and agriculture—in the recent totalitarian functioning of Nazi Germany despite its atavistic logic of "blood and soil," no less than in mechanized America or socialized Russia. Reaching down everywhere into the domain of the individual, it is apparent in an ever closer mesh of socialized patterns and institutionalized procedures. It is their function to bind, coordinate, define, and control his duties and activities, his purposes and behavior, in relation to those of his fellow men. Scientific research—once the happy hunting ground of the individual savant—is increasingly subject to co-ordinated control and organized purposes. Medical practice, with its traditional figure of the family physician, is rapidly becoming socialized; and even unemployment is embraced within organizational patterns. Significantly, the century opened with the organization in 1908 of the Boy Scout movement—the first international organization of children in history. And the century which has already witnessed the birth and demise of the League of Nations, and its resurrection in the United Nations organization, may well end in a vast and highly integrated system of similar organizations, world-wide in scope and all-inclusive in character.

The range and diversity of organization in the modern world defy recounting: the incidence of organization is universal, and its acceptance unquestioned. Nor has the trend toward further organization by any means exhausted itself. At every turn we meet with the demand for more extensive and closer organization; and no criticism is quite so shrill or insistent in modern ears as the cry that we are not sufficiently, or properly, or adequately organized. The occasional and incidental rumblings against "red tape," or the evils of bureaucracy, or the dangers of centralization, imply at bottom nothing more devastating than that the system either is not functioning efficiently or should be in other hands. It is true, decentralization, particularly of governmental functions, has often been urged, especially before the last war. But here, too, we are confronted with a criticism of the efficiency of certain organizational patterns rather than with that of the basic conception of organization itself. Likewise, the insistence upon minority rights, or the revolt against colonial usurpation,* or the demands of smaller nations in the concert of international affairs, are protestations against domination, not organization; and such movements generally seek to establish their position and their role in the functioning of some actual or incipient larger whole. Similarly, in another field, namely in that of antitrust legislation, the trend of events largely nullified the very effort to save the smaller units from absorption in the larger. "But while the antitrust

* Significantly, a world-wide organization of colonial peoples has recently been proposed.

laws prevented the cartelization of American industry," writes Peter F. Drucker, "they undoubtedly furthered the growth of the mammoth corporations in which management is as independent of stockholder control as is the executive of a cartel. . . . The antitrust laws which were enacted in order to protect the small fellow thus led in many cases to his actual extinction, since they made impossible noncompetitive survival as a member of a cartel." *

The trend toward increased organization is characterized by an internal movement of cohesion and adjustment as well as by an outward and more obvious movement of expansion. Combined, these movements adumbrate the status of the individual and the sovereignty of nations. They challenge the drift toward anarchic individuation, and by a kind of gravitational force strengthened in proportion to the area of its field, they deflect all isolate movements into a common course. Implicitly, they threaten the creative spirit of man. Thus, in the contemporary scene, for example, we find Virgil Thomson in his book *The State of Music* rising to the defense of the composer against the constrictions and limitations of the prevailing system of things. But his solution, it is interesting to note, consists of an *organization* of composers! The closing of the circuit is symptomatic: localized revolt ending, inevitably, in further organization. The basic challenge remains. For organization is inherent in the functioning of the system, its necessity compounded as the system itself expands, and this fact must profoundly affect, in one way or another, the artist's orientation. How far and in what manner the drift toward increased organization in every aspect of man's affairs will impinge upon the sphere of his cultural values is a grave and challenging problem. For the moment, however, it may be observed that, despite the far-reaching significance of the problem, protestations against the spread of organization are more often the wrenchings of internal adjustment than cries of opposition. The true opponents of organization as such are the individualistic anarchists, whose number is inconsequential, and whose influence is nil.

* Peter F. Drucker, *The Future of Industrial Man* (New York: The John Day Company, Inc., 1942).

Within the modern community the principle of organization constitutes an inherent and inevitable mode of operation. It is recognized as the necessary and axiomatic form of social procedure. This bland and unquestioning acceptance is a measure of its momentum—the promise of a mounting trend toward further organization. The force of that momentum is apparent in an insistent pressure toward ever wider and more inclusive social patterns and institutions, on the one hand, and for closer cohesion and greater penetration on the other. It is not a mere coincidence that our age has witnessed the ever more minute specialization of the individual, and, at the same time, a compelling impetus toward internationalism in the affairs of the world. Both phenomena issue from the same principle. The most challenging aspect of organization lies precisely in its universal applicability. If it embraces the farthest reaches and most diverse activities of life, that is but another way of saying that it operates beneath the plane of opposition: it unites, like a great geologic substratum, the endless range and diversity of the social scene under one compelling principle. It is the dominant *modus operandi* of contemporary civilization; an inherent and inescapable process spreading out into ever wider areas and reaching down into ever deeper recesses of contemporary life.

The meaning of the drift toward increased organization escapes us under the spell and sweep of its intrinsic practicality. Yet, as the compelling form in which our social operations increasingly take place, it must have for us a highly significant and basic meaning. What is that meaning? What bearing does the principle of organization have on the direction of life? What are the rules and laws of its functioning, the nature of its development, the logic of its implications? What, in particular, is the significance of its overwhelming acceleration in modern life? These questions challenge the self-evident and axiomatic character of organization; they drive toward its basic implications, and probe into its unquestioned and universal acceptance. And finally, what of the future? Toward what destination are we drifting in the course of this encompassing trend; what is the implicit goal of this deliberate procedure? Or are we in fact compelled, irredeemably, to accept the dictates of the principle of organization as the necessary and inherent framework of our social activities?

Such questions are certain to lead us into more or less abstract regions. The simplest phenomena are governed by laws or principles that are themselves often abstruse and enigmatic, their essential meaning obscured by their very generality. Behind the concrete necessity that justifies, in each instance, the acceptance of organized procedures, we may perceive the influence of broad historic movements, and beyond these, in turn, the operation of some all-inclusive morphological principle, implicit in the functioning of the social body. For the concept of organization reduces itself upon examination to ever more abstract terms, and its social significance, from this wider point of view, reveals itself as a principle based upon the inherent and obligatory nature of form and order in human affairs. In terms of such basic structural categories, the meaning of organization assumes indeed a universal bearing. Its implications carry us far afield into questions of cosmological order, and involve us, according to one school of thought, in the conception of a single, inclusive hierarchy of organizational planes uniting in one vast scheme of things the organic and inorganic realms. This more critical and abstract approach is reflected even in so remote a field as that of psychology, where the concepts of organization, pattern, and configuration have been studied in terms of form under the doctrines of the *Gestalt* philosophy introduced by Köhler, Koffka, and Wertheimer. Thus too, in the domain of biology, we may note the development of a new and fertile conception, advanced by such men as Needham, Woodger, and Bertalanffy, that the principle of organization, far from being a self-evident and a priori basis of all living matter, is itself one of the basic and central problems of life. The richest ore, it would seem, is to be found in the slag heap of the self-evident.

We are thus confronted with the question of how and in what sense the wider meaning of organization bears upon its more restricted social significance. Within the sphere of human relationships the principle of organization is concerned with the primary question of the status of the individual in relation to the functioning of the social whole; with centripetal trends in tension with centrifugal forces; with chaos and order; and, finally, with other, historically anterior modes of social cohesion. Plainly, our understanding of these aspects will come to depend upon our sense of the wider import of organization: only thus can we hope to establish the meaning of its historic development, or the cause of its present phenomenal expansion, or the probable trajectory of its momentum into the future. Such an approach will serve as a challenge to our bland and unquestioning acceptance of organized procedures in every aspect of contemporary life. And, because of its more generic and abstract character, such an approach will enable us to penetrate beneath the incidental conflicts, tensions, and disputes that necessarily veil the meaning of this unifying drift, which is everywhere advancing upon us silently and unacknowledged, like a vast historic transformation.

II

Organization is concerned with form and structure. Viewed as a purposive agency, it is a mode of procedure dealing with the systematic disposition of the parts in the functioning of the whole. It is concerned always with the arrangement of the parts as *means* toward the functioning of the whole as an *end*. These are dry and obvious truisms. But it is only necessary to probe beneath their manifest meaning to come upon certain inherent if less obvious implications. Thus organization, in the sphere of its social applications, is seen to consist of consciously contrived relationships; at every point the effective, coherent arrangements of the parts is dictated by the essential logic of intelligence in the service of a desired end. In its purposive aspects, organization is the child of intelligence. Conceived as a process, organization might be defined as the agency of attaining effective relationships; of marshaling means toward focused ends; of converting chaos into order. Clearly, the nature of our consciousness gives force to this mandate: the will to organize is an inherent and inescapable necessity imposed upon us by the need to operate within the locus of specific means toward the achievement of concrete ends. However daring our conceptual world in its infinite reaches, our mundane operations are limited to finite processes and concrete realities. Organization thus translates, under the influence of intelligence, the implicit possibilities of life into those explicit patterns of living that distinguish our conscious social processes and social relationships. It is the necessary form of conscious construction, of the deliberate marshaling of finite, explicit, and limited means, in the attainment of equally explicit and concrete ends.

Moreover, we can at once perceive certain inherent characteristics of the processes of organization. The functioning of the whole will inevitably demand ever closer integration and nicer adjustment in the disposition of the parts. Under the compulsion to seek the shortest distance between two points, as it were, organization is characterized by a sense of direction and is intolerant of detours. Transposed into the language of art, these concepts give rise to such basic aesthetic elements of abstract form as harmony, balance, and composition—whether set in static relations or poised in dynamic tensions. But in the moving sphere of social relationships, the more precise adjustment of the parts, implicit in the smoother, more efficient, ever more effective operation of the whole, demands at every turn the insistent reduction and elimination of friction. Hence, variation, spontaneity, divergence, must be eradicated in the set and appropriate subordination of the parts to the whole and to each other. Under the impact of these demands, organization tends implicitly toward standardization, and the calculable efficiency of fixed arrangements and predictable ends. The first of these conditions insures the elimination of detours; the second, the elimination of friction. These are internal characteristics. Externally, in respect to the medium in which it operates, organization may be said to create a field of influence which it seeks, in one way or another, to dominate or assimilate. Purposive in origin, its rigidly related parts add up to a dynamic whole; and organization may thus be interpreted as a basically extroverted mechanism whose meaning and justification range necessarily beyond its established domain. Its order, its systematized hierarchy of parts, its frictionless operation, are contingent upon an ever closer co-ordination and alignment between itself and its field of influences. Inevitably, *organization demands further organization*. For its order, its systematization, its frictionless functioning, constitute a kind of morphological determinism, imposing further order, system, and homogeneous action beyond its original confines. Organization absorbs chaos, inherently and progressively, as the day absorbs the night. Thus, organization tends as a matter of course to spread in converging patterns of ever greater extent; and perfected organization is conceivable only in terms of universal organization. By virtue of its internal mechanism and its external diffusion, organization tends necessarily toward an ever more penetrating and ultimately all-inclusive co-ordination; and from this converging trend stems its characteristic and profound tendency toward unification and centralization.

Speaking more freely, organization is a mesh, an ever expanding trellis, along which civilization expands and develops. The patterns of this network are complex and varied. They constitute an ever more comprehensive and explicit series of channels, so to speak, through which man's aims, efforts, and impulses are increasingly integrated. They are the forms and the framework through which the means of life operate, sharpened and clarified everywhere in our modern milieu through the agency of science and technology. And though these multiform patterns and channels are constantly changing, under an internal necessity of the system, they are never abandoned. To renounce the framework of organization is to expose ourselves to the winds of chaos. Even in periods when the force of social change reaches the intensity of war or of revolution, the implicit acceptance of organization remains unchallenged: the structural basis of social procedure is merely reaffirmed in terms of new forms and revised patterns. Organization is inescapable: it is the recurrent matrix within which social change takes place; and neither the tempo of events nor their direction affects this basic compulsion toward ordered relationships and consciously established arrangements. Thus, even the present series of world wars reveal themselves not only as vast organized enterprises but as movements largely motivated by even vaster organizational compulsions. Nor do major revolutions differ essentially in this respect from wars: they, too, engender more rather than less compact organizational patterns. Perhaps this principle has nowhere been more clearly illustrated in recent times than in the Russian revolution, followed by the Soviet regime, which has carried the implications of organization further than they had ever been carried before. Similarly, Nazi Germany, under cover of its myths, lost no opportunity in welding a singularly tightly woven mesh of organizational relationships of national, indeed totalitarian, scope. And, characteristically, these organizational patterns pointed, implicitly, beyond their national borders to world horizons. Nor has the aftermath of the recent war, with its chaotic, world-wide dislocations and disruptions, lessened in any degree the universal trend toward increased organization; and the apt slogan "One World or None," arising out of the terrifying reality of the atomic bomb, applies with equal force to every aspect of modern civilization.

The principles so startlingly apparent in totalitarian regimes are no less evident in the more democratically constituted countries. The balance of power between States' rights and the federal government in our own country, for example, is definitely shifting toward centralized control, while at the same time the province of government is constantly being extended everywhere beyond its original jurisdiction. Meanwhile the economic scene presents an even more striking illustration of the operation of organizational principles than the political picture. These two aspects of society, separate and distinct, relatively speaking, at the beginning of our course, show signs of merging under the pressure of events in a new and as yet uncharted synthesis. The rise, on the one hand, of modern corporations, mergers, cartels, and trusts, and, on the other, of labor unions, consumer co-operatives, and government finance institutions issuing subsidies, constitutes the preliminary stage in the organization of potentially greater and more inclusive units that will emerge inevitably as these others coalesce, absorb, and displace one another under their inherently expansive policies. In their exhaustive treatise on *The Modern Corporation and Private Property*, Berle and Means have ventured to make the following prophecy: "The rise of the modern corporation has brought a concentration of economic power which can compete on equal terms with the modern state—economic power versus political power.... The state seeks in some aspects to regulate the corporation, while the corporation, steadily becoming more powerful, makes every effort to avoid such regulation. Where its own interests are concerned, it even attempts to dominate the state. The future may see the economic organism, now typified by the corporation, not only on an equal plane with the state, but possibly superseding it as the dominant form of social organization." *

A similar trend is implied, however indirectly, by even so conservative a commentator as I. Maurice Wormser, in his book *Frankenstein, Incorporated*. "The franchise from the people which grants corporations their invaluable privileges and immunities," he writes, "involves the assumption of corollary duties and obligations.... They rest under a social obligation deeply implied both in fact and in law.... If they fail to heed and pay it, the community which created them will be justified in so regulating and controlling all their future acts and conduct that these shall not run contrary to the ends of sound public policy and social utility." † This cautious admonition, uttered nearly two decades ago, cannot in the nature of the case be heeded; and the larger corporations—if they will not eventually absorb the state—will certainly be absorbed by the state in some ultimate metamorphosis leading to a higher and more inclusive integration of both. The principle has long been apparent in our own economic and legislative trends, while in England it has engendered a policy of state control of public utilities that is but an entering wedge in the socialization of society.

As generalities these principles were already implicit in the

* A. A. Berle, Jr., and Gardiner C. Means, *The Modern Corporation and Private Property* (New York: The Macmillan Company, 1933), p. 357.

† I. Maurice Wormser, *Frankenstein, Incorporated* (New York: Whittlesey House, 1931), pp. 241, 242.

social and economic thinking of the nineteenth century; in the twentieth they are being realized. The prevalent discussions concerning the need of planning indicate a sharp change of direction in our approach to social problems: they preface the drift toward deliberate and co-ordinated enterprise in place of random enterprise; toward precise and scientific prediction in place of haphazard guessing; toward a balanced and functioning economy in place of the top-heavy, accidental, and bewildered economy still operative under the momentum of a laissez-faire attitude. This drift, plainly, is calculated to bring about political and economic patterns designed on "principles of sound engineering and the balanced load," in the phrase of Stuart Chase. The engineering approach to social problems is symptomatic: it is an expression of the principle of organization in that it implies the ever more effective co-ordination and adjustment of specific means in the attainment of concrete and defined ends. Such an approach has given rise to some specifically technological, if wholly provisional, solutions of our social problems; notably in the doctrines of technocracy, and more recently in such a prognosis of forthcoming events as James Burnham's *Managerial Revolution*. Doubtless these tentative excursions are limited and inadequate, but they reflect the direction of our basic tendencies and afford us, however distorted, a profile view of things to come. They are significant if only because they emphasize the unmistakable trend toward increased organization in the future condition of man. In this respect indeed they merely echo the axiomatic acceptance of organization implicit in all socialist and communist doctrines, and evident—less clearly, perhaps, but no less potently—in the desperate reactions to them. We may be certain that the future world, whatever its character, will have passed through the sieve of organization.

If we are unaware in any critical sense of the meaning of this condition, we are not unaware of its imminence; our literature of prophecy and prediction concerning the future state of man reveals a growing sense of this implicit development and an intuitive grasp of its encompassing sweep. The recognition of organization as a dominant principle in the further advance of civilization is already apparent in that prophetic classic *Looking Backward—2000-1887*, by Edward Bellamy. The sanguine mood of this book, inspired by an optimistic faith in progress common to the nineteenth century, was superseded in the twentieth by an increasingly critical and even satirical attitude; and, while the ever expanding role of organization was more sharply perceived, its consequences were pictured as a vast and threatening evil rather than the incidental and passing effects of a beneficent rationalism. The sinister nature of regimentation and automatism constitutes the theme of such a work as Karel Capek's *R. U. R.* (Rossum's Universal Robots), and a like moral, based upon a satiric projection of Soviet experience, is voiced in Eugene Zamiatin's novel *We,* in which the characters are no longer indentified by names but merely by impersonal numbers, and in which we read derisively of a time "... when human beings still lived in a state of freedom, that is, in an unorganized primitive state. One thing has always seemed to me the most improbable: how could a government, even a primitive government, permit people to live without anything like our Tables,—without compulsory walks, without precise regulations of the time to eat, for instance?" *—or again, in an even more heightened and conscious sense, in Aldous Huxley's *Brave New World,* or, more recently, in the rather strained pages of such a novel as *That Hideous Strength* by C. S. Lewis, in which the dire evils of unflinching rationalism are satirized in the machinations of the "National Institute of Coordinated Experiments." Far more significant in its direct approach to the meaning of this challenge is that rising body of literature concerned with the fateful struggles of the individual in the toils of an impersonal, arbitrary, and, above all, increasingly organized world of deliberately established norms of conduct—of the individual in a collectivized world.† Thus, not

---

* Eugene Zamiatin, *We* (New York: E. P. Dutton and Company, Inc., 1924), p. 15.

† Cf. *Nineteen Eighty-Four* by George Orwell (New York: Harcourt, Brace and Company, 1949), in which this theme is explored with ruthless consistency. Here there is no romantic escape at the end; the climax of the novel consists, indeed, in the smooth, unruffled functioning of an all-powerful organization whose primary objective is summed up in these dire and significant words: "But the purpose of all of them was to arrest progress and freeze history at a

alone in the critical writings of the social philosophers but in the literature of the novel, in essays and sermons, has the impact of organization been accepted—in its specific aspects if not in its generality—as a theme of challenging and profound implications. The defense of individualism—whether it is urged in opposition to the threat of communism, or as a political strategem designed to guard the depredations of the few against the many, or as a corollary of political freedom, or, finally, on the basis of the infinite worth of the person as an inviolate spiritual entity *—betokens always and everywhere a fateful sense of an all-encompassing transformation of life, of an emerging social determinism. And that determinism, coordinating at every point the life of the individual in terms of mass patterns, is not a nameless force; it is implicit in the obligatory drift toward organized procedures in every aspect of our civilization.

Under the momentum of this universal trend, the individual will indeed find himself churned into an ever smaller particle, into a minute and at length irreducible atom of the social system. As the significance of the individual is thus steadily diminished, his status and identity must necessarily approach that of a statistical average, while at the same time the mass will become correspondingly enlarged and dominating in its new and terrifying totality. Under pressure of this transformation we will have crossed the threshold of a collectivist age. The meaning of this transformation, however, is not to be encompassed by the contemporary use of the term "totalitarianism" —it is at once more basic, more sweeping, more deeply rooted in the profound momentum of man's historic development. It is a universal phenomenon, moving under the impetus of its overwhelming surge toward a far vaster and all-inclusive configuration of world affairs. For the collectivization of man, though it will necessarily affect his political, social, economic,

---

chosen moment" (p. 204). The same ominous thought is expressed in a further passage (p. 216): "...The Party has been able—and may, for all we know, continue to be able for thousands of years—to arrest the course of history."

* Cf. W. T. Stace, *The Destiny of Western Man* (New York: Reynal and Hitchcock, 1942); Erich Fromm, *Escape from Freedom* (New York: Farrar and Rinehart, 1941).

and cultural development in all their diverse aspects, presaged indeed by the totalitarian systems of today, is not to be understood apart from a consideration of that *morphological determinism,* that organizational compulsion, under which it is even now taking shape. Organization is the key to our understanding of the future.

III

Modern thought perceives in collectivism something more than an imminent historical stage. Viewed from a strictly morphological point of view, collectivism, which has long been anticipated, is implicit in the historic development of man more in the nature of a summation than as another phase or interim in a continuous process. This bald statement clamors for vindication. To substantiate it involves us not only in a critical study of the historic process seen as a whole but in a more searching analysis of organization as the ultimate, inherent, and inescapable form of social procedure. For collectivism is nothing but the social application of organization. But in affirming this simple definition we are at once confronted with certain grave and basic questions concerning the relation between form and content in the checkered course of history; with the relative dominance of means and ends in the far-flung activities of man. For clearly, as the means of life have multiplied and proliferated in the long course of man's development, while his ends have remained comparatively fixed, like a polar star in the firmament of his myriad activities, he has been driven to seek an integrating principle or means for the functioning of other means in all their vast and overwhelming diversity. This necessity leads us to ask in what manner and to what extent form itself implicitly molds historic forces? Does the very structure of social procedure, by virtue of some intrinsic principle, coerce the course of events? In brief, are we justified in speaking of a morphological determinism in the affairs of man—of an inevitable manner of procedure, following its own course, its own laws and principles, which point, necessarily, to collectivism?

And if such a principle can be discerned in the long and

tortuous course of history, why, we may ask, should it seem to emerge clear and dominant today? The challenge of this question involves us in a multitude of further problems: the question of other modes of social integration and the historic function of organization; the distinction between the concepts of organism and organization—vital and profound in scope; the impact of the phenomenal increase in world population upon the forms of social control; the crucial role of the machine and of a machine technology; the advent of science and the inherent effects of the principle of cumulative knowledge; the relation of the individual and the mass under stress of organizational forces. And finally, granting the premise of such a sweeping and inescapable structural determinism, what bearing would this implicit course have in defining the future condition of man?

In approaching these problems it will be wiser to avoid rather than to welcome the well-plowed controversies, interpretations, and elaborated doctrines of socialism, communism, and fascism; the capitalist system and economic determinism; the inevitable dictatorship of the proletariat, or the managerial revolution of the industrialists. It will be better—not because these more or less crystallized concepts, bequeathed to us largely by the nineteenth century, are irrelevant, since in fact they point toward intenser co-ordination of the social fabric, but because a more abstract approach to these problems may reward us with fresh horizons and a deeper insight into the operations of the historic process. Soviet Russia gained much inspiration from capitalistic America, to the surprise of theorists who had failed to perceive the potency of organization as a determining factor in the development of technological procedures: the parallelism between them revealed a common and basic direction beneath their economic divergence. Similarly, collectivism may in the future develop in a much more universal sense than anything the totalitarian countries have thus far envisaged. Even the theoretical contributions of specific social and economic systems are apt to be rooted in concrete historic institutions, and to reflect more or less isolated economic, political, or social conditions. The accelerated drift toward increased and perhaps ultimately universal patterns of organization is likewise subject to historic eventualities; but, more profoundly, it molds these actualities and rises, as we have seen, out of an inherent and inescapable mode of procedure. The problem is to disentangle and observe precisely the naked and primary force beneath the tortuous course of the drift, like the impact of the force of gravity, molding the sharp windings of a river within a given terrain. Organization can only be comprehended in its widest meaning on the basis of its abstract significance—that is to say, its most universal interpretation, its deepest, most sweeping and comprehensive function.

If collectivism was spoken of as though it were virtually synonymous with organization it is only because collectivism, as we perceive it today, is an incipient stage in the inherent development of social organization conceived as a process. It may itself be transmuted in the future through the further operation of the process into ever more rigorous forms of world-wide scope and universal significance. But to understand the dynamics of this situation, it will prove more rewarding for the moment to look in the opposite direction, and to inquire how the principle of organization came to insinuate itself, unobtrusively and as it proved unavoidably, into the affairs of man. For plainly mankind did not enter upon the scene of history aware of this principle, though it pervaded his actions and his designs with increasing clarity, like some distantly approaching *deus ex machina,* from the very beginning. The idea of organization, like that of progress—with which, unfortunately, it is sometimes loosely confused—came to be accepted as a definite and conscious principle only in relatively modern times. It is true of course that the Romans, for example, displayed a high degree of order, system, and organization in their vast engineering works and architectural monuments, in their clearly articulated legal system, and in their far-flung imperial conquests. Likewise, other even earlier, closely woven civilizations, so to speak, such as that of ancient Egypt with its highly complex, rigidly hierarchical forms of life, must have manifested a definite, conscious sense of organization. But it is only in our own period, taken in a wide sense, that the principle of organization has come to permeate life intensively and extensively; and it is only today that we are beginning to suspect the inherently dynamic nature of this expanding phenomenon. How then, we may ask, did man fare in the remote past without its supporting guidance, innocent alike of its need and its meaning? By what mechanism did organization as a principle of operation come to establish itself ever more firmly in the fabric of life?

In thus seeking to trace the meaning of organization against the background of the historic process rather than within the framework of specific historic phenomena, however expansive, as for instance in the rise of the Roman Empire or in the institutional development of the Catholic Church, we are inferring that its principles are somehow rooted in the very depths of our behavior as rational beings—a kind of inexorable technique which we follow rather than invent. Yet primitive man, plainly, showed little sense of consciously planned organization; and it is clear that the principle has emerged in ever stronger and more explicit forms as mankind itself has advanced. Anthropologists, to be sure, would be quick to point out that man in his primitive estate was subject to a high degree of social integration; that virtually the whole of his life was envisaged within rigidly fixed patterns and established norms; and that, far more than the individual of today, he was bound by inexorable habits and customs. Social form, however, was achieved by a wholly different technique from our own consciously contrived and explicitly codified laws, agreements, and procedures. The difference between primitive society and our own in respect to their mutual modes of integration and cohesion is essentially the difference between a state of *organic wholeness or unity,* on the one hand, and a state of *organized totality or unification,* on the other. The one evolves by innate growth; the other by deliberate and conscious expansion. That is not to say, however, that the primitive group constituted an organism in the biologic meaning of the word; or that our institutions are free of traces of their origin and prototypes. The distinction is intended to emphasize the contrast between unconscious, long-accepted forms of social cohesion, and our own deliberate, analytical, and conscious modes of attaining social integration. A perceptible trend carries mankind from a primordial union with nature, a condition of instinctual harmony with the established and inherited patterns of living, toward an ever more premeditated program of action, an ever more deliberate recourse to purposive, rationally affirmed procedures. This drift encompasses the basic principle of man's development. And under pressure of this drift, he finds himself compelled to integrate anew, in each age, his changing mores. But the principle of guidance in this process of reorientation likewise changes, slowly but irrevocably, from an unquestioning acceptance and mystical identification with the powers and forces of life, to their conscious and masterful manipulation. These principles, moreover, apply equally to the development of Eastern as well as Western civilizations, even though, in a sense, they have followed divergent introvert and extrovert directions: both have affirmed the doctrines of consciousness in the solution of their problems.

The distinction here developed between the approaches of primitive man and of ourselves toward the problems of social cohesion and integration has far-reaching implications through which we may come to a more basic understanding of organization. For in this distinction we may perceive in man a fundamental cleavage in his mode of approach to the problems of life that conditions his entire development and lies, apparently, at the very root of his being. Indeed, this dichotomic approach may well account in the first instance for his dramatic divergence from the biologic series, resulting in his unique status in the scheme of nature. It is for this reason primarily that the social developments observable in the animal kingdom, particularly among the social insects—the ants, termites, and bees —do not afford a basis of comparison with those of man despite their often highly intricate structural forms and functional patterns. To quote from Julian S. Huxley, the analogy between insect and human societies, "...however obvious and however often applied, must be rejected out of hand. The two rest on different bases—those of ants, bees and termites on the fixity of the instincts, those of man on the plasticity of intelligence." * According to Huxley the insects have been shut off from further progress by the nature of their breathing mechanism, which has restricted their size to the point of not allowing for the necessary brain mechanisms required by intelligence.† It is not surprising that ants have thus been found imprisoned in Baltic amber, essentially identical—indeed, "practically indistinguishable from those now living in Northern Europe and North America"—dating back some fifty or sixty million years. ‡ In contrast the plasticity and flexibility of man, thanks to his intelligence and an adequate brain mechanism, resulted in rapid and profound changes. But here it is well to bear in mind that man is the unique inheritor of a kind of compound progression. For not only was the development of his brain mechanism relatively rapid in an evolutionary sense, according to Huxley; § his social development bypassed, as it were, the slower biological principles of hereditary changes, advancing on the basis of the material and cultural transmission of his cumulative knowledge and achievements.

The progressive development of man was thus doubly assured. But in this very fact we may discover a principle of disharmony in his development, a natural cleavage in his procedures that must inevitably hobble his efforts as he advances from one unstable equilibrium to the next. Speaking of the plasticity and potential variety of which man is capable, Huxley says: "This increase of flexibility has also had other psychological consequences which rational philosophers are apt to forget: and in some of these too, man is unique. It has led, for instance, to the fact that man is the only organism normally and inevitably subject to psychological conflict." ‖ And further on he adds this revealing reflection: "In close correlation with our subjection to conflict is our proneness to laughter. So characteristic of our species is laughter that man has been defined as the laughing animal. ... But biologically the important fea-

* Julian S. Huxley, *Man Stands Alone* (New York: Harper and Brothers, 1941), p. 235.
† *Ibid.*, p. 11.
‡ William Morton Wheeler, *Social Life Among the Insects* (New York: Harcourt Brace and Company, 1923), pp. 6, 7.
§ Julian Huxley, *Man Stands Alone*, p. 21.
‖ *Ibid.*, p. 22.

ture of human laughter seems to lie in its providing a release for conflict, a resolution of troublesome situations.... True laughter, like true speech, is a unique possession of man." *

To return once more to the condition of primitive man, it is plain in the light of our more advanced status that his modes of procedure, seemingly fixed and static, were in reality in a state of flux. Viewed in terms of the whole development of man, they represent in fact a transitional phase between the purely instinctual urges of his remotest progenitors and those ultrarational procedures toward which his descendants appear to be moving. These vistas are so immense, however, that the distinction between primitive man and ourselves is seen to be merely a matter of degree within comparatively narrow limits. For actually, in a schematic sense, these limits might be said to define and encompass the story of human history—a transitional period of uncertain duration in the course of which man's intelligence has at length come to challenge the dominance of his instincts. Thus defined, history is seen as a specific process of continuous conflict and dynamic change arising out of the ever varying relation between instinct and intelligence in the structure of our world. If primitive man differs from ourselves it is in the ratio of these shifting forces. Under the impact of their changing relationship the panorama of history unfolds itself; and under stress of their influences our more primitive, organic forms of social cohesion became transformed, slowly but inexorably, into the consciously directed patterns and institutions of our prevailing social systems. In place of organic cohesion, which arose out of and gave expression to the binding force of the instincts, organization emerges as a necessary surrogate: it is the scaffolding which intelligence erects to sustain the social structure.

IV

Man did not begin his development with a history; in time he acquired a history. Thus, we speak of a prehistoric age in the sense not only of a time before man had a written record

* *Ibid.*, p. 27.

of his achievements but of a still more remote time when he had virtually no achievements to record. It is difficult to encompass the profound depths of this transition. For us, at the moment, the significant point in this vast change is the fact that man, rising out of the fathomless dark of instinctual behavior, entered upon a new and conscious mode of approach to the problems of life. His divergence from the biologic hierarchy took aeons of time, but it was marked from the beginning by a numb intelligence that carried him from one change to another in his deeply ingrained ways and habits. That man stumbled upon a new mode or principle of operation, rather than upon a fortuitous series of purposeful events, is amply clear if only because each advance, instead of assuring him prolonged periods of stability and contentment, actually precipitated him, with ever increasing momentum, into further change. Gradual as the process must have been in its inception, it followed an accelerating tempo. When at length man became aware of change as such, he had stepped upon the stage of history; he became a historic being. He entered the world of choice, of conscious decision, or—perhaps it would be better to say—he enjoyed a consciousness of direction; and therewith the unity of his instinctual responses was forever destroyed. Henceforth he was to pursue his course under a twofold compulsion: that of instinct and that of intelligence. But a strange fatality now descended upon him: the two forces proved unequal, and he thus found himself diverging ever farther from his instinctual harmony along a precarious path of unstable syntheses. And that path is history.

If history is indeed the conscious and possibly culminating phase of this disparity, it may be viewed as a vast and complex movement of transition in the total perspective of man's development. And as the process or conflict of history had its origin in the remote depths of the past, so its ultimate resolution may conceivably be protracted into an equally distant future. In any event, the character of the process as we have come to know it in the light of our limited insight and experience appears self-contained: the arc of its trajectory, far from pointing to some boundless transfiguration in the destiny of

man, gives evidence, on the contrary, of a set span and a defin-
able course. Only in the high moment of this transition, projected through the supreme consciousness of mystic and seer,
has it been given to mankind to glimpse a vision of transfinite
being. But thanks to the sweep and surge of overwhelming historic forces, this vision, it is clear, is destined to be dimmed and
perhaps forever extinguished. For the vision is not yet reality;
and man is free only in the sense of perceiving his bondage
under the impact of forces beyond his control. In their farthest
reaches man's aspirations are but tangential projections of his
ardent insight; and as his fate traces the curve of its appointed
path, the dream of an otherworldly destiny will fade and disappear—a Fata Morgana of his will to unattainable perfection.
In its place we will see, ever more clearly, the established direction and set course implicit in the drift of history.

Thus chastened, we may return once more to the question:
what is the meaning, the direction, the extent of that vast
transition in the development of man we have defined as history? If the question seems presumptuous, the answer here
entertained is confined to factors inherent in the trends out of
which it arose, and in the course of which the flowering of our
diverse civilizations took place. Basically, as we have seen, the
process of transition had its genesis in the conflict between instinct and intelligence: the one dominant by virtue of its evolutionary priority; the other challenging that sovereignty by virtue of its inherently cumulative power. In a sense the process
is one of more or less continuous exfoliation—of older forms,
habits, customs, concepts falling by the wayside as they are
replaced, under pressure of intelligence, by new constellations
of thought, insight, and experience. Earlier, naive patterns of
behavior carry with them something of the binding character
of instinct; they serve to integrate primitive society by the
force of their enregistered validity. These undefined, instinctually fixed responses represent a pristine, unconscious acceptance of life that is slowly but irrevocably transmuted by an
ever more deliberate and conscious awareness. Innate behavior
is gradually transformed into explicit and consciously formulated relationships, laws, and institutions. The deeply im-

planted mores of primitive man thus suffer a progressive externalization in the course of which the erstwhile organic unity of society is gradually dissolved and at length supplanted by a deliberate principle of unification—in brief, by the conscious integration of organized procedures. Thus always there is a drift from *unconscious participation* in the accepted rituals and dogmas of primitive life toward an ever more *conscious conversion* of their form and substance into the rationalized and purposive institutions of civilized society.

The compelling trend of this transition is already present in the nature of language—one of the earliest, as it is probably one of the most potent, forces of social integration. For language is essentially a social medium, converting innate feelings and instinctual responses into explicit symbols and tangible expressions. Through language the individual is united with his fellow-men in the common enterprise of living; and through the gift of communication the thought processes of man are enriched by an instrument of incalculable range. Language thus furthers that process of conversion from instinctually given, primitive responses to those increasingly mature analyses upon which intelligence builds its subsequent constructions of civilized procedures. As this process of conversion approaches its goal, a certain parallelism between conscious and unconscious modes of behavior emerges: the predominantly communal structure of primitive society, for instance, has its counterpart in the transposed logic of contemporary collectivism. The instinctual solution has been replaced by a rational solution. But whereas the earlier approach presents itself as a harmonious whole in which the means and ends of life are fused in the functions of living, consciousness splits this happy amalgam asunder, rendering the formulated counterpart into a means for the realization, not infrequently, of itself as an end. Thus, religion gave rise to an array of symbols culminating in the church, but it is the church which now hopes by means of these very symbols to give rise to religion. Consciousness breaks down the whole into its component parts, only to re-establish them once more in transmuted form. In the course of this change a new mode of operation in the social life of man is born. For the means of life, no longer merged and embraced within the organic harmony of primitive existence, require a procedural framework of their own, a wholly new mode or principle of structural integration. That principle, fashioned by intelligence, is organization. It is the vehicle for the conscious functioning of the means of life.

Consciousness tends to polarize life, as it were, into a series of explicit means, demanding, as we have seen, their own intrinsic system of order and coherence in the service of implicit and ultimate ends. In the degree in which man establishes this sequence of means and ends, he diverges ever further afield from his primordial estate. But this excursion into ever wider experiences of life was implicit in the nature of intelligence, which not only endowed man with a twofold approach to the problems of survival and adjustment but led him, in time, to dominate his environment in a drastic and purposive manner. If instinct served as the vehicle of adjustment previously, intelligence, responsible for this deviation, now increasingly shouldered the task. But the endless complexity of nature afforded no ready solution to the problem of adjustment; under the impact of intelligence it engendered an ever expanding series of means. The fixity of the instincts, in their essentially ingrained character, thus serves to enhance by contrast the purposive mobility of intelligence. In consequence man finds his life characterized by a growing complexity; the tempo of change increases; and the means of life multiply in an expanding series, until man is confronted by the dilemma of his own protean inventiveness. Thus the conflicting trends of instinct and intelligence are accentuated as their paths deviate, leaving man in the precarious position of courting disaster in the act of straddling divergent modes of survival. In the turmoil of adjusting himself to the demands of life in a sea of change of his own making, he looks forward, in the barely acknowledged desperation of his transitional position, to an ultimate solution in universal organization, or backward to a fancied "golden age" of erstwhile harmony—to the encompassing security of his instinctual origin.

The trend of events, however, is set, it would seem, irrevocably. Whether men choose to stand still or attempt to recover an earlier status, mankind is being ushered relentlessly through a series of unstable equilibria, through changing empires and mutable civilizations, toward an ever more stringently organized state. Man's instability is the sign not of his freedom but of his discordance under the impact of opposing forces. But these forces are not equally balanced; and it is this paramount fact that gives to history its sense of directed movement and unique significance. For there is a grain to the texture of events; a significant direction to the course of human development. The undeniable drift of historic forces toward a more crystallized status of man, within ever wider and more compelling forms of organized procedures, testifies to the inequality of the conflicting elements and presages the dominance of intelligence over instinct—of the later over the earlier technique of adjustment in the problems of human achievement and survival.

But that is not to say the progression will run its course in a line of undeviating precision; on the contrary, history has ever been a terrain of unimaginable contradictions and incredible contrasts. Even today life exhibits a range in status from that of prehistoric man to the sages and prophets of tomorrow. Nor need we search the seven seas for this diversity; it exists within the confines of our most advanced communities, certain of whose members may be planning for the future according to the dictates of science, while others are consulting their astrologers! Such disparities only confirm the thesis that the forms of life, at once implicit and inescapable, mold its course and control its direction. For the integrative power of these forms, emerging in organized patterns of social procedure, reduces such divergencies in the course of time to statistical averages, to a common denominator. Similarly, on a vaster plane, the intricate panorama of history may possess a unity of direction despite its diversity, as the stormiest sea may be wind-swept from one quarter. Leibnitz, creating, out of zero and one, a number system that embraced infinity, was led to observe: *Omnibus ex nihil ducendis sufficit unum* (One suffices to draw all out of nothing)—and history, for all its apparent chaos, may arise out of an infinite complexity, a vast and challenging profusion, rather than a meaningless confusion. Man may appear to move through history in all directions at once; yet history itself, though it mirrors the boundless range of human enterprise, reveals in its totality an underlying drift of all-encompassing scope. And that drift, issuing out of the dichotomic nature of man's development, is perceptible in ever sharper outline as a kind of morphological determinism embracing every aspect of the human scene.

Looking at the picture more closely we have reason to believe that this drift will run its course to a predestined goal, because of certain intrinsic factors in the dissonance between instinct and intelligence out of which it arose. While the operation of instinct is essentially static, changing only with the slow rhythm of biologic evolution, that of intelligence is mobile, depending upon the cumulative character of knowledge as a fulcrum for its expanding power. Hence the dominance of intelligence over instinct as a primary faculty of guidance does not come to depend upon a biologic principle so much as a social principle: it is implicit in the fact that social inheritance outstrips biologic inheritance since it is built upon successive accretions to human knowledge—upon a cumulative system whereby the individual is endowed, so to speak, with the benefits of humanity as a whole, and humanity with the contributions of its component individuals. Human knowledge is thus compounded on an increasingly rapid basis; and it is knowledge, acquired experience socially transmitted, that assures the ultimate dominance of intelligence over the deep-rooted and ingrained instincts. The process may be said to have burgeoned in the rise of science, that body of "organized knowledge," as it has been significantly termed, through which man not only succeeded beyond his fondest hopes in ordering and controlling his environment, but through which, in an even more profound sense, he has learned to adapt himself to the invariant laws of nature rather than to nature direct. In this change of orientation, man has necessarily abandoned, in a new and significant sense, the technique of instinct for that of intelligence. And just as the instincts guided the organism through the hazards of the environment under an earlier dispensation, so intelligence, utilizing hitherto unsuspected principles of control and prediction, now insures survival and achievement on a new and far more commanding plane.

In this transition the machine * plays a highly significant and dramatic role. Before indicating its nature, however, it may be well to emphasize once more, at the risk of reiteration, that intelligence, in the very measure in which it supplants the instincts, must weave a mesh of its own fashioning to bind and integrate the activities of man into a coherent whole. Thus, organization is embedded, inherently, in the functioning of intelligence. But the machine, defined in its most abstract terms, constitutes in itself a unique and perfect paradigm of organization: it consists of a series of interrelated means contrived to achieve an explicit end. The deepest significance of the machine, in its effect upon the social fabric of man, lies precisely in its own rigid organizational structure. Thus conceived, it is possible to assign a profound historic meaning to the machine —a role in the transitional phenomenon of man's development.

The effective functioning of organization, as we have seen, rests upon a principle of predictability that inherently demands the further organization of all contiguous regions of the system. Order demands order. And just as, in the realm of physics, there are in fact no "isolated systems," so too, in the domain of social relations, all systems, however arbitrarily defined, exist not in a social vacuum but in relation to adjacent systems. There is always an interaction between a set scheme of things and its environment, so to speak, that awaits translation into deliberate and consciously contrived relationships. This involves an extension of organization beyond its previous locus till a new unity is achieved—which demands, in its turn, still further expansion. Organization, dissolving chaos and incoherence in ever wider arcs of life, moves toward universality; and nowhere has this inherent drift been more compelling in its sweep and more peremptory in its demands than in the ex-

---

* In speaking of "the machine" the term is intended to convey more than its restricted nineteenth-century connotation. It is intended to cover the entire range of possible applications of natural laws to the manipulation of external phenomena, and includes such more recent ventures as the developments in the field of electronics and nuclear physics.

pansive claims of the machine and its technology. For the machine—conceived in its most generic terms—may be compared to a primary crystal of perfect organization: having been introduced into the social system at a crucial phase in its development, when the influences of intelligence are attaining ascendancy over those of instinct, the machine, like a crystal, has brought about a unique, sudden, and profound change of structure in the fabric of society—the crystallization of society in the patterns of a collectivized and ever more intensively organized world.

If the machine has already produced a vast transformation in the character of our civilization during the relatively short period of its incipient stages, we may well anticipate a far more profound transformation of life and values in the course of its continued impact upon our development. Nor need we picture this evolution in the spectacular terms of unimaginable discoveries to come and undreamed-of inventions to be perfected: startling as its wholly unexpected projections have been in the past, it is the basic nature of the machine as an organizational agency that will prove most potent in transmuting the structure of socialized life and therewith our values, our culture, and, indeed, the whole orientation of our civilization as well. Yet it is true that already, in the early decades of the present century, the so-called machine age gave way to the power age,* and, before the full repercussions of this change were realized, we had reached the threshold of an even more enigmatic electronic age, to be followed, almost simultaneously, by the atomic age! In speaking of the machine it is clear that we must endow the term with its fullest possible implications —with a pregnant sense of the widest technological explorations of nature. In accepting this inclusive approach we can readily grant the momentous significance of the change that is upon us, and the even more momentous transformations in our social structure that the expanding impact of the machine must inevitably produce. The theory that the manifold powers of the machine, perfected and enhanced far beyond our present achievements, will eventually free man and provide him

* Cf. Walter N. Polakov, *The Power Age* (New York: Covici-Friede, 1933).

with the leisure necessary for a wider enjoyment of his creative faculties may in time prove correct. But it is well, in this connection, to bear in mind the necessary price that a machine technology will exact: against the boon of a nicer balance between labor and leisure we must weigh the subtle question of the meaning and quality of both under an ever more intensified technological dispensation. And here it is clear that the machine will exact increasing loyalty to its own rhythm as the price of that very freedom. For the expanding complexities and increased co-ordination of a machine technology will inevitably exert a peremptory demand upon society; and both the leisure gained through the further development of the machine and the freedom to use it creatively will be decisively conditioned by a more general and more insistent mechanization of life.

The machine is accelerating the emergence of organization in every phase and turn of life; in its subtlest expressions no less than in its most patent aspects, in ever wider arcs and more penetrating depths. In considering the effect of the machine upon our values and standards, our habits and ideas, it is well to remember that as an agency of organization the machine is an index of the dominance of intelligence over instinct—as organization itself is a modulus of change from one mode of procedure to another in the development of mankind. This shift in our basic technique of procedure, accelerated and concretized by the machine, will in time be reflected, under pressure of its necessitous character, in a universal transmutation of values in every aspect of existence—in our ends and aims, our aspirations and conceptions, our faiths and beliefs. Society fashioned progressively under the strictures of organized procedures will be unlike society functioning as a purely organic entity; and, as man moves toward a more conscious dispensation, we are confronted not only with the question of his changed destiny, but with the inescapable price that such a divergence from his erstwhile estate must inevitably exact.

The structural reorientation of life implicit in the drift toward increased organization tends to approach a natural limit in universal organization. But this ultimate goal can only be interpreted as a static condition of "fixity and permanence"

—a state that may prove no less enduring perhaps than the long aeons of time which elapsed before history may properly be said to have begun. Thus conceived, as the province of man's changing status, history may be looked upon as a highly charged transitional phase in man's development; and its span, coincident with the ultimate and final organization of his activities, may conceivably taper off into an unchanging condition of perfected adjustment. Devoid of movement, such a condition of stability marks the end state of growth, where life is purchased at the price of further development. But such a state is not altogether incongruous with the basic if minimal intention of life as the longest possible detour to death—an interpretation that may conceivably apply to the whole course of organic evolution interpreted as a vast projection against the ultimate triumph of cold, inanimate matter. Man's consciousness, rebelling against the set arc of this fate, may well succeed only in hastening its approach—to vanish as it arose —in the decline of tension between conflicting forces. Thus far, at any rate, we have no reason to believe, however bleak the prospect, that man is exempt from a fate that appears universal; and though it may be his destiny, long after the heightened awareness we call consciousness has been dissipated, to extend the final chapter of his life into some immeasurable future, he will never circumvent its end. Yet for us, seeking to fathom the course of events, it is not the final denouement of the process, but its nature, that alone will afford guidance to a fuller comprehension of its meaning and a clearer understanding of its operation.

The impending collectivization of man, vouchsafed by the organizational trend we have been discussing, is sufficient evidence of a profound change of status in the condition of humanity. Before entering upon the nature of the consequences such a vast reorientation of life will entail—whether we choose to view it from the vantage point of values established in the past or attempt to assess it imaginatively from the heights of a remote future—it may be well to confirm its apparently necessitous character and to examine, however abstractly, the inevitability of its course. Nothing will be more essential in clarifying the direction of this drift than to satisfy the question of its obligatory course; but to establish this point it will be necessary to analyze more clearly the relation between instinct and intelligence in their bearing upon the development of mankind.

II

INSTINCT AND INTELLIGENCE

...The very essence of an instinct is that it is followed independently of reason.—CHARLES DARWIN

I

INSTINCT CAN BE traced back in the biologic series to elementary tropisms—those involuntary responses to stimuli that characterize life in its most rudimentary stages. The more complex the organism, the higher in general will be its instinctive processes and responses. This parallelism hides a truism: namely, that the functioning of the organism is in fact its instinctual behavior. Thus the perfection of the instincts is but another way of speaking of the high degree of adaptation of the organism. Moreover, the instincts, as Henri Bergson expressed it, are "...necessarily specialized, being nothing but the utilization of a specific instrument for a specific object." * Our difficulty in apprehending the nature of instinct arises from a transferred frame of reference: we judge instinct on the basis of intelligence. The instincts appear to us at once marvelous in their perfection and mysterious in their origin; but this is only to assert that instinct and intelligence are different modes of approach, and that the perfection and nescience

* Henri Bergson, *Creative Evolution* (New York: Henry Holt and Company, Inc., c. 1911; Arthur Mitchell, c. 1938), p. 140.

of the one seem unfathomable in terms of the conscious but often halting procedure of the other.

Biologically speaking, it is intelligence that is mysterious and challenging. The instincts, it is true, are baffling precisely as life itself is baffling in distinction to inorganic matter. But within the scope of the organic realm, intelligence arises as a surrogate of the instincts or, rather, as a supplementary principle that in time usurps the function of the instincts in the higher adjustment of the organism. Perhaps, indeed, we should not speak of "the instincts" as though they existed apart from the innate functioning of the organism, though we may legitimately speak of intelligence as a definite and precise instrument of action, a cerebral mechanism. Intelligence is a directing agency superimposed, as it were, upon instinctual behavior. It is a late arrival in the evolutionary hierarchy. Indeed, it is as though evolutionary development had found in this principle a certain freedom from the rigorous and static demands of instinctive adaptation, a method of meeting chance contingencies denied to blind instinct. Accentuated in man far beyond the tentative excursions manifested in the case of the higher primates, intelligence finally liberated us from the constrictions of enregistered behavior. Thus, intelligence may be said to have eclipsed instinctual behavior as a directive force; and, in establishing a wholly new technique of adaptation, it endowed man with a new relation to nature. Under the pervasive drift of intelligence man entered upon a different time-principle in his adaptations: in place of random mutations, blindly fortifying the organism against the hazards of the environment—a process often requiring aeons of time—man now proceeded boldly and analytically to the task of fortifying himself. He entered a world not only of conscious relationships and conceptual thought but, at the same time, of cumulative change.

The potential significance of this altered status has been forcibly expressed by Julian Huxley in his admirable essay entitled "The Uniqueness of Man." "The first and obviously unique characteristic of man," he writes, "is his capacity for conceptual thought; if you prefer objective terms, you will say his employment of true speech, but that is only another way of saying the same thing. This basic human property had many consequences. The most important was the development of a cumulative tradition.... But in no case [of animals] is the tradition cumulative.... In man, however, tradition is an independent and potentially permanent activity, capable of indefinite improvement in qualities and increase in quantity. It constitutes a new accessory process of heredity in evolution, running side by side with the biologic process, a heredity of experience to supplement the universal heredity of living substance." * In a passage further on he says: "Thus man is more intelligent than the animals because his brain mechanism is more plastic.... The essential fact ... is that the change has been profound and in an evolutionary sense rapid. Although it has been brought about by the gradual quantitative enlargement of the association areas of the brain, the result has been almost as abrupt as the change (also brought about quantitatively) from solid ice to liquid water. We should remember that the machinery of the change has been an increase in plasticity and potential variety: it is by a natural selection of ideas and actions that the result has been greater rationality instead of greater irrationality." † And in a final passage he sums up certain unique qualities of man as follows: "Those of man's unique characteristics which may better be called psychological and social than narrowly biological spring from one or other of three characteristics. The first is his capacity for abstract and general thought: the second is the relative unification of his mental processes, as against the much more rigid compartmentalization of animal mind and behavior: the third is the existence of social units, such as tribe, nation, party, and church, with a continuity of their own, based on organized tradition and culture." ‡

This interpretation is doubtless sufficiently orthodox. It may be interesting in this connection, however, to mention that of

---

* Julian Huxley, *Man Stands Alone* (New York: Harper and Brothers, 1941), pp. 3, 4.
† *Ibid.*, pp. 21, 22.
‡ *Ibid.*

an earlier authority, Sir E. Ray Lankester: "Man is born with fewer ready-made tricks of the nerve-centers—these performances of an inherited nervous mechanism so often called by the ill-defined term 'instincts'—than are the monkeys or any other animal. Correlated with the absence of inherited ready-made mechanisms, man has a greater capacity of developing in the course of his individual growth similar nervous mechanisms (similar to but not identical with those of 'instinct') than any other animal.... The power of being educated—'educability' as we may term it—is what man possesses in excess as compared with the apes. I think we are justified in forming the hypothesis that it is this 'educability' which is the correlative of the increased size of the cerebrum." The quotation ends with this significant passage: "... The character which we describe as 'educability' can be transmitted, it is a congenital character. But the *results* of education can *not* be transmitted. In each generation they have to be acquired afresh, and with increased 'educability' they are more readily acquired and a larger variety of them. ... The fact is that there is no community between the mechanisms of instinct and the mechanisms of intelligence, and that the latter are later in the history of the evolution of the brain than the former and can only develop in proportion as the former become feeble and defective." *

But it would be as grievous an error to suppose that man had escaped from his instinctive impulses as to imagine them reincarnated under the guise of intelligence. Deeply ingrained, the heritage of an almost illimitable biologic past covering possibly fifteen hundred million years, the instincts lie virtually impregnable at the heart of man's being. "The cardinal error," says Henri Bergson, "which, from Aristotle onwards, has vitiated most of the philosophies of nature, is to see in vegetative, instinctive and rational life, three successive degrees of the development of one and the same tendency, whereas they are three divergent directions of an activity that has split up as it grew." † The main emphasis of this passage is on the distinction

---

* Sir E. Ray Lankester, *Nature,* LXI (1900), 624, 625.
† Henri Bergson, *Creative Evolution* (New York: Henry Holt and Company, Inc., c. 1911; Arthur Mitchell, c. 1938), p. 135.

in kind between these three phases of life, but the statement might lead us to believe that intelligence has as long and honorable a heritage as the instincts themselves. In a later passage, however, Bergson qualifies this thought. "On the other hand, intelligence has even more need of instinct than instinct has of intelligence; for the power to give shape to crude matter involves already a superior degree of organization, a degree to which the animal could not have risen, save on the wings of instinct. So, while nature has frankly evolved in the direction of instinct in the arthropods, we observe in almost all the vertebrates the striving after rather than the expansion of intelligence. It is instinct still which forms the basis of their psychical activity; but intelligence is there, and would fain supersede it. Intelligence does not yet succeed in inventing instruments; but at least it tries to, by performing as many variations as possible on the instinct which it would like to dispense with. It gains complete self-possession only in man, and this triumph is attested by the very insufficiency of the natural means at man's disposal for defense against his enemies, against cold and hunger. This insufficiency, when we strive to fathom its significance, acquires the value of a prehistoric document; it is the final leave-taking between intelligence and instinct. But it is no less true that nature must have hesitated between two modes of psychical activity—one assured of immediate success, but limited in its effects; the other hazardous, but whose conquests, if it should reach independence, might be extended indefinitely.... Instinct and intelligence therefore represent two divergent solutions, equally fitting, of one and the same problem." *

That instinct precedes intelligence is affirmed in very positive terms by William McDougall; indeed, he implies that intelligence would be functioning in a void but for the necessary presence of the instincts. "Intelligent behaviour," he writes, "thus always involves modifications of instinctive modes of behaviour, and intelligence presupposes instinct, for unless a creature possessed instinct of some kind, all basis for the play

* *Ibid.*, p. 142.

of intelligence would be lacking, there would be no tendencies to be modified, and modification of pre-existing tendencies is the essence of intelligent activity." *

On the other hand, man might well have evolved without pain or conflict had instinct simply been displaced by intelligence. Such was not the case, and the dynamic force of intelligence, the decisive power of this new approach, is revealed precisely by the redoubtable nature of his instinctual heritage. Everywhere the titanic conflict is conditioned by the biologic priority of the instincts, and by the same token the character of the struggle is one of ascendancy rather than outright displacement. For the primary ends of life, however elaborated, are reducible to instinctual urges, which intelligence seeks to satisfy according to its own means. The apprentice would discard the master's technique. Thus intelligence triumphs in the domain of means; it tells us "how," but instinct, retaining always the inmost kernel of our ends, tells us "what." This manner of speaking, however, hides the travail of their mutual interactions. The immense complexity of their relation, the wavering, uncertain influence first of one and then of the other in the confused and discordant affairs of man, the struggle of conscious and unconscious impulses at the root of his being, merging into coherence and diverging into opposition, creating and destroying, but ever changing his culture, his values, his civilizations, characterize every aspect of his development and give color and form to his history. Clearly, under the sanction of intelligence, man has diverged from his primordial, instinctual harmony with nature, and by an inherent necessity of his development he now finds himself launched upon an uncharted course.

II

In our attempt to trace the influence of instinct and intelligence in the historic development of man, two basic principles are immediately apparent. The first is the biologic priority of the instincts; the second is the cumulative time-principle under

* William McDougall, *Psychology, the Study of Behaviour,* "Home University Library" (New York: Oxford University Press, 1912), pp. 163, 164.

which intelligence operates. The first anchors man to the past; the second projects him into an ever changing future.

The situation appears paradoxical if not contradictory. Yet, bearing in mind the differences between instinct and intelligence, we can readily see that man, progressively developing new means for the realization of his basic ends, wanders ever further afield to achieve his original aims. This extravagance is imposed upon him by the divergence between his essentially static, fixed instincts and his dynamic, purposive, and exploratory intelligence. The activation of the one is unconscious; of the other, conscious. The instincts, moreover, as we have seen, are congenitally fashioned patterns of behavior, whereas intelligence implies an active principle of deliberate relationships—a mode of operation rather than an established circuit of responses. Thanks to this unique freedom, enhanced doubtless by man's gregarious nature and above all by his faculty of articulate speech, the relationships established by intelligence are gradually formulated into a superior body of knowledge, into pragmatically verified traditions. And, however primitive and animistic these traditions may have been originally, they are subject to continuous change under the constant impact of intelligence. Thus, in contrast to his instinctual adaptations, man's intelligence furnished him not only with an ascending stairs, as it were, but with a kind of accelerated medium—an evolutionary escalator of ever increasing speed. This is not to say, however, that man changed as a biologic entity, or that his individual stature as an intelligent being was augmented during the relatively brief period of his history—if we accept the pronouncements of anthropologists—or, finally, that, having acquired a history, he had entered upon the certain path to perpetual progress. What he did do, under the cumulative impact of his intelligence, was to engage upon a grand readjustment in his relations to nature, based upon conscious reactions in place of unconscious responses.

This change, however, had profound implications, some of which are not yet fully apparent. It involved, in the first place, a new time-ratio of change. That is to say, man now improvises changes quite apart from the slow sculpturing of biologic forces, and his habits and customs, his ways of doing things, his patterned responses in every aspect of life change not only in character but in an ever increasing tempo. Despite regressions, despite his often long and recessive static periods, his progressive deviation under the pressure of intelligence is impressive and unarguable. As we ascend from the earliest periods of prehistoric man to the present, the course of change has by and large been characterized by a striking acceleration that indicates in itself the presence of a new and dynamic principle. When we bear in mind that so primitive an ancestor as Neanderthal man lived some fifty thousand years ago, while his ancestors—Heidelberg man and Pithecanthropus—lived, in turn, some five hundred thousand and a million years before that, more or less, we can already perceive the evidence of a variable ratio between time and change at the beginning of man's deviation from the biologic series. But as we ascend from Neanderthal man to the early Neolithic period and onward to the dawn of civilization we see clearly the full ferment of this new principle. Alfred Kroeber has summed up the matter in the following passage: "Metals were first used in Asia and Egypt about 4000 B.C. and in Europe about 3000 B.C.—say five or six thousand years ago. The most conservative authorities, however, would allow forty or fifty thousand years for the Stone Age; while others make it a quarter million. The assumption, which is here followed, of the intermediate figure of a hundred thousand years gives the Stone Age a duration twenty times as long as the Age of Metals. When one remembers that hand in hand with metals came the art of writing and an infinite variety of inventions, it is clear that larger additions have been made to human civilization in the comparatively brief period of metals than in the tremendously longer time that preceded it. Progress in the Stone Age was not only slow, but the further back one peers into this age, the more lagging does the evolution of human culture seem to have been. One can definitely recognize a tendency toward the acceleration of evolution: the farther advancement has got the faster it moves." *

* Alfred Kroeber, *Anthropology* (New York: Harcourt, Brace and Company, 1923), p. 141.

Nor did this cumulative process come to some arbitrary halt with the advent of historic times. On the contrary, it persisted unabated. It is true that our clearer understanding of man's historic period with all its vast and complex changes enables us to distinguish periods that were static, races that have declined, empires that have disappeared, and even knowledge that has become lost to us. But the steady advance has nonetheless proceeded until, in our own time, its vertiginous pace overwhelms our most daring expectations. The totality of man's awareness might be likened to a pool, which, though it was muddied by his ignorance and his superstitions, cleansed itself by the steady flow of new knowledge and new experience. Language enabled man not only to transmit but to store his experience, until this body of knowledge became a social heritage that increased in cumulative fashion throughout the course of his history. Man, building upon his advances, gained in time unsuspected rewards. Thus we may speak of progress—or rather of a progression—in the ways and means by which he encompasses the demands of life. This progression he owes to his intelligence. "In one respect," writes Franz Boas, "we may well speak of progress. Since earliest times knowledge and control of nature have received constant additions without any serious losses. New powers have been acquired and new insight has been opened. The ability of man to cope with his environment has improved, and new resources have been made available. At the same time the progress of knowledge has led to the elimination of error. The conflict between rational thought, on the one hand, and emotional reactions and rigid tradition, on the other, has tended to lead to the supremacy of reason, although the emotional elements have continued and still continue to shape the form of our culture." *

III

It is doubtless in his relation to his environment that man has made the most obvious if not the most profound changes

* Franz Boas, *General Anthropology* (New York: D. C. Heath and Company, 1938), pp. 676, 677.

in the slow course of his readjustment. Long before science finally confirmed this changed relation, man had already established his conscious independence from the biologic scheme of things: indeed, the direction was set and the process begun with his first flint implements, and, in a later stage, in Acheulean days, celebrated, no doubt, with his first fires. The decisive step, however, was probably the addition of agriculture to his meager repertoire. Here he supplemented nature by skillfully utilizing her ways to further his own ends. But this in fact was his constant formula; and, no matter how far the trajectory of his divergence has taken him, he has always paid homage to nature the better to free himself from her constant spell. The process ultimately rewarded him with science; and it is through science that man at length came to a precise turning point in his relation to his environment. This relationship has actually passed through three phases: in the first stage he was himself part of the natural panorama, dependent wholly upon his instinctual, unconscious adaptations; in the second stage he diverged from the biologic series into conscious awareness of his environment, guided now by his intelligence to ever greater mastery over his surroundings; in the third stage, which he has reached only today, science has enabled him to adjust himself to the basic laws of nature rather than to nature in her immediate and visible presence. But to dwell upon this last phase is to anticipate somewhat the argument that is to follow. Meanwhile, however, it is clear that man has become the master of his environment rather than merely occupying the dubious eminence of its highest ornament.

Man was from the first a gregarious being—a characteristic that is but the primitive version of his maturer sociality. From the beginning his environment was not merely nature but the horde, the group, the tribe. Man originally was bound within the mores of his group with something of the same instinctual bondage that characterized his relation to nature. In the course of his development this deeply compelling but wholly unconscious relationship changed significantly. The group widened out into a confederation of groups and ultimately into vaster national aggregates, while the position of the individual

changed constantly in the direction of a more conscious, formulated, and explicit membership. Just as his changed attitude
toward nature involved a transvaluation of instinctive patterns
of behavior in terms of conscious modes of approach, so, too,
in the intimate environment of his fellow men, he found himself drifting into ever more conscious sanctions and formulated relations. Customs became transformed into laws;
ancient rites and habits became explicit practices and codified
ordinances. If the process in this case was more confused and
halting, it was because man was himself the theater of conflict,
while in the other case nature offered no resistance. His readjustments to nature seem always to precede his readjustments
to himself; witness the lag between his technical triumphs and
his social efforts. The courses followed by these twin changes
in man's environmental relations, though interconnected, were
in no sense parallel. Yet they stem from the same source and
follow a similar logic. However maladjusted the internal structure of man's civilization may have been at any given moment
in his history, his continuous adaptations—whether to himself
or to nature—follow always a similar pattern, a common principle.

What is that principle? We have already traced it in terms
of instinct and intelligence, of conscious and unconscious responses. In man's readjustment to nature the trend is patent
and the direction obvious. In his more intimate, mutual, and
human relations, the same principle encompasses deeper realities; it lies hidden behind the vast superstructures to which
man's attributes of faith and imagination, fear and hope,
thought and feeling, have given form. It embraces his history.
To subsume this vast, incredible, contradictory, immemorial
panorama as merely a battle between two forces may well seem
presumptuous. But that is only to say that we have not yet become fully awakened to the all-embracing depths of our changing status.

IV

We are confronted with a broad question. Man is thought not
to have changed physically to any appreciable extent during

the last one hundred thousand years, while mentally, according to Franz Boas and other eminent anthropologists, he shows no greater native capacity than his early prehistoric ancestors. Robert Briffault states the matter thus: "Evolutionary development has, in the human species, been transferred from organic elements physiologically inherited to social *tradition*. It may be doubted whether the modern civilized individual differs greatly as regards inherited capacities from his ancestors of the Stone Age; the difference between savagedom and civilization is not organic, but cultural. The increase in our knowledge of ancient types of man has, in some respects, accentuated rather than attenuated the abruptness of the transition from animality to humanity; the oldest human remains and the tools associated with them indicate a brain-capacity which is not markedly, if at all, inferior to that of existing races.... The problem has, for the most part, been considered in a false light; it has been regarded from the point of view of the individual organism, whereas the human mind is from the first essentially a social product." * Thus, despite his organic stability, man has changed more, in his mode of living, during historic times than in all his previous phases taken together. In what manner has man changed? Does history itself sustain the idea of some dominant direction, of some appreciable trend?

If the natural endowment of the individual has not undergone a change commensurate with that of man viewed historically and collectively, we are justified, as Briffault suggests, in seeking an explanation of his extraordinary series of changes in a principle that has affected mankind as an entity, as a continuous social whole. Such a point of view, though sustained by the facts, may seem highly aloof to the historian, overwhelmed by the task of explaining in turn each minute aspect and episode of the evolving picture, let alone the whole of the historic panorama. Spengler, for instance, as noted below, rejected such a conception and approach along with the term "mankind" as a zoological designation. It is true, of course, that during his-

* Robert Briffault, "Evolution of Human Species," in *The Making of Man; An Outline of Anthropology,* edited by V. F. Calverton (New York: Modern Library, 1931), p. 763.

toric times, amidst all the immense diversity of races and peoples and the staggering complexities of man's varied civilizations, no unilinear development is directly discernible. But this is only to say that counteracting influences have diverted its dominant direction into all the multifarious play of time and circumstance—into the ceaseless gyrations of man under the impact of opposing forces. Like an inundating sea, change has broken in where it may, accepting the contours of existing conditions here, flooding barriers there; but the fact remains clear and undeniable that mankind has been borne onward by a decisive and all-encompassing principle whose origin is lost in the far instinctual past, and whose final effects, geared ever more to the impact of intelligence, have yet to be discerned. In its sweep it is calculated to absorb the manifold influences of many civilizations, of individuals as well as peoples; and, once absorbed, their momentum is carried forward by mankind as a whole. Only less manifest in other aspects of man's activities, this character is well illustrated in the case of mathematics: here the contributions of different cultures have been absorbed in a vast body of common knowledge accessible to mankind everywhere. The same point applies to other phases of our cultural heritage: to science and technology, to agriculture, to cooking, to education, and to building. Behind these consummating activities lies a principle that belongs to mankind as a whole. To plumb its depths and trace its levels at every point in the vast expanse of history, like a geodetic survey of man's activities, would constitute a fascinating and significant task, but one altogether beyond the scope of the present inquiry. The basic fact and character of that principle have already been indicated; it is time to explore further its larger meaning and its fundamental implications.

If the influence of that principle has not always been directly and continuously apparent, nonetheless its operation has been ceaseless. Neither the urgency of man's intelligence nor the stream of his knowledge has ever been known arbitrarily to have ceased and disappeared. On the contrary, they are part and parcel of his permanent possessions, as it were: like language they constitute his specifically characteristic equipment.

Together with these essentially cultural instruments of survival, man carried along, as we have seen, his inherited instinctual background of traditional ways and immemorial habits. Thus prepared for survival, his equipment seems indeed more powerful than his need, biologically speaking; and this may well account for the innate optimism that has led him to believe, not unnaturally, in panaceas, utopias, and paradise itself! Small wonder that man came to have faith in survival after death when survival itself was thus doubly assured. His surplus energies were consumed in the creation of his varied civilizations, whose values, spiraling into supercharged structures under the surging influences of chaotic feelings and confused thoughts, often enough collapsed under the impact of that very battle of attrition out of which they arose. For his instincts and his intelligence, however he contrived to hitch them together, were not set to go in the same direction. That is the crucial fact of his history. Their relation, their eternal conflict in all its diverse facets, might be said to constitute his history—the endless search for new forms within which they might be harnessed in some happy equilibrium. That man has never found that equilibrium, that civilizations have arisen and then perished, that his most cherished beliefs have been abandoned, reluctantly, under the urgency of new ideas and new concepts, that his most vaunted structures have fallen into decay and collapsed while he moves restlessly toward unknown goals, like Rasselas, ever unhappy in his present estate—all this is but evidence of a persistent dichotomy in his approach to the problems of life. Yet the significant point in the ebb and flow of this conflict is the fact that the center of the struggle shifts ground: there is a perceptible movement, an unarguable drift. For the struggle is unequal. The static pressure of the instincts must give way under the dynamic impact of intelligence, reacting with ever greater force through the fulcrum of cumulative knowledge. If man as an individual is no more intelligent than his remote ancestor of prehistoric days, mankind is. Under this progressive acceleration, the nature of the conflict changes like that of a solution, drop by drop, step by step, endowing history with an unmistakable trend. But history gives evidence of more than a progressive trend: it constitutes a change of direction as well.

However we define the qualities that served to differentiate primitive man from the biologic series, it is essentially an extension of these same qualities that in turn distinguishes historic from prehistoric man. Thus we are presented not only with a certain continuity in the development of man but also with an increasing departure or divergence from his instinctual background. The general character of this deviation was indicated by the contrast between unconscious responses and conscious reactions. But this terminology, though it may serve to convey the idea intended, is inexact, if not faulty. To be unconscious is to presuppose a condition of consciousness; it would perhaps be better to speak therefore of a *preconscious* state as correlative with the primary, instinctual stage of man. His psychic evolution may thus be defined as a progression from a preconscious to a conscious state.

In turn, this progression may be correlated with many parallel or analogous developments in the psychic structure of man. Their course sheds further light upon the idea that history constitutes a change of direction in man's ways and habits. We have already spoken of the translation of customs into laws, of a process transmuting implicit relations into explicit formulations. The phenomenon can be defined in more basic terms as a movement from innate, preconscious responses to acquired, explicitly defined, conscious reactions. These more or less abstract terms take on specific meaning within the framework of history; they apply to the course of events and reveal themselves in the trends of man's behavior and institutions. As instinctual patterns of behavior are transmuted into or supplanted by those of intelligence, faith and belief recede before advancing knowledge; religious views of the cosmos shrink before the world-picture of science; primitive cultures become transformed into the higher intricacies of civilization; the slow development of earlier societies becomes translated into the measurable progress of today; and everywhere, in all aspects of life, our instinctual ends are preceded by an ever increasing procession of contrived means. Universally, the more introverted values and attitudes of man give way before an expanding extroversion. And whereas man was originally bound within the locus of deeply ingrained values and innately accepted rituals and modes of behavior, he now finds himself increasingly in a transmuted world of external compulsions and arbitrary patterns of conduct. Man, the puppet, animated from within by the hand of instinct, becomes a marionette controlled from without by the compulsions of intelligence. The social structure, once comparable in its functioning to an organism, has been converted by slow degrees into an ever more detailed and comprehensive system of organized means and purposes. History thus marks a change of direction in the social structure of man, which may be subsumed as the transmutation of society as an organism into an organization of society. The characteristic qualities of one phase are reflected in equivalent attributes in the other phase. Thus, under the headings of Organism and Organization we may list related groups of qualities and attributes that bear in each case a similar correlation to each other:

ORGANISM	ORGANIZATION
Instinct	Intelligence
Innate	Acquired
Implicit	Explicit
Preconscious	Conscious
Faith and Belief	Knowledge
Religion	Science
Customs	Laws
Culture	Civilization
Ends	Means
Growth	Progress
Introversion	Extroversion

Such pairs of equivalents doubtless might be multiplied. Those here given are neither exhaustive nor perhaps adequately phrased. But they serve to indicate a general direction in the historic process from organic to organizational forms and patterns, qualities and attributes. This morphological transformation is deeply and inherently correlated with the change from an earlier, essentially instinctual, and preconscious stage to a later, purposive, intelligent, and conscious phase. Thus these equivalents indicate a time sequence from earlier to later stages —not necessarily in their actual historic order or confluence, but in their basic meaning and trend. The process, plainly, is at once sweeping and inescapable—and, by the same token, irreversible. We may thus speak of a definite change of direction in the development of man: a change that reveals in turn a comprehensive determinism behind the whole panorama of historic events.

V

To say that history follows a definitely determined course comes close to implying that its processes are amenable to specific laws. This thesis has often enough been maintained but perhaps never satisfactorily demonstrated. If such laws are comparable to scientific laws, they should afford a basis for prediction; but even allowing a wide latitude for inaccuracies, the prognostications that have been ventured in the field of history have been either wide of the mark or at best tentative and generalized rather than specific and positive. Certainly no "laws of history" have ever been stated with sufficient precision to invite application to past or future with anything approaching scientific standards. The situation is all the more embarrassing in comparison with such a field as biology, since history affords us not only a knowledge of specific events but an inward approach to a fuller understanding of such events. Though historians have thus the inside track, as it were, they are among the last to aspire to the status of scientists in their approach to their own field. Possibly this very fact prevents them from attaining not so much an objective view of their domain as a comprehensive view: the nature of their study confines them to the trees while hiding the forest. Despite increasing attention to this major problem, it would almost seem as though a whole field of inquiry had been silently passed by; and the study of history lost in the tangled web of histories.

Even physicists, dealing with supposedly immutable material, find themselves constantly obliged to revise their findings or supplement their theories. On this basis historians, working with far less tractable and precise phenomena, might readily be excused from attempting to reach final and irrefutable laws. Science, of course, as F. J. Teggart says, "is not a body of beliefs and opinions, but is a way or method of dealing with problems." Here the historian may take refuge, however, in the fact that one of the basic methods of science, namely experimentation, is denied him; he is reduced by the nature of his material to observation and such theories as his observation may sustain. Thus reduced, he has often succumbed to the questionable aid of deduction by analogy, and more especially by analogy drawn from the field of biology. But here, unfortunately, the cardinal fact about man is precisely his divergence from the biologic series in ways that have endowed him with a history! Thus the door would seem to be closed upon ready analogies between human and insect societies, or between evolutionary development and social progress, or, indeed, upon any direct inferences based upon mere biologic evolution. The quandary of formulating a science of history may thus appear forbidding, but the prospect is nonetheless inviting; and the courageous attempts made in the face of doubt and skepticism to achieve a science of history attest to a deep intuition of its ultimate possibility. The art of flying was conceived by man long before the motor, which made it feasible, was even imaginatively entertained; in like manner the processes of history may be found susceptible of scientific statement even though the material seems to us, at the moment, intractable and chaotic. Indeed, it may be that not until man himself has emerged from what may prove to be the chaos of a transitional phase in his development will he be able to formulate the laws of his historic course.

Meanwhile, if the history of humanity, conceived in broad outline, is an irreversible process indicative of an explicit and basic determinism, it should be possible to establish points of reference and a "gradient" by which to measure it. The suggestion is not too fantastic. But the difficulties are formidable. Chronology itself becomes hazy as we recede into the remote past; points of reference imply standards of choice involved in the very process we would measure; and the process itself, far from being a direct and unilinear affair, appears to be a complex of ill-defined, at times confluent, at other times contrary, influences. But this is only to say that we have not yet resolved the complexities of the problem. Nonetheless certain facts emerge clear and adamant above the dark sea of ignorance that now hides their possible interconnections.

We have first, then, to consider the basic fact of man's divergence from the biologic hierarchy. This initial accomplishment was due to a number of contributory factors, chief among them his marked superiority in intelligence. But it would be a mistake to suppose he emerged from his earlier instinctual stage as from a chrysalis: primitive man rose very slowly, as we have seen, from an essentially instinctual status within the biologic series to a position of increasing imbalance under the cumulative pressure of emerging intelligence. Man thus entered ever further into an era of opposition and conflict between factors of "fixity and persistence," as Teggart calls them, and factors of change. In this struggle the factors of change slowly triumphed, because of the impact of an inherent and cumulative acceleration in man's knowledge and experience. Deeply correlated with this transition, man changed from a preconscious to an ever more purposive and conscious phase. And this shift in values was marked, chronologically, by an increased tempo in the rate of change; for, though detached and specific dates may be difficult to establish with precision, the mounting flow of historic events reveals unmistakably an ever accelerating movement from the virtually unchanging vistas of primitive man to the ceaseless changes of today. Viewed as a single sweeping movement, the whole panorama of man's development, following an ever accelerating rate of change, plainly reveals a correspondingly intensified deviation from the primal status of man—a deviation that can be identified only with the emergence and growing dominance of intelligence. We may thus speak of man's development as a movement characterized by direction; and of his history as a specific phase of that movement.

In its sweep this movement transformed the whole complex

of primitive life and culture into the varied civilizations of history, while man's primal and intimate relation to nature changed into an extroverted conquest of his environment. The nature of the process called for a steady transmutation of values and modes of procedure: morphologically speaking, the process demanded, with all the force of an inherent determinism, the translation of organic forms into organizational formulations. Thus, as we have noted, customs were translated into laws; implicit beliefs into explicit explanations; and the intuitive, closed relationships of primitive life became in time the highly externalized and deliberate procedures of civilized man. The identity with nature broke down, and man entered upon "the deliberate and systematic mastery of the physical world," in the words of Carl Becker. The process is thus seen to be a vast, oscillating struggle between the primary urges of the instincts and the imposed but inescapable compulsions of intelligence. And though the struggle wavered throughout the complex movements of history, the conflict was basically uneven: while the instincts held sway over the primary ends of life, intelligence dictated the ever changing means for attaining them. The principle involved in the first case is static; in that of the second, dynamic. The union that exists between means and ends in the intimate functioning of purely instinctual creatures was ruptured by intelligence in the case of man; and this rift was carried forward, under the all-pervasive force of intelligence, until means and ends became separate entities in a conscious world of explicit values. Thus the basic movement of history is one not of choice but of an inherent and inescapable drift. In its incipient stages, man must have been wholly unaware of its direction, or indeed of its existence; and not until the struggle had reached the historic stage of a conscious conflict could man have perceived its significance. In the historic phase of his development man at length awakened to the heroic but fateful struggle between those factors of "fixity and persistence," established by instinct, and those ever encroaching factors of change, inherent in the functioning of intelligence. These factors were in opposition long before he was aware of them, and they may eventually reach a condition of static equilibrium in the triumph of intelligence and the consequent, if gradual, cessation of change. But such a condition will likewise be equivalent to a gradual ebbing of historic consciousness, when man may once more enter upon a state of rigid and continuous stability under the crystallized formulations of intelligence. History must then be looked upon as a transitional stage in the evolutionary development of man.

During the course of man's history the relationship between the influence of instinct, on the one hand, and that of intelligence, on the other, is not readily disentangled. Yet it is clear that if we represented their influences graphically, by means of lines or curves,* that of instinct would show a relative descent and that of intelligence a correspondingly relative ascent during the course of history, or certainly—to make the picture more complete and revealing—from the earliest period of primitive man onward. And though we cannot readily establish points of reference in the development of man as a whole, or within the specific confines of historic eras, it is sufficiently clear that the influence or domination of instinct and intelligence in the affairs of man are in inverse ratio to each other, and that their diagrammatic lines would fall in the one case and rise in that of the other. Needless to say, such a simplification is justified only on the ground of its general convenience. Yet it reveals at once a striking and significant fact. Whether we have established specific reference points or not, and however we choose to draw the lines or curves representing the influences of instinct and intelligence upon the course of man's development, we come, sooner or later, upon an inevitable point of intersection—an era of balance between their influences. To assign such an era to a specific period of history would be to anticipate the argument that follows; but even a cursory guess would lead us to place it well within the unfolding process of history itself. Such a point would constitute a crucial moment in the entire development of man. And certainly, in the immense time-scale of that development, it is not

---

* The curves that present themselves most readily to mind (see page 55) turn out, not unnaturally, to be similar to the asymptotic S-shaped curves familiar in graphic studies of organic growth and decline.

unreasonable to believe that even a point of intersection between two such basic elements as those here considered must
be allowed extension in time, and be accepted in the sense of
an era or historical period rather than some specific date of
uncertain validity. But plainly, in any case, this moment of
tremulous balance will mark a unique reference point in the
entire range of man's changing course—a basic turning point
in his direction.

Nothing could be more helpful in the effort to determine this
illusive point than some system of measurement, proper to the
occasion and recording for us at a glance the relative dominance of instinct or intelligence in the tangled affairs of humanity. Man has applied measurement to almost everything but
his own history, with gratifying results in the further manipulation of his universe. His propensity for measuring is
an essential asset in achieving order and establishing precise
relationships—in a word, in the processes of integration and
organization. That organization itself, however, should prove
to be a modulus of measurement is perhaps less evident but
equally valid. To serve as a modulus of measurement, an entity
must bear a direct and invariant relationship to the object of
measurement: thus the yardstick becomes a measure of distance; the radius at the base of a classic column the modulus
of the whole order; and, in a like sense, organization, arising
directly out of the functioning of intelligence in the purposive
manipulation of specific means to particular ends, becomes inherently an accurate and effective measure or modulus of its
influence.

Here, though we have shifted the difficulty of measurement
from one process to another, we have at least arrived at a more
tangible and precise yardstick. Moreover, the static nature of
instinctual responses, in contrast to the dynamic character of
intelligence, would lead us to believe that their relative influences upon the course of history might far more readily be
reflected in terms appropriate to the functioning of intelligence
rather than to that of the instincts. Obviously, it is the pressure
of intelligence that has molded life in its divergence from its
instinctual base. But how to apply the yardstick of organiza-

tion to this problem remains to be determined. That organization is a basic and characteristic element in the functioning of intelligence is clear. As the necessary structural framework, the purposive order, coherence, and arrangement through which available means are co-ordinated in the attainment of their ends, organization is inherently correlated with intelligence and synonymous with its operation. Yet the extent and intensity of organization in any given period are not readily gauged; the relative advance or recession of organization as a principle of action or knowledge remains a formidable historic problem that has never received the critical attention it merits. Even the immensely accelerated expansion of organization in our own day has been passed over with little more than casual notice as a sign of the times. Nowhere has it been recognized as the profound signal of a climax in the affairs of man—as the signpost of a new direction in the course of man's historic development. Only negatively, so to speak, has modern man sensed the powerful drive of events as though he were standing, helpless and ignorant, in the backwash of his own epoch. Advancing with unprecedented strides, the trend toward organization in every aspect of life is a reality and a portent—a portent of a crucial change of direction; a portent of that illusive moment we were seeking. And thus we may ask what precursors and auguries of change, commensurate with the event, have we at hand. What signs, if any, of some climactic, high moment in the drama of history have been vouchsafed us? By what logic shall we recognize a moment which, if it has passed, has eluded us, and, if it lies ahead, must now rest, vague and incipient, in the womb of time? To these questions we must now attempt to find an answer.

III

THE CRUCIAL EPOCH

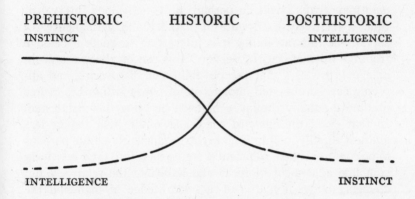

PREHISTORIC   HISTORIC   POSTHISTORIC
INSTINCT   INTELLIGENCE

INTELLIGENCE   INSTINCT

THE MOVEMENT FROM instinct to intelligence is seen to exhibit a kind of determinism—historic or morphological but inherent, in any case—in the evolution of man's development. In no sense is this trend his choice: rather it is his fate, his inescapable direction, rooted in his very nature. Three conditions were noted in respect to this trend: first, that at some point, tentatively assumed to lie within the historic era, the weight of influence of instinct and intelligence upon the affairs of man would reach an unstable equilibrium; second, that such a point would constitute a vital moment or era of transition dividing man's development into two phases—an earlier phase under the dominance of the instincts, and a later phase under that of intelligence; and, finally, that organization was a modulus of the increasing dominance of intelligence. Armed with these abstract conditions, we were to seek a more precise epoch for the critical point of balance between instinct and intelligence—with the hope, implicit in the argument, of gaining a

55

limited insight into the future phase of man's development based on the direction and momentum of his past.

A glance at the diagram above reveals the fact that the thesis here outlined contemplates a final *posthistoric* phase, more or less symmetrical with the prehistoric phase. History itself is thus marked off as a transitional interregnum—a period of ever increasing change, tending toward a climax, after which man may again attain, in perhaps an equally long interval of time, a relatively fixed state of stability and permanence. In support of this possibility it is interesting to quote a passage from the work of Carl L. Becker. "It is conceivable, even probable," he writes, "that the possibility of discovering and applying new sources and implements of power will in the course of time gradually diminish, or even be altogether exhausted. In that event the outward conditions of life will change less and less rapidly, will in time become sufficiently stable perhaps to be comprehended, sufficiently stable therefore for a relatively complete adustment of ideas and habits to the relatively unchanging body of matter-of-fact knowledge of man and the outer world in which he lives. In such a stabilized and scientifically adjusted society the idea of progress would no doubt become irrelevant as progress itself becomes imperceptible or nonexistent." * Thus we contemplate a period of "stability and permanence" symmetrical with, if not precisely equivalent to, that of man's earliest period. But before venturing into these unknown regions we must substantiate the thesis indicated above upon which such a sally into the future comes to depend.

Meanwhile, in an enterprise of this scope it will be well to bear in mind that the eras and epochs, the various stages and phases of man's development here referred to, encompass long periods of time; and that the hope of establishing accurately some microscopic point in a macroscopic landscape will prove to be futile. History itself, in all its inextricable complexity, is here presented as a transitional stage or phase between epochs of far longer duration. Within the scope of this wider thesis lies a more restricted conception—namely, that history, as the

* Carl L. Becker, *Progress and Power* (Alfred A. Knopf, Inc., 1949), p. 112.

stage of this transitional conflict, must sooner or later reveal
a significant climax or basic change of direction in the course
of man's development. It is upon the validity of this conception that the larger vista of the future is predicated. But even
such a crucial turning point will hardly emerge from the tableau of history, tagged with a specific date to gladden the
hearts of children with another commemorative holiday. Such
an occasion will more likely resemble an undefined epoch
stretching imperceptibly into the surrounding terrain of historic events. For our purposes it will suffice to discern and
identify such a region, trusting to more competent explorers to
map its exact topography.

I

The task of distinguishing between the influences of instinct
and intelligence upon the course of man's development seems
altogether forbidding. As we recede into the past it is clear that
man was ever more under the dominance of his instincts; but
even at the dawn of history, when man first immortalized his
deeds in writing—or even earlier, when he first cultivated his
fields—we are already in the presence of a degree of intelligence comparable to our own. It is rather in the extent and
complexion of our knowledge that the contrast between ourselves and primitive man is decisive. In our conscious appraisal
of its values and its function, we can isolate intelligence in
ways that primitive man could not; but the power of this instrument of the mind comes to depend always upon the body of
knowledge with which it operates. Yet, knowledge itself is not
an apodictic ladder to reality—an infallible and frozen presen-
tation of facts. Knowledge shifts, changes, and grows. And, in
a manner of speaking, the potency and effectiveness of intelligence are dependent upon the degree of acceptance which nature, no less than we ourselves, bestows upon our knowledge.
For it was not until nature accepted, as it were, the interpretations man put upon her that she rewarded him with miraculous
powers. That is merely to say that knowledge is efficacious in
so far as it is based on the actualities of nature rather than
upon man's preconceived and purely subjective conceptions of

nature. Just as the instincts are fashioned in the interaction of organism and environment, so too does intelligence demand a body of knowledge forged by man's mind in contact with impersonal and objective fact—with nature. Thus only could intelligence function with the certitude vouchsafed the instincts. But whereas the instincts—set, fixed, and unchanging—function best within a locus of established relations, intelligence is capable of viewing man and his environment as mutually susceptible of change and adaptation. Thus intelligence has a far greater range and power of penetration: if the instincts enable the organism to adapt itself to the environment, intelligence enables man to adapt himself to an ever wider theater of operation—to the whole panorama of nature. For while the instincts obey nature, intelligence penetrates to the laws of nature: therein lie its freedom and its power.

Early in his development man appears to have sensed that nature was an orderly system of things. But it was only very late in his development—indeed, only in his immediate past—that he succeeded in formulating this knowledge. If he once supposed that nature followed invariant laws, he now set about discovering what these laws were. And in the degree in which he succeeded nature rewarded him with unstinted bounty. This revelation came to him, however, only after he had learned to retreat in order to advance; only after he displaced his "subjective arrogance," in the words of Rudolph Eucken, by a "humble recognition of limits." Not until he had rejected his preconceived ideas, his uncritically accepted dogmas, his authoritarian beliefs, indeed, not until he was *conscious* of his ignorance, his nescience, did he begin to gain that impersonal and objective knowledge we know as science. Man had, as it were, to clear away the accumulated furniture of his mind before he found room for this new manner of knowledge.

The scientific outlook marks a significant change in man's orientation. Its derivative effects are, even now, wholly incalculable; its ultimate effects wholly unpredictable. In its basic divergence from man's previously held attitudes and modes of approach to the problems of life, the scientific outlook marks not so much a culmination of as a deviation from long-sustained habits of thought. Its emergence was due not to the development and flowering of component elements but to the paring away of superimposed and long-entwined modes of apprehension, of thought and belief. The scientific outlook did not add to man's faculties of comprehension; it separated them. That is the secret of its power and its universal acceptance. That accounts in some measure also for its relatively belated emergence in the history of man, at a moment when the heavily laden, instinctually rooted vine of medieval Christianity fell away, revealing once more man's native, virile, and free intelligence. For long, medieval theology had drained the intellect into the cul-de-sac of Aristotelian scholasticism while sanctioning the irrational under the perverse banner of Tertullian's *Certum est, quia impossibile est* (It is certain because it is impossible). It may be true, as Alfred Whitehead argues in *Science and the Modern World*, that the Church, by its avowal of a God-created and therefore ordered universe, prepared men's minds for the scientific conception of natural law, for an ordered rather than a capricious world. Certainly the very conception of the miraculous implies an ordered universe as a necessary backdrop. Such preparations, however, must be counted wholly adventitious: the hearts and minds of medieval men were turned toward a heavenly abode, and it was only in the dissolution of that dream that they embraced the earth with a new and wondering ardor. In this awakening they found themselves, suddenly, free and unencumbered; they attained, as man had never before attained, the clarity of first principles, and with almost childlike simplicity they felt and saw and tasted the world about them. For the scientific outlook which sprang from this pristine experience succeeded for the first time in separating at one drastic bound the long-accumulated residue of instinctual values and traditional modes of thought from the clear and unimpeded functioning of intelligence. The result was profound and sweeping. Man now entered upon an era of coordinated experience and thought, of objective experiment and *conscious* ignorance, no less than of *conscious* knowledge. He thus uncovered, rather than discovered, a mode of approach available to man everywhere; and in the relatively short period of a few centuries this singular procedure dominated and unified the whole of mankind in its acknowledged means and its avowed aims. No other system of thought or belief has thus encompassed the world. Science, by virtue of its essential universality and its unarguable basis in human rationality and intelligence, marks a definite turning point and change of direction in the affairs of mankind. For it heralds the triumph of intelligence over instinct as the decisive principle of guidance in all the conscious adjustments of life.

This qualification might well seem to leave intact the vast areas of unconscious behavior. But quite apart from the advances of psychology, and particularly psychoanalysis, in throwing light upon unconscious motivations in human behavior, science by its critical analysis has everywhere narrowed the power and extent of unconscious responses and unconscious adjustments. Through the agency of science man has made immense strides precisely in that process of translation from unconscious modes of behavior and perception to conscious power and knowledge. Analysis and experiment have everywhere proved superior to conjecture and surmise; and the pragmatic justification of science rests squarely upon the cornerstone of its power of prediction. The soothsayer and the clairvoyant have given way to the statistician, and man relies implicitly upon the scientific trajectory of facts rather than upon omens and oracles. Science may indeed be said to be the dictionary by means of which man translates in time the entire body of unconscious valuations into conscious formulations. Nor is this trend limited to man's perception of external nature. The domain of human values, nourished in the soil of instinctual responses, is likewise subjected to a process of transmutation. Like all else, these responses are thrown into the rationalistic hopper, ground fine by analysis, and consciously reconstructed into more pragmatic forms. For everywhere the sanction of the instincts shrinks as the influence of science expands. The triumph of science accelerated the trend upon which in fact it was largely based—the trend, namely, of freeing intelligence of all instinctual adumbrations. But this drift hastened the dissolution of human and cultural values in favor of the more consciously and purposively determined ends and aims of our predominantly technological civilization. Thus science completed a cycle of rational values into a more or less self-contained system with which, like a lasso, man sought to encompass the world.

The strength of science is due to its ever more rigid exclusion of assumptions. This self-cleansing process, however, cannot be carried to a final and absolute conclusion: science can only approach such an aim as a mathematical limit, as an ideal. But by this rigorous exclusion of all modes of apprehension other than those of precise observation and logical deduction, science leads to a world view sharply different from all previously held cosmologies. For science alone, disavowing belief, unfolds through concrete experiment and hypothetical theories, through suppositional and tentative conclusions, in its ever closer approximation to reality. In consequence, science does not present us with a closed picture of the universe, for it is itself but a mode of apprehension—an organized system of provisional constructs.

The scientific analysis of the world, however far-reaching and valid, remains therefore at best a chart of operations, an abstraction composed of diagrammatic and generalized formulations. It is the virtue of this abstract picture, however, to reveal a world of definite contours and implacable construction; in giving explicit form to the world, science has enabled man to manipulate it. This principle was clearly recognized by Francis Bacon when he said: "We cannot command nature except by obeying her." Perhaps his dictum that "Knowledge is Power" comes closer to summarizing the age that was to follow than any number of subsequent critical analyses; here, in brief, we come upon that fructifying attitude which gave science its world-wide acceptance and set in motion the sharpest, the most comprehensive, and the gravest transformation in every aspect of life that man has yet experienced. The scope and temper of this change cannot well be conceived as other than a basic change of direction in the history and development of man.

II

This change of direction cannot be ascribed to science alone. The development of technics with its concomitant political, economic, and social influences was likewise involved. Lewis Mumford in his *Technics and Civilization* has carefully traced the wide correlation between these diverse aspects of a movement that long antedated the Industrial Revolution and embraced indeed a far wider and more profound transformation. Under the impact of this change the whole orientation of man in his attitude toward himself as well as toward the world at large was altered. Everywhere he threw himself into the task of discovery and expansion. The realm of external fact captured his mind and his imagination; he came to believe in progress and reason; and at all points he applied himself with high energy, thought, and purpose to the exploration of his world and the magnification of his ego. Man became individualized and his values correspondingly focused in a vast program of extroversion. "More than ever before," wrote Rudolph Eucken in reference to this period, "is thought the impelling and guiding force in our civilization. Ends and means are all discussed beforehand, possibilities all considered, life mapped out in advance and lived in anticipation." * The means of life were incalculably extended. Time—the medium within which the means of life function—became a new dimension. Knowledge had expanded far beyond the capacities of the individual. Mathematics, developing into unimagined regions, penetrated ever more deeply into the texture of life. Invention and technology converted the world into a machine civilization. Power became available to man in forms and magnitudes beyond his fantasy. The population of the world, relatively stable up to the middle of the seventeenth century, more than quadrupled itself. And along with this prodigious increase man envisaged for the first time a potential world of plenty. Man felt he had indeed conquered nature. In power and control, in means and in knowledge, the world, viewed in historic perspective, may be

* Rudolph Eucken, *The Problem of Human Life* (New York: Charles Scribner's Sons, 1910), p. 306.

said to have been fabulously realized; and the vastness of these changes, the immensity of this tableau, were attained within the span of some ten or twelve generations of man!

This reaching out into time and space gave man a sense of limitless possibilities: a point of view which he summed up in the dynamic idea of indefinite progress. He had attained unsuspected results, unimagined victories, unsought triumphs. He had reached pinnacles of unforeseen and unbelievable vistas; and he matched these accomplishments with unwonted pride. The past, moreover, was but the prologue to an even more glorious future; and his vertiginous speed led him to believe that he had stepped upon a magic escalator that would carry him, story upon story, to incredible heights. The vision was far from apocalyptic. His accomplishments justified his expectations: all the more so since man felt that his efforts did not quite merit his achievements. Somehow, somewhere, the benefits of the system had surpassed man's most sanguine hopes. If he had any doubts, they arose from a sense that he was perhaps not so much the master as the recipient of these unearned benefits, and that, in the natural course of events, they might vanish as quickly and mysteriously as they had appeared. Progress, however tangible, carried with it, even in the day of its most substantial gains, a faint element of surprise and unreality.

The matter is of particular interest to us, for obviously so audacious a philosophy of change as the idea of progress would seem to lend support to the conception of a profound and inherent change of direction in the affairs of man. Its optimistic tone, its expansionist trend, its basis in fact, and its emphasis upon rationalism, all seem to substantiate such a close relation. Finally, its marked emphasis upon the future and its sharp divergence from previous philosophies add to this plausible testimony. It may be well, therefore, to examine the idea of progress more carefully, and in this task we can not do better than to lean upon the treatise of J. B. Bury: *The Idea of Progress*.

It is not surprising that the immense acceleration in the rate of historic change should have been reflected in a philosophy of change. The idea of progress, like that of science, and even certain primitive conceptions in the technology of the machine, were not wholly foreign to the ancients. The idea remained embryonic, however, and it was not until about the middle of the seventeenth century that it emerged once more in tentative and uncertain form. With the bolder advances of science and technology, the triumphant spread of the machine, and, finally, the advent of the theory of evolution, the idea of progress came into its own. Strictly speaking, evolution is a theory of organic change and not of progress in a beneficent sense. But the notion of a continuous and indefinite amelioration of human affairs seemed nonetheless sustained by this philosophy of change, especially in view of man's unparalleled triumph over nature, and the creation of a new world of machinery. In place of an immutable order of things, man now envisaged the hope of indefinite perfectibility; and in place of an uncertain and vague paradise in the hereafter, he foresaw, in some attainable future, a vision of heaven on earth. Thus the idea of progress constituted the crowning doctrine in the whole conception of human development—a vast, optimistic vista embracing the entire panorama of man's past neatly balanced by an ever more alluring future. The present was always the highest pinnacle attained from which new vistas unfolded themselves, and the idea of progress harmonized the shortcomings and failures of humanity in the past with promises of fulfillment in the future.

Even as the idea was receiving its final polish—a phase that so often in the course of human affairs betokens merely a premature patina—the more critical minded began to question an edifice that had risen beyond man's most sanguine expectations. Some feared what obviously they could not control; others surmised that progress was wholly external, arbitrary, and spiritually impervious. They looked askance upon a structure of such gratuitous proportions and unbalanced composition; and they feared, not without reason, that what appeared to be an unending dream would reveal itself as a headlong rush toward some fateful climax beyond which lay chaos and destruction. The edifice of progress seemed to them like a tower of Pisa—an imposing structure precariously tilted on shallow foundations.

The very idea contained the seeds of its own eclipse; and Bury in an epilogue to his book asks: "But if we accept the reasonings on which the dogma of Progress is based, must we not carry them to their full conclusion? In escaping from the illusion of finality, is it legitimate to exempt that dogma itself? Must not it, too, submit to its own negation of finality? Will not that process of change, for which Progress is the optimistic name, compel 'Progress' too to fall from the commanding position in which it is now, with apparent security, enthroned? ... A day will come, in the revolutions of the centuries, when a new idea will usurp its place as the directing idea of humanity. Another star, unnoticed now or invisible, will climb up the intellectual heaven, and human emotions will react to its influence, human plans respond to its guidance.... In other words, does not Progress itself suggest that its value as a doctrine is only relative, corresponding to a certain not very advanced stage of civilization; just as Providence, in its day, was an idea of relative value, corresponding to a stage somewhat less advanced?" * Thus, from all sides, this idea, which seemed solidly substantiated in the material advancement of man no less than in his scientific progress, was under fire even before the evidence on its behalf had been fully presented; and before long the very word came to suggest a grandiose mirage of perpetual motion—the panacea of those who prefer not to move at all!

Clearly, the idea of limitless development, though based upon spectacular and unarguable advances, challenged common sense. Goethe, in a wise saying, had observed that the trees do not reach the sky. The second law of thermodynamics, if not indeed a critical scrutiny of the theory of evolution itself, would have sustained such a thought. A law of diminishing returns seemed somehow to be operative in the sphere of progress as well as elsewhere—if only because man could not keep up

* J. B. Bury, *The Idea of Progress* (New York: The Macmillan Company, 1932), pp. 351, 352.

with his own accelerated pace. Actually, the matter went deeper. Advances of the kind upon which the idea of progress was based are still going on; indeed, they promise to go on for a long time to come. The momentum of change has perhaps not even reached its apogee, and life may witness new revelations beside which the surprises of the past may fade into insignificance. But even such a state of affairs is a far cry from an unending progression, a vista of indefinite advance. Yet this essential continuity is the distinguishing feature of the conception of progress. As Bury pointed out, it is a theory built upon a synthesis of the past and a prophecy of the future—a future of limitless potentialities. Implicit in the idea is the presence of a unilinear, continuous, and progressive evolution. But in these very aspects the idea of progress is to be sharply distinguished from the notion of a basic change of direction marking a fateful climax in the historic process: at best the one idea is seen to be merely a tangential and premature projection of the other.

Their identification has, nonetheless, a momentary validity. This fact is readily explained. The foundations upon which the idea of progress rests—namely, the reorientation of values that began during the fifteenth and sixteenth centuries and came to fruition in the fuller development of science and technology—this basic recasting of values must likewise be recognized as the locus of a change of direction in world history. The ideas thus share a certain coincidence in time. But their paths soon diverge. For the idea of progress is a tangential conception, born of a high moment in that basic change of direction, and projected forward into the illimitable spaces of wishful thinking. The cumulative force of that change of direction was accepted as a token of endless change; the momentary slope of the curve of events was interpreted as its final direction; and the hopes of the moment carried the promise of indefinite and limitless advancement. Thus the sources and origin of the idea of progress are in fact related to the changes that herald the crucial turning point we are seeking; but the character and significance of that change will have to be defined in terms wholly independent of the idea of progress.

III

In contrast to the notion of sustained continuity, implicit in the idea of progress, two conceptions of a quite different complexion support the conjecture of a change of historic direction. For such a change of direction must be viewed in the light of a more or less abrupt break, of an interruption or climax, in the basic compulsions and primary forces of man's development. Nor need such a phenomenon astonish us: nature not infrequently displays limits beyond which new phases appear—witness the freezing of water; the formation of coal; the birth of a nova in the skies. Continuity is but one aspect of natural processes; and, along with unilinear growth, evolution embraces the phenomena of climax and culmination, change within change, and transformations as unexpected as they are amazing. The readily accepted notion that history will inevitably follow a continuous course without break or climax, devoid of any possible comprehensive transformations, any basic and significant changes of phase, must be held to be as arbitrary, dogmatic, and essentially unimaginative as the contrary notion that history is a directionless chaos. Moreover, such an assumption neglects the drastic transition encompassed by man in the evolution of his development from a prehistoric to a historic status. The cumulative forces within the locus of historic events alone assure us that history cannot forever mirror the identical drama against the admittedly changing backdrop of local customs and random fashions. Seen in their totality, historic events constitute a historic process. The significance of that process, however, cannot be apprehended until, as with a mathematical curve, we have established its formula and determined its inherent characteristics. Meanwhile, the supposition that a decisive turn in the course of historic events has at length afforded us an unexpected profile view of the past, so to speak, is augmented by the relatively recent efforts to define the meaning of history, to establish a science or, at the least, a philosophy of history. Like the first established pieces of a jigsaw puzzle, the historic process gives evidence of a pattern—intimations of a significant design.

The virtue of a sound hypothesis consists in subsuming a thousand facts while predicating still other and undisclosed relationships. The conception of history as the arena of a vast struggle between the forces of instinct ,and intelligence, in which, sooner or later, mankind will find itself compelled to accept a change of direction in its course, is sustained not only by the visible triumphs of intelligence but by certain emerging aspects of the historic picture that herald a basic and profound confinement and limitation of human endeavor. The notion of a continuous progression is thus limited by the attainment of these ultimate conditions which, for want of a better term, might be called *perimeters of the future*. If the development of man has come within sight of such ultimate aspects, it is plain that to this extent his condition in the future will be one of fixity and permanence rather than one of change. Nor can we doubt that the impact of these boundaries will in time be reflected throughout his domain; and that in adjusting himself ever more closely to such insurmountable barriers he is already defining ultimate patterns of living. But another and totally different set of conditions lends support to the notion of a crucial turning point in his affairs. If the development of man has in general exhibited a deepening of consciousness, the historic aspect of the process has been characterized rather by a steady translation of instinctually rooted values and concepts into equivalent patterns erected on a purely rationalistic basis. This *principle of equivalence*, which in itself must be held accountable for an unending series of clashes and conflicts throughout history, gives promise not so much of a drama of ceaseless opposition as of signs of an emerging climax, after which the whole drift of human existence must once more inevitably move toward goals of "fixity and permanence." Thus there are elements of finality rather than continuity in the development of man that are emerging in ever clearer and more decisive forms.

Man has already achieved in this respect certain limits within which his future development must take shape. Such limits define his potentialities and serve as boundaries for his efforts and his aims. In respect to such perimeters he has no choice but to conform; and in these ultimate landmarks the world of the future—however it may finally shape itself—is already determined and brought to focus. Thus, the circumnavigation of the globe in the early years of the sixteenth century confined the world; and the implicit consequences of that limitation have not yet been fully absorbed. The impact of this spatial perimeter doubtless caused man to deflect his creative energies and his imagination toward more intensive explorations of the dimension of time. In this effort he evolved a world of machinery. Meanwhile, the actual circumnavigation of the globe gave a natural impetus to the notion of ultimate world unity; and it is not surprising to find Jean Bodin, a French historian, who wrote just a few decades after Magellan's voyage, already aware, according to Bury, of these implications in all their modern meaning. "He had a conception of the common interests of all the people of the earth," writes Bury, "a conception which corresponded to the old ecumenical idea of the Greeks and the Romans, but had now a new significance through the discoveries of modern navigators. He speaks repeatedly of the world as a universal state, and suggests that the various races, by their peculiar aptitudes and qualities, contribute to the common good of the whole. The idea of the 'solidarity' of peoples was to be an important element in the growth of the doctrine of Progress." *

Four centuries later the unification of the world became a critical and pressing problem. The major political, social, and economic aspects of the world today are related in one way or another to the basic need for universal integration and a single, comprehensive, world-wide organization of man both as consumer and producer. The trend in this direction, already realized in certain respects, is emerging in ever clearer form as an inescapable necessity under pressure of world events. The transition of a world of national states into a single, international fraternity of peoples on a world-wide scale involves a conflict between instinctive responses, based upon age-old residues of thought and feeling, and the reactions of intelligence confronted by the immediate realities and pressing implications

* J. B. Bury, *The Idea of Progress* (New York: The Macmillan Company, 1932), pp. 43, 44.

of the situation as it exists today. Behind each specific element in this problem we may detect the converging drift and insistent pressure of that universal trend toward organization which, as we have seen, is inherently correlated with the dominance of intelligence in the affairs of man. The fact of a bounded world gives form and focus to this trend, as a container enables water to find its level. With the establishment of a terrestrial perimeter, internationalism became an implicit reality; and, ever since, the tentative steps toward its attainment have carried the conviction of its ultimate achievement. It is not unlikely that, before the present century will have run its course, we shall be privileged to witness the crystallization of this idea; and in time internationalism may well reach the same degree of development, of internal co-ordination and integration, that we now associate with the idea of nationalism.

Incidentally, it is worthy of note in this connection that the idea of a consciously contrived international or universal language emerged in response to the general trend toward greater unification and cohesion in world affairs.* Of the many phases of life affected by internationalism, the idea of a universal language carries with it a symbolic significance, an avowal of the essential unity of mankind. Actually mathematics has served to fulfill this integrating function in a wholly abstract but perhaps therefore all the more telling sense. Because of its aloof character it penetrates all boundaries, establishing a universally acceptable framework for the expression of its endless developments. The role of mathematics in the transformation of the modern world is truly incalculable: not only is it the language of science, it is an essential instrument of technology, and perhaps esthetically as well as logically the ultimate language of mankind. As the highest expression of the intellect, mathematics is at the very antipodes from the instincts; and from our point of view it is not without significance that the triumphant developments of modern mathematics, overshadowing the entire heritage from the ancient world, should have

---

* It is interesting to observe that virtually all efforts to establish a universal language took shape during the nineteenth century. Esperanto was initiated in 1887. A very early effort, however, by Bishop Wilkins bears the date 1668.

been ushered in during the early years of the seventeenth century. The immense burgeoning of mathematical thought during the ensuing centuries may thus be looked upon as the essential vehicle without which neither the progress in science nor that in technology could have materialized. Through mathematics the generalities of nature are garnered into the laws of nature; and man has thus gained an instrument of exploration which permits him to fathom the world of possibilities in ways completely inaccessible to the instincts. And as a consequence the universe has become his environment.

Intelligence, indeed, may be said to bear the same relation to the universe at large that the instincts bear to our immediate environment. As an instrument of adaptation the instincts bear a relation to nature; intelligence, as we have noted, to the laws of nature. This distinction does more than mark the difference between the unconscious adaptations of instinct and the conscious adaptations of intelligence: it establishes a new environment in which man now finds himself and to which he must now adapt himself. By orientating himself according to the laws of nature—however he may see fit to change their statement and formulation—man has in a sense completed his divergence from nature through the agency of his intelligence. And to the degree in which he comes to adjust his ways of life to the unchanging verities of these laws he will approach fixed perimeters in his future development. It may well be, as Bertrand Russell suggests, that the so-called laws of nature "... have turned out to be in some cases human conventions, in others mere statistical averages." Nonetheless, they approximate, even if they do not express with final exactitude, an underlying invariance in the processes of nature. The acceptance of these laws as an inevitable basis of adaptation constitutes in itself a perimeter of man's behavior; and, in conforming to the unvarying laws behind the changing façade of nature, he will of necessity tend toward ever greater uniformity and stability in his reactions. The point may be illustrated by the vast range of effects imposed upon him by the natural diversity of climate and topography in contrast to the undeviating character of such a force as electricity, which presents at all times and everywhere the selfsame aspects. Its universal identity has an inherently unifying effect; in a similar manner the laws of nature will enforce upon man identical, primary, and comprehensive adaptations along with his incidental adjustments to variants of such character as climate or locale. The laws of nature, however subject to revision and restatement, may thus come to constitute in time a new and far more compelling environment than nature itself. And in the degree in which they become crystallized and final—because of some irreducible statement of their relationships, or because man no longer has the power of further penetration into unknown regions— they will inevitably come to function as fixed perimeters of the future.

In adapting himself to the so-called laws of nature, man has mastered an entirely new gambit in the game of survival: he has learned to adjust his environment to himself. Perhaps, indeed, his earliest efforts in agriculture already foreshadowed a change in this direction; but the fuller mastery of nature began in fact only with the advent of science. Looking upon the matter from a wide perspective makes it clear that this incredible deviation from the biologic hierarchy set man apart and insured his supreme triumph. But it also reveals, from the very beginning, a dichotomic approach to the problem of adjustment and survival: clearly man's extraordinary audacity, his unique success, are due not to his instincts but to his intelligence. When he has at length insured his triumph by establishing an environment more readily adapted to himself, it is evident that his instinctual equipment must sooner or later prove inadequate, if not extraneous and obsolete. The dominance of intelligence and the decline, relative or actual, of the instincts will thus be assured, if only because the medium within which the instincts can function will have been supplanted by one far more suitable to the operations of intelligence.

Perhaps the most striking perimeter of the future that science has already vouchsafed us lies, significantly enough, in the field of communication. Little more than a century ago man's means of communication differed little if at all from those of the ancient Babylonians and Phoenicians. Only yesterday, in one magnificent leap, as it were, man attained world-wide scope combined with ultimate speed in his methods and systems of communication. The radio, the telephone, and television may doubtless be improved; their speed, which is that of electricity, can never be exceeded, since it is virtually instantaneous. With the temporary exception of television, their reach is already world-wide and cannot be extended. It was the faculty of communication which started man in the first place upon his long course of development; and again it was the invention of an alphabet, and later of the printing press, that profoundly accelerated this development; while in our own day the achievement of universal and instantaneous vehicles of expression must certainly be counted as one aspect of his ultimate development. The full effects of having attained this perimeter have not yet been realized, but they promise to be overwhelming and decisive. Certainly the sudden realization of this ultimate goal must greatly hasten the dissemination of knowledge and the unification of the world. But knowledge, as we have seen, is the fulcrum of intelligence; its wider diffusion will only intensify the dominance of intelligence over instinct as a guiding principle, and this inherent trend must hasten the ultimate organization of mankind. In the long run knowledge can be neither perverted nor limited arbitrarily, and in the final accounting no force will be able to subvert either its power or its range. Mankind will share its inheritance in this respect with unequivocal freedom, whatever the obstacles, if only because knowledge springs up anew behind every barrier. The limitations in this direction—if such limitations should eventually disclose themselves—will be due wholly to the not unlikely possibility of some future perimeter to human knowledge itself.

The idea that knowledge may have ultimate limits is not new. Intimations of such inherent boundaries have already been sighted, particularly in certain recondite fields of research such as the so-called indeterminacy principle in physics. Knowledge of the infinite, as in mathematics, is naturally not to be confused with infinite knowledge; and it is questionable whether the human mind as the instrument of knowledge must not sooner or later reach its own finite and inevitable limitations. But quite apart from direct restrictions in this sense, it may be questioned whether the span of human life could ever be sufficiently prolonged, as Bernard Shaw contemplated in *Back to Methuselah,* for man effectively to co-ordinate his knowledge into a significant and workable whole, assuming that his advances in any given direction were not in themselves limited. The indications that man must thus at some time or other come upon certain inherent boundaries to his knowledge, or to his ability to assimilate and co-ordinate into a significant whole the cumulative knowledge of mankind, give rise to the notion of an ultimate perimeter in this quarter of human endeavor. Such a perimeter is by no means a fanciful limit, like the ancient conception of the edge of the world, but an implicit possibility that has indeed already been anticipated. While such a condition may perhaps never be fully realized, it is plain that as knowledge expands toward an inherent saturation point, like a mathematical variable approaching a limit, it will no longer operate as an effectual instrument of change; on the. contrary, it must then become itself a factor of increasing fixity and permanence in the affairs of man.

Meanwhile the cumulative increase in knowledge must tend to shift the balance in man's attitude toward a rational in place of an instinctual solution of his problems. The conscious trend toward such a change was already clearly in evidence in the eighteenth century—the century of enlightenment—and perhaps indeed much earlier.* Man's acceptance of this principle, however, was far more apparent in his relationship to nature than to himself. Such a lag in his development might have been anticipated, since the rational approach was made easier by half where objective facts rather than subjective feelings were involved. But the phenomenal and wholly unexpected success that crowned the clarification of man's relation to nature sanctioned a similar approach in the more subtle, complex, and intimate field of his social relations as well. The power of

* See J. B. Bury, *A History of the Freedom of Thought* (New York: Henry Holt and Company, 1913).

analogy, in what came to be regarded as basically a homogeneous universe, was all but conclusive; and even today the social sciences, in their efforts to penetrate more fully into the nature of man, are deeply motivated by analogies based upon hypotheses in the physical and biological sciences.

The often painful evidences of lag in the social life of today reflect the immense tension under which the conflict between instinctually rooted values and rationally based concepts takes place. The notion of lag implies a delay—a temporal hiatus that will be healed in time. But in truth it arises out of an inherent cleavage, a divergence in direction, that will only increase with time. The reduction of lag implies thus always a triumph of one element of conflict over the other, rather than their convergence; and the whole process, as we have seen, is effected by a colossal transformation of values in every aspect of life and society. In that transformation the body of objective knowledge—accumulating according to some geometrical progression—exerts an implacable pressure in favor of intelligence. Knowledge, it is clear, has not only changed man's relation to nature: inexorably it will change man's relation to man.

IV

The transition from a preconscious to an increasingly conscious mode of existence involves a process of translation, so to speak, in which certain aspects of life reappear in equivalent, if modified, forms. Such transformations will be characterized by a kind of symmetry, since they represent identical realities under divergent modes of operation. Man's temporal awareness under the dominance of instinctual values, for example, expresses itself in an emphasis upon the past; under that of intelligence, upon the future. It is not surprising that primitive peoples, looking upon a state of fixity and stability as natural, should face toward the past—toward that which is established; while we, on the contrary, accepting change as the invariant condition of life, turn toward the future—toward that which is not yet realized. Their temporal orientation points toward a still more unconscious state in comparison with their own; ours toward increasing consciousness. This complete transposition is illustrated in the contrast between the high ceremonial devotion accorded the dead throughout antiquity, and our own increasing concern with the yet unborn. It is shown in such matters as the formal educational system of the Egyptians, which, according to Flinders Petrie, centered largely in a "routine of memory" *—in the establishment of a confining wall of set ideas and fixed rituals. For the Egyptians, as indeed for medieval Christianity, only the dead had a future. Believing in rigid ancestor worship, they were deeply concerned with the life of the departed, as revealed in their burial tombs and pyramids, their hieratical art, their mummies, and their endless funeral rites. In contrast, modern man, hounded by the pressure of increasing change, reinforced by a consciousness of time itself, is becoming ever more aware of some imminent climax in his affairs; and never before has he been so conscious of or so curious about his future, not individually but in the collective generations to come. It is a commonplace of modern literature to be concerned with the nature of that future and to venture predictions concerning it: witness the title of such a symposium as *Whither Mankind.* The classics of ancient Egypt, on the other hand, were concerned with the ritual of the departed, and bear such titles as *The Book of the Netherworld,* or *The Book of Coming Forth by Day,* known to us as *The Book of the Dead.*

Man, it is reasonable to suppose, must originally have been wholly adjusted to the tempo of nature itself—to the serene turning of the heavens, the even flow of the seasons, or the sudden flash of his prey. But, as he was weaned from his earlier communion with nature, he gradually came to experience time in a new sense and to establish a tempo of his own fashioning. Time was no longer the passing moment accepted with unconscious compliance; it became a pressing reality hurrying him onward from one instant of unstable equilibrium to the next. If primitive man accepted the movement of time without challenge, we have become conscious of time as a medium

* See W. M. Flinders Petrie, *Social Life in Ancient Egypt* (Boston and New York: Houghton Mifflin Company, 1923).

within which all our activities are realized: for us it is an endless backdrop against which we measure all other changes.
And as the rate of change itself has advanced enormously during the course of history, we have become increasingly aware
of the passage of time—the future melting ever more rapidly
into the past. Time has become for us, so to speak, a malleable
entity. Our timepieces are not only devices by means of which
we establish a rhythm of our own, independent of nature, but
a tally enabling us to measure the extent by which we have
"gained upon time." Timepieces are instruments of temporal
order—through them man can organize his affairs in respect
to the dimension of time with something of the same precision
he had long applied to space alone. It is significant that clocks
were among the first mechanical contrivances, such timepieces
having been in use, according to Lewis Mumford, since the
thirteenth century. Ever since, as he points out in his fascinating volume on *Technics and Civilization,* they have served not
only to "synchronize the actions of man" but to symbolize the
world of mechanics; and it is interesting to note in this connection that Samuel Butler uses the incident of wearing a watch
as the opening theme of *Erewhon*—a satiric legend based on
the calamitous consequences of mechanization.

The organization of time required an instrument of arbitrary
and methodical regularity; in this respect the clock proved as
precise and objective as the yardstick. And in establishing
Greenwich time, a co-ordination that was perfected and accepted only toward the end of the last century, man sanctioned
the idea of a universal perimeter or fixed standard of time—a
unifying rhythm of world-wide scope. Thus in the categories of
both time and space man has enveloped his world in a mathematical mesh: his every activity is embodied within a Cartesian
system of time and space references. Such a systematization
facilitates the ultimate organization of mankind on a global
scale: it constitutes the necessary unifying and co-ordinating
framework within which all else may be measured and correlated.

The consciousness of time made man aware of events in a
new sense: he no longer views them as discrete happenings but

as related in connected sequences, in series and processes. Events are seen to possess relationship and continuity: we speak of a "chain of events"; and the idea of evolution, the conception of history as a sustained and connected panorama, like all ideas of development and progress or of dissolution and retrogression, involve, in one sense or another, the conception of time. Science is inconceivable without the notion of time, as religion is without the idea of eternity. In centering his attention upon mundane affairs, in deepening his sense of time and widening his consciousness of events, man at length lessened his concern with eternity; and, along with this slow transition in which he focused his thoughts upon the foreground of his perspective, science usurped the interest if not the devotion formerly accorded to religion. And in harmony with this changed horizon man transferred his reliance upon implicit values to a new faith in explicit knowledge. The conscious discipline of science thus served as a kind of equivalent approach to the intuitive perceptions of religion, even though the incommensurable world of values could not be directly translated into the measurable values of the world. The change in emphasis from religion to science—quite apart from any metaphysical question of their compatibility—thus marked a definite drift from man's faith in intuitively established evaluations to an ever more deliberate and conscious procedure in the solution of his problems and the assuagement of his doubts.

A number of characteristic pairs of equivalents were indicated in a previous chapter by way of clarifying the notion of an inherent drift from preconscious to ever more conscious modes of procedure in the course of history. The emergence of such equivalents marks the span of a vast transition that must be interpreted at its high moment as a definite change of direction in the final development of man. In its comprehensive sweep this drift has affected virtually every facet of human existence, and illustrations of the principle are everywhere at hand. Thus, for example, even in the much disputed nature of the changes and developments in land ownership and tenure, we may clearly trace the general pattern and characteristic stages of this process of transformation. Despite the immense diversity in customs and folkways concerning land usage, and the formidable differences of opinion among anthropologists concerning the interpretation to be placed upon this vast body of often conflicting data, it is nonetheless possible to discern a general trend in harmony with the overwhelming drift from instinctual modes of operation to increasingly rational conceptions and procedures.

In a relatively recent critical survey of this much disputed problem, Melville J. Herskovits states the matter as follows: "The concept of primitive land tenure as a kind of 'inherited use ownership' clears a good many points. This is the reason, for instance, why rent is so rarely encountered, while this approach would seem to settle once and for all the controversy regarding private as against communal holding of land. For as far as the land itself is concerned, while it is in the vast majority of instances tribally controlled or, where this is not the case, owned by families, the right of the individual to retain it for his use gives tenure the complexion of ownership. Private ownership of land, however, implies greater rights than are generally accorded in primitive systems, while communistic tenure assumes that the individual has fewer rights than are found in practice. Primitive folk are concerned with the products of the land, not with land itself; and this is perhaps a reflex of the lack of economic surplus, production thus being for use and attention being focused on yield rather than on land as such." *

The intensification of individual private ownership with exclusive rights of disposal and absolute control in the uses of land tenure is characteristic of modern capitalistic society in a degree virtually unknown to primitive society. Primitive land tenure, even where it is individual, has a definitely social complexion, accentuated by the universal custom of sharing in the produce when conditions dictate. The return to the idea of land as a prime factor in the principle of production for use bridges the individualistic attitude and relates an earlier, more or less communal approach to the meaning of the land as the

* Melville J. Herskovits, *The Economic Life of Primitive Peoples* (New York: Alfred A. Knopf, Inc., 1940), p. 329.

source of supplies for the group at large with modern, rationally derived, communistic principles of land ownership and tenure. Needless to say, modern technological advances tend to reduce individual cultivation of the land to an anachronism. Thus, under primitive conditions, land was generally owned in a group or communal sense—even if it was individually worked and the produce individually owned;—whereas the social tendency today favors a collectivist use as well as ownership of land, because of modern machine methods of agriculture.

John Gunther, speaking of Mexico in his book *Inside Latin America,* contributes an interesting confirmation of this idea of equivalence in respect to land ownership and tenure. "The basic problem of the revolution," he writes, "is to make a successful land reform on *ejido* principles.... Its implications go back at least four hundred years to Aztec times, when clans owned land in common. The peasants worked the community area jointly; they pooled their resources and efforts, and shared the results. And it is the *ejido* system which the Mexican land reform attempts essentially to recreate. It resembles, as is obvious, such highly modern experiments as collective farming in the Soviet Union. Yet the inspiration for the Mexican procedure does not derive from Marxist doctrine. It is a throwback to the commun*al* (not commun*ist*) practice of the Aztecs." * The equivalence of communal practice and communist doctrine—the one instinctually derived, the other rationally—so clearly enunciated here, explains what seemed to many observers of Soviet Russia a mystery: namely, that a relatively primitive people should have been able to advance into the future at one step, as it were. But the essential identity of communal and communistic principles, operating under divergent modes of procedure, the one instinctual, the other rational, as indicated above, explains this apparent anomaly.

Man's societal relations and obligations in their more primitive forms, fashioned by his instincts, emerge in the guise of unconscious participation in long-established habits and customs. Under the guidance of intelligence these relationships

* John Gunther, *Inside Latin America* (New York: Harper and Brothers, 1941), p. 67.

tend to find expression through conscious consent or explicit regulations, proscriptions, and laws. Primitive man, turned inward, expelled those who transgressed his accepted norms; modern man, facing outward, incarcerates those who transgress his established patterns and laws. Such equivalent behavior patterns might readily be multiplied, tracing always a course from less conscious to more conscious forms and conceptions. Increasingly, the relation of the individual to society is reflected in manifestly deliberate forms of association and organization. Expansion, fact, work—sustained by a vast mesh of conscious relationships—characterize the modern world. Implicit participation, faith, habits and customs unconsciously established, distinguish the life of primitive man. In the conscious interrelationships of modern life we may perceive a converging movement embracing ever wider arcs of life, as though the slowly accelerated shift from instinctual values to those of intelligence transformed the whole of human existence into ever more sharply focused, explicitly articulated elements of a vast and co-ordinated design.

Oswald Spengler, with characteristic vehemence, has made much of this antithesis. But he conceives the distinction as applicable more to the various stages of culture and civilization, characteristic of all peoples, than to mankind as a whole. Indeed, limiting the operation of these forces to the histories of specific peoples, he has arbitrarily chosen to ignore mankind as a meaningful historic concept and to deny, in fact, the possibility of its development under the impact of the same basic principles. But this is to deny a life history to the forest while granting similar life cycles to the trees. The truth is that his incisive characterizations of culture and civilization as inherent stages in the evolution of human societies are clearly based upon the operation of universal principles whose scope embraces life forms in all their range of scale and complexity. Under the restricted formula of his particular philosophy of history, he has nonetheless plumbed the depths of this antithesis with sharp precision; and his statements, if capriciously limited in their meaning, are worthy of quotation for their penetrating distinctions.

"...Not external life and conduct, not institutions and customs, but the deepest and last things are in question here—the inward finishedness (Fertigsein) of megalopolitan man, *and* of the provincial as well. For the Classical world this condition set in with the Roman age; for us it will set in from about the year 2000.

"Culture and Civilization—the living body of a soul and the mummy of it. For Western existence the distinction lies at about the year 1800—on the one side of that frontier life in fullness and sureness of itself, formed by growth from within, in one great uninterrupted evolution from Gothic childhood to Goethe and Napoleon, and on the other the autumnal, artificial, rootless life of our great cities, under forms fashioned by the intellect. Culture and Civilization—the organism born of Mother Earth, and the mechanism proceeding from hardened fabric. Culture-man lives inwards, Civilization-man outwards in space and amongst bodies and 'facts.'

"Scientific worlds are superficial worlds, practical, soulless, and purely extensive worlds.... Life is no longer lived as something self-evident—hardly a matter of consciousness, let alone choice—or to be accepted as God-willed destiny, but it is to be treated as a problem, presented as the intellect sees it, judged by 'utilitarian' or 'rational' criteria.... The brain rules, because the soul abdicates. Culture-men live unconsciously, Civilization-men consciously." *

Behind this somewhat awesome manner of analysis one perceives the conception of a definite historic trend. According to Spengler this trend will presumably reach its culmination for Western civilization between the years 1800 and 2000. This climax, however, will more likely signify a change of direction for mankind as a whole. For the trend here indicated, as we have seen, is plainly an inherent and inevitable drift characteristic of the development of man irrespective of its special manifestations within particular cultures. If the fate of Western civilization seems to have been identified, in the course of this argument, with that of the world at large, it is because

* Oswald Spengler, *The Decline of the West* (New York: Alfred A. Knopf, Inc., 1926), pp. 352, 353.

today Western civilization reveals decisive factors of world-wide scope—not the least of which is the likelihood that the destiny of the Orient will become absorbed and entwined with that of the Occident in the very act of a wider synthesis, in a world coalescence. And in this connection it is worthy of note that, in the slow mutations from unconscious or preconscious patterns and customs and habits of life to their equivalent conscious formulations, man has not infrequently skipped all intervening stages and accepted a far more advanced level of development with primitive ardor, as in Soviet Russia, or with renascent vigor, as in modern China—examples that may well be followed in time by a modernized India. The explanation of this far-ranging phenomenon is doubtless to be ascribed to the well-nigh miraculous powers of transformation inherent in the machine; but in any event it heralds the ultimate unification of the world under the inexorable influence of a predominantly rational dispensation.

The antithesis between culture and civilization indicated above depends wholly upon the interpretations we choose to place upon these terms. Generally speaking, they are held to be synonymous; and certainly, however sharply defined, their meanings overlap and interpenetrate. As here used they are intended to emphasize the inherent shift in dominance between those life-forces rooted in instinct, in feeling and intuition, on the one hand, and the more rational, analytical faculties associated with intelligence, on the other. In what might be deemed a literary as distinguished from a purely anthropological use of the term, culture has come to signify an amalgam of ideal values expressive of the highest achievements of a civilization. In this sense culture represents a profound ideality: the goal of attaining a higher approach to life by integrating in a fused synthesis the contradictory facets of instinct and intelligence. The delicate balance of thought and feeling, the ever shifting emphasis and conflict of values, the underlying urge to achieve a significant harmony and a wider correlation of the values of life—all these desired ends testify to an inherent and unstable movement within the cultural complex itself. The ·iage of its elements in all their endless diversity dissolves

as soon as it is formed; and the kaleidoscopic changes that accompany this mirage of unity in the guise of fashions and
styles, periods and schools, movements and cults, trends and
countertendencies—all the febrile activities and restless seeking of values and forms, of truths and principles—are in fact
the unstable aspects of an impossible harmony. For culture
and civilization, like instinct and intelligence, in which they
are respectively rooted, are divergent and not confluent elements in the life of man. It is this fact that may account in
part at least for the decline of individual peoples and cultures
throughout history; but it is not to be assumed that the same
significance can be attached to this antithesis for mankind as
a whole. That constitutes a problem of another order to which
world history alone can give a final answer, and to which, meanwhile, only a world-view of history can contribute.

V

Culture, in the sense here indicated, attains its ultimate vehicle of expression in an anarchic, self-sufficient individualism
—the clear manifestation of a transitional philosophy. For the
higher synthesis which culture implies is itself unstable and
hence incapable of sustaining an established system of values;
only the individual as such can be sufficiently agile and eclectic
to follow its shifting sanctions. Arising out of a dualism of essentially incompatible forces, culture represents at every stage
a momentary and fleeting fusion that dissolves into one or the
other of its major components in the very act of being realized
and acclaimed. As the power and influence of instinctually
rooted ideas, conceptions, feelings, and values are finally coun-
terbalanced by those based upon intelligence, life assumes its
richest and ripest glow: and it is not surprising that such a
high moment in the development of cultural individualism
should have its sunset flare in the heroic figure of Nietzsche's
Superman. Individualism could go no further: thereafter the
philosophy of anarchism, as of individualism, was forced to
fight a rearguard action, harassed at every turn by the cumulative power of events that converged, as by some inherent de-

sign, toward an opposite pole. For the ideal of individualism shunned by implication the elementary gravitational force of humanity; and, unlike the medieval conception of the infinite worth of the individual—or rather of the individual soul—cultural individualism called for the development of the self as an isolated atom, distinct, unique, and valuable only in so far as it might be distinguished and set apart from the social mass.

The expansionist trend that accompanied the heightened consciousness of the Renaissance and its ensuing periods reached its zenith in a philosophy of individualism, of a zealous aggrandizement of the self; and significantly the explorer became the symbol of men of courage and independence in all fields alike, whether of art or science, commerce or politics, industry or philosophy. The conception of the self as a dynamic and irreducible entity called forth those doctrines of freedom and liberty that in turn nourished the cultural and political, no less than the religious, salvation of the individual. Freedom and liberty, however, must be recognized as tangential ideals; projections of an individualistic and transitional philosophy silhouetted against a background of events moving in an opposite direction. The true nature of the present is perhaps nowhere more clearly revealed than in the frantic efforts now prevalent to harmonize the ideals of freedom and liberty with the will and sweep of a nameless determinism, mistakenly identified with the will of the masses but in fact due to the pressure of an inescapable reliance upon intelligence in place of instinct in the affairs of man. That is the underlying theme of the twentieth century—the century of transition. For the lever which, from time immemorial, has been held down by instinctually rooted habits and customs is slowly being brought to a precarious balance by the ascending power and pressure of intelligence; and in this moment of unstable equilibrium life has reached a kind of incandescent pitch of intensity, of conflict, of immense and overwhelming contrasts. In the catastrophic hurry and confusion of this moment, mankind is busily translating the societal constraints and customs, the experience and insight of the past into new patterns; and in this interim individualism, whether that of the man of genius or of the entrepreneur, of the artist or of the scientist, of the gangster or of the dictator, arose and flourished as never before, while mankind is moving bag and baggage, despite untold dislocations, from an earlier domain to the house of the future.

It has been the supreme era of the individualist, and once past will never again return. Growing out of the moment of balance between two conflicting forces, individualism must vanish upon the resolution of that conflict as quickly as it arose. In broad, historic terms the changing status of the artist and the scientist may serve to illustrate the stages of this transition. Thus, primitive man, though often achieving a superb art, knew little or nothing of the artist; we, on the contrary, abounding in artists, know little of the grand traditions without which great art cannot flourish. The magnificent sculpture of so relatively advanced a people as the Egyptians was virtually all anonymously executed according to strict hieratical principles throughout the incredibly long era of their history. It is true the unsurpassed, primitive boastings of their Pharaohs would seem to indicate a high sense of individualism, but such outpourings cannot be appraised apart from their context within the accepted scheme of things. J. H. Breasted in speaking of Ikhnaton—the one Pharaoh in the long history of Egypt who sought to reform religious concepts in the light of reason —significantly calls him "the first individual" in all history! Egyptian art, like all early, primitive, and archaic art, is the more or less formal expression of the ethos of a folk. But a somewhat parallel or perhaps equivalent interpretation is to be placed upon certain tendencies in the art of Soviet Russia, where large-scale, anonymous enterprises are not unknown. Such manifestations serve to illustrate the principle of equivalence mentioned above—of the conscious translation and acceptance of preconscious or unconscious values, habits, and ways of thought and action. From the time of these earlier periods in art—including indeed the profound monuments of the deeply felt medieval tradition of the Christian era—to the very moment of a consciously motivated return to communal efforts accompanied by anonymity in modern times, art became increasingly a vehicle merely for the personal expression of the individual artist. Originality, a modern virtue, was neither sought nor possibly understood by the marvelous artisans and craftsmen responsible for the impressive monuments and noble sculpture of ancient Egypt. In time, however, individuality became the hallmark of excellence in art; and not only did the artist strive for a personal style, an individual idiom, he became increasingly concerned, as has often been remarked, with portraiture—not merely of distinguished personalities but, in a closely related sense, of everything else as well. In a word, he became the realistic reporter whose fidelity to fact alone was the *sine qua non* of his art. The abstractionism of today is a revolt against this trend; but it is also a harbinger of a return to a more universal, more deeply representative and therefore more abstract conception of expression. The art of the future, like that of the remote past, may well again be profound, direct, clear, and impersonal; it will doubtless reflect once again the basic attitudes of a people rather than the individualism of the artist. For the artist will himself become a vehicle of expression for the people, a voice, an articulate artisan, whose creative impulses will demand the suppression of his personality as the condition of his art. And as a symbol of his comprehension of this role he will remain anonymous.

In a somewhat different yet comparable sense the scientist follows a similar metamorphosis. During the Renaissance the scientist was indeed the greatest of "explorers," and as such his work reflected the individualistic character of the age; but from another point of view his work was always, in the nature of the case, integrated with that of others. Thus it presaged a pattern of thought and analysis affording a kind of counterpoint to individualism. The nature of science, as well as the trend of the world at large, for that matter, tend to emphasize the latter aspect of the scientist's work and relations; and it is not surprising to find that research is increasingly left to organized groups designed to eliminate the uncertainties of individual enterprises. The creative artist lurking within the man of science is thereby circumvented, as it were; and collective methods, within limits, are challenging if not displacing the individual genius in the field of scientific research. Thus, in a sense not altogether unlike that of the artist, the scientist may himself become merely the vehicle for the operation of the scientific method, and his function, like that of the artist, will be to serve the will of the social community quite apart from his own in the direction and execution of scientific enterprises. It is a portent of the times that while we may know the name of the president of the telephone system, for example—himself a symbol of its internal and external organizational setup—we are likely to be in ignorance of the anonymous scientists upon whose knowledge the perfection of the system comes to depend. The individual scientist, as such, having aided in the coming of age of ever larger co-operative enterprises, may be among the first casualties of the new dispensation, and, though science may prosper and develop, it will be without benefit of the individual geniuses of its pioneering days. For the scientist of the future, like the artist of the future, may conceivably work only within the framework and discipline of controlled and communal enterprises.

The eclipse of the individual is implicit in all the trends that point toward the future: indeed the tendency has already gone so far that we are likely to believe an inevitable reaction must set in, disproving the entire principle. But though such a contrary movement is already in evidence, its effects will prove illusory. In the confusion of forces that confront us nothing is plainer than the steady drift toward ever wider and more inclusive social relationships and, by the same token, a corresponding pressure upon the individual toward greater conformity, coherence, and compliance in ever wider arcs of life. All of this has been duly commented upon, but it may be worth reiterating if only because it establishes in still another aspect that principle of equivalence emphasized above. Thus, the earlier, unconscious mode of participation, based upon instinctually rooted habits and customs, is displaced at the other end of the scale by conscious and explicit behavior patterns demanding or imposing individual compliance with all the force of law or even, if need be, of physical coercion. But beneath this more obvious aspect of the modern picture, another factor of operation emerges, less apparent but ultimately far more potent—*the principle of predictability*.

Predictability is the child of science. Here too, however, we may speak of equivalence since man from earliest times peered into the future, or rather the unknown, by methods that, for all their weird unreality, nonetheless revealed an intuitive faith in the possibility of exploring the dark and hidden world—a possibility that science justified and realized in wholly unexpected measure. In time the blind and fumbling mysteries of magic and thaumaturgy, astrology and alchemy were duly translated into the concrete terms and focused visions of science. Not only did man gain incomparably in power and precision; he gained in a sense of mystery as well, and the ancient lore concerning numbers and dreams, for instance, seems trivial beside the depth of insight that psychoanalysis has vouchsafed us, or the awe-inspiring systems of number and space relations that mathematics has bequeathed to us. Science has been defined as applied common sense, but in fact it is the deliberate and conscious exercise of intelligence in the solution of the problems, practical and ideal, concrete and abstract, that beset man. If previously he used the chisel of intuition, now he would add the hammer of reason to sculpture a world more explicit, defined, and interrelated. In that process the idea of predictability emerged as the watchword of his efforts. By implication it rests upon those laws of nature which it is the object of science to unfold; but in the world of human affairs the principle of predictability rests upon nothing more substantial than the vague "hunches" and inexact guesses known as the lessons of experience or, in larger matters, the examples of history.

Now the important point in this picture is that, as science and technology advanced, man alone appeared a wayward and unpredictable entity in an otherwise ever more tractable universe. Such a situation becomes in time intolerable as the world is subject to increasing change; and the intelligent operation of human affairs thus required man to look upon himself objectively as part and parcel of his own system: he, too, had to become amenable to engineering calculations like his steel beams, his dynamos, and his turbines, to the end that men and machines might be correlated with the same nicety and precision achieved in their design. The attitude, new to man, of viewing himself in terms of averages, probabilities, and ratios; the immense extension of the use of numbers by way of identification, integration, and efficiency; the stark increase in the prevalence of the straight line, the circle, and other geometrical forms in modern life; and the introduction of modules and standardized units everywhere, from packaged bread to modernized houses, indicate at every turn a vast and interlocking trend toward greater predictability and organization. The whole conception of a planned economy, of a balanced system of production, distribution, and consumption marks the clear-cut impress of intelligence in the higher administration of man's affairs. But such a system cannot be realized without profound reverberations in the social relationships of man, resulting in wholly new structural and collective implications based always and everywhere upon the tacit principle of predictability. The effects of this principle upon the philosophy of individualism have not yet been fully realized; but in the solution of the mass problems of today it is plain that the individual *per se* will receive ever shorter shrift, and his subtlest and rarest contributions to life and values may in time appear so far out of line as to be considered evidence of unbalanced psychic deviations from the norm. The efficient functioning of the system will call for the ever more stringent reduction and elimination of friction; and the individual as such will either have been altogether submerged or, in the interest of higher predictability, pulverized like a grain of sand into nothingness.

Thus, the idea of equivalence in respect to the relationship between the individual and the group would seem to be substantiated: the absence of a dominant individualism in primitive life will be repeated in the mass patterns of the future. The self-conscious traits of individualism are seen to be the expression of a transitional and unstable cultural amalgam that must inevitably dissolve in the final dominance of intelligence over instinct.

VI

In exploring the reasons for believing that mankind has come upon a crucial epoch in its history, we have encountered certain perimeters of the future and certain equivalent modes of behavior expressive of the transition from an essentially preconscious past to an ever more conscious present. The evidence that mankind is passing through a nodal point in its development is equally patent in a series of trends that are approaching their culmination in our time or, even more significantly, that are arising out of the momentum of their past into wholly new and revolutionary phases.

Thus the rate of historic change, which considered over large periods of time has certainly followed a definitely accelerating rhythm, dependent doubtless in some remote way upon the cumulative aspects of knowledge, now appears to be nearing a climax in a state of virtually ceaseless change. Obviously such a situation justifies the assumption that we are approaching a nodal point in the course of history beyond which we may not unreasonably expect a corresponding decline in the rate of historic change. In harmony with this possibility it is well to remember that the wealth of cumulative knowledge, already exceeding in each defined subdivision the capacity of our most gifted minds (and this in itself is tantamount to a warning that we are approaching a saturation point) is plainly reaching a near, or perhaps even distant but nonethelesss definite, human limit. But such a limit would necessarily slow up the rate of historic change, presaging an increasingly stabilized condition in human affairs as man adapted himself with ever greater precision to his furthest boundaries, as to some mathematical limit toward which he would move with ever more mincing steps.

The idea that historic changes reveal a progressive rate of acceleration while at the same time shaping themselves into a significant world pattern is perhaps, thus stated, too neat and pat to be acceptable without a lengthy detour of scholarly reservations. The matter must needs be left in the hands of historians, but it is amply clear that throughout prehistoric times change followed a progressively accelerated time-rate. Recorded history covers a span of not more than some six thousand years, and, even though a further extension be allowed this period, plainly, in comparison with the prehistoric era, the whole of this historic period is in reality a singularly brief and effervescent affair. But the rate of change, rising steadily during the earlier period to a conscious pitch, now shot upward in the period of recorded history with unprecedented acceleration, until today man is breathlessly trying to keep up with himself in an ever faster cataract of changes. To gauge the degree of acceleration we need only bear in mind that Egyptian history alone covers a period of almost three thousand years, or virtually one half of recorded history. Yet it is dissociated from ourselves by the vast panorama of ancient, medieval, and modern history. The rate of historic change may indeed follow no precise law; yet, taken by and large, the tempo of history certainly appears to be mounting in an ever hurrying spiral. Periods of relative stability or stagnation are followed by epochs of exceptional activity and ferment, as though history suffered no lagging. Thus, the Renaissance followed upon the Middle Ages with the power of a force long dammed. Once the dykes of scholasticism were broken down, man entered with renewed vigor upon an era of fruitful thought and far-flung enterprise. Similarly, Russia, after the revolution, awoke, as it were, in the future; precisely as China and India, arising from their slumber, face today a new and challenging reality. Viewed in a sufficiently comprehensive perspective, history itself seems like a released force in the progression of man's development. For man, conscious of this progression, history becomes a distillation of experience in which change is seen to induce still further change with ever increasing velocity. Man has telescoped time; and the whole of history reveals a quickening pulse, an animated procession, an awakening into deliberate, inevitable, and conscious relationships of ever wider scope.

Now one aspect of this picture is of particular interest to us: namely, that the *rate of change* apparently increases with time, and that, under this accelerated schedule, either the trend must end in some ultimate limit or saturation point beyond which lies a new phase in the development of man, essentially different from that of his past, or the hurrying drift of events must end in meaningless chaos—in a final cacophony of change devoid of all direction. Before attempting to resolve this drastic alternative, it may be well to look at another curious and indeed paradoxical aspect of the process. Since history represents the rise of man into the field of conscious relations and conscious change, it is plausible to suppose that in general each new departure represents in turn an improved status over the immediately preceding condition; and that in consequence change might reasonably be expected to exhibit a definite slowing up rather than an acceleration with the passage of time. But precisely the reverse obtains; and we may see in this phenomenon the signs of an increasingly prevailing pressure or force, an inexorable and obligatory drift animating the whole historic process. Faced with this situation it would seem as though man is either blindly racing downhill to some ultimate perdition, despite his conscious participation in the process, or that he is in the grip of a compelling principle hurrying him onward toward a fate beyond his ken—indeed toward a state that can only be abstractly conceived as a wholly new phase of unknown potentialities. Plainly, man rushes onward with unwonted speed as change generates change. But what, we are forced to ask ourselves in the face of this undeniable acceleration, can be the principle upon which this inexorable development takes place?

The increasing speed of historic change, with its alternative implications of meaningless confusion or of a transition into some wholly new phase of human destiny, resolves itself into a problem of chaos and order, into a conflict of centrifugal and centripetal forces. Now it is interesting to note that not only change has increased with the passage of time but equally the socially inheritable knowledge that must be counted among the prime factors distinguishing man from the biologic hierarchy. That they are interrelated is self-evident. The very speed of historic changes has aided in bringing about a balancing centripetal drift toward increased organization; and as knowledge approaches an inherent limit so, too, change may reasonably be expected to subside and become in time progressively retarded. Clearly the rate of change tends toward a climax: at its zenith it may well mark the high point in the arc of man's development beyond which he will tend, inevitably, toward increased stability, fixity, and permanence. There is thus a kind of grand equivalence in the vast perspectives beyond the era of historic drama—one aspect reaching backward into the remote past; the other stretching forward into perhaps equally remote vistas of the future.

Meanwhile, in the immediate present, in our own age, we have come upon the threshold of new and unexplored vistas, of processes and trends that have attained wholly new and revolutionary aspects. For the first time in his history man stands on the threshold of an age of plenty. This extraordinary prospect is vouchsafed to us as a first fruit of attaining the status of a power age in place of a machine age—a status that, as Walter Polakov * has shown, must affect every aspect of our economy, our political order, and our social structure. In biology and its related fields we have only just achieved possibilities of organic manipulation that promise to outrival our far-flung triumphs in the world of chemistry and mechanics. Thanks to basic work in genetics and biochemistry, not only our food supply but we ourselves are destined to undergo profound changes. Indeed, genetics touches upon wholly unsuspected regions whose potentialities may well transform life beyond anything we now contemplate. The possibilities inherent in ectogenesis, or artificial insemination, already familiar in animal breeding, may well be extended to the human family in practices that go far beyond its present usages, with wholly new and startling results. Readers of *Daedalus* by Professor Haldane are acquainted with this development in the field of biologic invention. But the possibilities in this field

* Walter N. Polakov, *The Power Age*. For a contrary view concerning the "age of plenty" see F. A. Hayek, *The Road to Serfdom* (Chicago: The University of Chicago Press, 1944), p. 98. The argument that the productive capacity of the world has virtually reached its zenith seems, on the face of it, fallacious if not disingenuous.

have perhaps nowhere been explored more comprehensively and authoritatively than by Professor Hermann J. Muller in his prophetic analysis *Out of the Night;* and a hardly less spectacular and far-reaching perspective has been presented to us by Julian S. Huxley in his book, *Man Stands Alone.* In these essays we are invited to view the vista of evolution, consciously directed, rearing itself in sharp antithesis to the whole development of organic forms throughout the endless aeons of the past. Professor Muller has pictured for us not only the unique significance of this conscious divergence from the long-established order of nature but the sudden "explosive speed" of the change. "...And so our view changes, and we now see that, for the species as a whole (as the biologist looks at species), the possibilities are really unique and inexpressly stirring. The recently innovated process of social evolution, confined to man alone, has enabled him to push himself up into an isolated position, fraught with potentialities barred to any other animal. And within a paltry few centuries this process has entered into an utterly unprecedented phase, which makes it incomparably more potent still. For in this phase, man, and man alone, is acquiring the eyes of science wherewith to see the structure of nature and to guide his inventive hands towards the intelligent control both of the bits of cosmos immediately encompassing him and that within himself. If he would continue to raise himself, it must still be by his own efforts, but the productivity of his efforts is being indefinitely augmented. In terms of geologic time, this extension of power is going on at an explosive speed, with a volcanic violence unparalleled in all past evolution; and the reaches to which its conquests may extend, a trivial thousand years from now, seem utterly beyond romance." *

The last few centuries have indeed opened up unsuspected vistas, and the full implications of science, technology, and the world of machinery are so vast as to defy, even in our advanced day, the possibility of sensing their ultimate meaning or their final impact upon our ways of life and thought. Only

* Hermann J. Muller, *Out of the Night: A Biologist's View of the Future* (New York: Vanguard Press, 1935), p. 35.

today, after the world of the machine has already revolutionized man's whole manner of living, his economy, his political dogmas, his social values, does he deem the machine, as such, worthy of critical thought and appraisal. The facts of its implications had to overtake him before he believed in their powers and their effects. In an age of science man applied his newly acquired knowledge to everything but himself; and in time he found himself more ill-adjusted in a world of his own creation than in his previous, more natural condition. This reluctance to change as regards himself and his social attitudes is due wholly to his emotional, instinctual approach to the problem of human relations. But the growing disparity of his own maladjustment places him under an ever more stringent compulsion to accept a drastic reorientation, involving vast structural changes, as his present status vanishes in the birth of a universal and collectivized society. The climax of man's historic changes, at once imminent and inevitable, will be realized in its incipient stages through this basic, all-embracing transformation.

The most phenomenal, the most rapid and far-reaching change that mankind has ever experienced is unquestionably due to the development of the machine. This comparatively recent acquisition in the long history of mankind seems somehow alien, despite its authorship, to man's innate character, as it is alien and external, unlike the tool, to his bodily self. Nowhere do animate and inanimate nature appear to react upon each other more subtly or more strikingly. Two worlds meet in man and the machine, at once interdependent and incommensurate. Obeying man's will and at the same time every law of nature, the machine presents a kind of externalization and symbol of man's own dichotomic character—of his need for submission to nature to gain his freedom from nature. The tension, it is clear, can be resolved only by intelligence: it alone, pragmatically speaking, can dissolve the antinomy of freedom and determinism. And in this fact we may glean a reason for the apparently belated appearance of the machine in the long development of man. For it was not until late in his history, when intelligence had at length freed itself from the instinctual penumbra still clinging to its garments, that man could at long last draw a direct line between his means and his defined ends. Before he cleared away the tangled undergrowth of emotional and instinctual values that obstructed the foreground of his vision, he had concerned himself all too hopefully with timeless aims and illimitable ends: once he eschewed this search for the unattainable he found ready to hand the instruments of his mind for the solution of his more mundane problems. And of a sudden, upon the retrenchment of his wandering spirits, the machine answered his humbler prayer for release from the burdens of this world without recourse to the myth of a fairer world in the hereafter.*

But in this transaction he incurred a new and hidden debt which demanded payment in a subtle but inescapable conversion of his values. In the course of this profound change he came to doubt and distrust his most cherished ideas and his most acceptable dogmas. The anomaly was heightened by the fact that the machine, at once a source of pride and doubt, was after all the offspring of his own mind—or was it indeed a Frankenstein monster threatening its creator? This sense of being overwhelmed by the machine and its accompanying technology, of surrendering to the machine for good or ill, has

---

* Erich Kahler in his book *Man the Measure* (New York: Pantheon Books Inc., 1943) has an interesting passage supporting this point of view (pages 235, 236):

"Why did the great ancient cultures, especially the Greek and Roman, with their high development of the intellect and of political, social and commercial life, never focus their attention on nature as an object of human exploration and exploitation? Why did they not achieve a technical civilization, such as that of the modern world?

"It seems that there is only one answer to this problem: the prerequisite for the tremendous technical and industrial progress of our era is the modern concept of nature, and what prevented the ancient peoples from forming this concept, was religion, and the power it exerted over their minds throughout all ages and stages of their development. Religion is the one great antagonist of technology and economy. Religion presents the world as a consistent and coherent universe including both man and natural forces, connecting and uniting them intrinsically through a common divine order. And religion ties man down to rituals and customs, and thus deters him from giving his uninhibited and undivided attention to worldly aims. So it was the crumbling of the idea of a sanctified universe and the withering of the power of religion over man, it was, in brief, the process of secularization that divorced man from nature and freed his reason for mastering, exploring and exploiting the forces of the profane and material world...."

animated the thoughts of every critical and sensitive mind with fear or hope, ranging from the ironic pessimism of Samuel Butler's *Erewhon* to the arid optimism of Edward Bellamy's *Looking Backward*. For good or ill, the machine is obviously here to stay in an ever closer compact with life; and it is not accidental that this irresistible alliance should coincide with an overwhelming trend toward increased organization in every phase of our existence. In this connection it may be well to quote in full a passage by Lewis Mumford from *Technics and Civilization:*

"To understand the dominating role played by technics in modern civilization, one must explore in detail the preliminary period of ideological and social preparation. Not merely must one explain the existence of the new mechanical instruments: one must explain the culture that was ready to use them and profit by them so extensively. For note this: mechanization and regimentation are not new phenomena in history; what is new is the fact that these functions have been projected and embodied in organized forms which dominate every aspect of our existence. Other civilizations reached a high degree of technical proficiency without, apparently, being profoundly influenced by the methods and aims of technics. All the critical instruments of modern technology—the clock, the printing press, the water-mill, the magnetic compass, the loom, the lathe, gun-powder, paper, to say nothing of mathematics and chemistry and mechanics—existed in other cultures. The Chinese, the Arabs, the Greeks, long before the Northern European, had taken most of the first steps toward the machine. And although the great engineering works of the Cretans, the Egyptians, and the Romans were carried out mainly on an empirical basis, these peoples plainly had an abundance of technical skill at their command. They had machines; but they did not develop 'the machine.' It remained for the peoples of Western Europe to carry the physical sciences and the exact arts to a point no other culture had reached, and to adapt the whole mode of life to the pace and the capacities of the machine. How did this happen? How in fact could the machine take possession of European society until that society had, by an inner accommodation, surrendered to the machine?" *

Historically, according to Mumford, it was the clock more than any other early mechanism that ushered in the world of machinery. For it was the clock that gave concrete expression to the precise sense of order and routine upon which the discipline of the monastery depended; and in turn it was the need of regular prayer and devotions, and the presence of order throughout the institutions of the Church itself, that set the stage for that "inner accommodation" upon which the ultimate ascendancy of the machine depended. The order and systemization of church and counting house may well have developed those underlying modes of thought that sprang into material realization in the machine—though this gratuitous psychological preparation, this disciplining of mind and hand to the mechanical routine of the machine, cannot, by its very character of ingrained habituation, have furnished the spark that engendered the new world of the machine. What is new, Mumford admonishes us, is the fact that mechanization and regimentation "have been projected and embodied in organized forms which dominate every aspect of our existence." But the increasing incidence of organized forms is an expression, as we have seen, of a direct, inherent, and unavoidable compliance with the dictates of intelligence. Clearly, the triumphant development of the machine and of a machine technology had to wait upon the emergence of an unencumbered intelligence operating in a world of circumscribed and pragmatic values. In consequence the world of the machine, like the mechanisms from which it springs, presents a hard and rigid aspect in contrast to the subtle and intimate world of human values—and this essential incommensurability presents a problem that is but one aspect in the basic cleavage between instinct and intelligence. Today that problem presents itself to us in the anomaly of an impoverished inner life in the midst of an enriched world. Lewis Mumford raises this very issue in the concluding paragraph of his introduction to *Technics and*

* Lewis Mumford, *Technics and Civilization* (New York: Harcourt, Brace and Company, 1934), p. 4.

Civilization by asking whether the apparently mechanistic determinism of the modern world is inherent or merely the "turbid residue" of an earlier form of technology. The same question, in somewhat different terms, is implicit in the present inquiry.

VII

Despite many efforts to define and understand the machine, it seems nowhere to have been studied and interpreted as a type and example of organization. Yet, unquestionably, it is the most sharply contrived, the purest instance of organization the mind of man has conceived: a world that satisfies in every aspect the demands of intelligence wholly divorced from instinctual values. The machine consists always of specific means to precisely defined ends; of the coherent assemblage of its related parts toward the highest possible efficiency in the functioning of the whole; of interrelationships marshaled wholly toward a given result, a preconceived, precisely determined objective. In the degree in which the machine approaches perfection there can be neither extraneous parts nor extraneous movement: all is set, part for part, and motion within motion, toward the functioning of the whole in a given direction and the accomplishment of a fixed purpose. This perfect adjustment of means to a specific and defined end is the work of pure intelligence.

When the machine is thus defined and comprehended, it is clear why it did not arise in the course of human history until long after man had already achieved the necessary mental capacity and the necessary techniques for its consummation. He needed first to find himself at ease within the locus of intelligence apart from instinctual overtones and emotionally conditioned ends and purposes. The mental instrument for the successful development of the machine was at hand but not in a form suitable for its direct use. Not until intelligence could function in unalloyed freedom could the world of the machine arise in anything like its full potentialities. To become mechanical-minded meant not so much to achieve a new aspect in our thinking as to free our thought processes from extraneous feelings and sensibilities devoid of a valid role in the causal chain that led from a preconceived end to the means for attaining it. The conditioned attitude of mind that accompanied the rise of the machine age is evident in the curious survival of ornamental motifs in the earlier design of machine parts. The tentative, crude examples of the very earliest types of machines, however, lack this telltale adornment, much as very primitive furniture has a direct and honest simplicity of design; but it was not until the machine had come into its own, and mechanism became an accepted category of abstract ideas, that the machine designer freed himself altogether from these extraneous atavisms suggestive of an earlier age and another attitude. Indeed, the logic of this trend is discernible in the curiosity bestowed in the early days of mechanism upon automata whose mechanical principles were hidden beneath the human form, while today our curiosity is aroused by the spectacle of "Mechano, Marvel of the Age," whose human attributes are hidden behind a machine-like exterior. And, significantly, standing at the threshold of an age of universal mechanization, we have projected into the future the myth of the Robot, a creature half human, half mechanical.

This logic of function reveals itself in a clear and decisive manner in the development of modern architecture. Once called "the mother of the arts," architecture is rapidly becoming a science of rationalized forms devoid of all decorative counterpoint in its strict and barren formality. Divesting itself of style in the traditional sense of the term, architecture for the first time in the history of man reveals everywhere the same sheer and functional nudity. We have come, it is clear, not to a new synthesis of architectural elements but to a new divestment of all but the structural and functional requirements of design. The house, according to Le Corbusier and his school, has itself become a mere machine for living. This mechanical approach, eschewing the expression of all introvert values, has given rise to a characteristic mode of architectural expression—hard, direct, logical, and uncompromisingly puritanical. Needless to say, a reaction set in, a counterrevolution the purpose of which was to restore to its rightful place and ancient dignity the expression of human emotions. Curiously enough, Russia led in this counterrevolution, asserting in formal decree that the machine existed for man, not man for the machine! Yet this gesture, clothed in semilegalized form, gives more than a hint that no persuasion, no critical edicts can stem the tide of style and events, so interwoven in the language of architecture. It is noteworthy that, in the disappearance of those characteristic national style traits which have distinguished architecture in the past, we are witnessing the search for more basic and universal forms: the language of logic and of function endows architecture everywhere with the same stark similarity of form and treatment. We are approaching an internationalism in architecture as indeed in most other matters; and it is not surprising that an effort was made to establish the term "international style" for what is essentially a modern, functional, and above all severely rational solution of the architectural problems of today.*

The machine age, then, may be said to mark in at least one domain of our complex existence an achieved and conscious divergence between instinct and intelligence. Meanwhile, as intelligence asserted itself with increasing force in the new

---

* Modern architecture might be defined as the science of space organization. The logic of this approach is concerned not only with the functional relationships of the various space areas within a building structure; it involves equally the spatial and functional relationships of buildings to each other. Hence modern architecture, encompassing in its sweep the entire range of environmental and sociological relationships of the community, is basically concerned with the science of town planning. This larger approach to architecture has been well expressed by Sigfried Giedion in his volume, *Space, Time and Architecture* (Cambridge: Harvard University Press, 1941), p. 25:

"Architects today are perfectly aware that the future of architecture is inseparably bound up with town planning. A single beautiful house of a single fine residential development accomplishes very little. Everything depends on the unified organization of life. The interrelations between house, town, and country, or residence, labor and leisure, can no longer be left to chance. Conscious planning is demanded."

But this emphasis upon conscious planning and organization, upon the functional solution of space relationships, tends inevitably toward a purely rational approach, devoid of those intuitive expressions of feeling which, in the past, have entitled architecture to be considered an art as well as a science. The schism between feeling and thinking, so characteristic of the architecture of today, is but a reflection of a basic trend in our orientation toward the future. Speaking of this schism, Giedion wisely observes: "Thinking is trained; feeling is left untrained.... Knowledge and feeling are isolated from each other. So we arrive at the curious paradox that in our period feeling has become more difficult than thinking." (*Ibid.*, p. 585.)

world of technological development and scientific thought, its triumphant sanctions in these fields led man to hope that its dominance might be extended over the entire range of his conscious reactions and purposive responses. But history moves onward only through the resolution of opposing forces. Against this trend man attempted to reaffirm and re-establish that amalgam of values which reflected the range of his whole being and which was lost, at least for Western European man, with the dissolution of what has been aptly termed "The Great Tradition." In somewhat different terms Henri Bergson, in a famous passage, touches upon this same dichotomic aspect of man's nature. "Consciousness in man is preeminently intellect. It might have been, it ought, so it seems, to have been also intuition. Intuition and intellect represent two opposite directions of the work of consciousness: intuition goes in the very direction of life, intellect goes in the inverse direction, and thus finds itself naturally in accordance with the movement of matter. A complete and perfect humanity would be that in which these two forms of conscious activity should attain their full development." * Pragmatically, however, man developed his civilization at the expense of his culture—that is to say, he found himself compelled, in the irreversible drift of the historic process, to accentuate the cleavage between instinct and intelligence, or intuition and intellect, rather than to transcend these faculties in some higher synthesis. For culture—in the sense of a union of man's highest intellectual and emotional aspirations—rested precisely upon the hope of attaining, in ever more significant and expressive forms, a living synthesis of instinct and intelligence. But this ideal, however we may state it, had inherently only a passing validity. The trend of historic events soon showed that it blossomed only as the influences of instinct and intelligence reached a momentarily balanced status; and once that passed, the ideal vanished with it. Increasingly civilization came to represent the impact of intelligence upon the instincts, as former phases in man's development had represented the dominance of instinct over in-

---

* Henri Bergson, *Creative Evolution* (New York: Henry Holt and Company, c. 1911; Arthur Mitchell, c. 1938), p. 267.

telligence. The crucial turning point in this sweeping and profound reversal in man's approach to the problems of life was coincident with the conscious acceptance of the methods and aims, the values and perspectives, of the world of machine technology. For the machine marked the irreversible triumph of intelligence.

To gain an insight into the fuller meaning of this change it is necessary to understand the nature and significance of the machine, rather than to rehearse in admiration the never-ending mechanical and scientific innovations and inventions that have so miraculously transformed life. Confined wholly within the material sphere that constitutes, according to Bergson, the special province of the intellect, man has achieved in the machine a type of organization which surpasses in its orderly operation and functional design anything he has yet achieved in the more intimate realm of his own human relations. The machine, indeed, represents, as we have seen, the ideal embodiment of the principle of organization; and it is primarily from this angle that its ultimate contributions to the historic process must be weighed and apprehended. For therein lies its most potent and basic significance as an agency of transformation in the processes of history.

Before attempting to define the historic significance of the machine on the basis of its unparalleled organizational patterns, it may be well to recall certain basic aspects of the nature of organization itself. In this connection it may be remembered that the functioning of organization is inherently and universally marked by expansive tendencies. In a world partly ordered and partly disordered and haphazard, the operation of the ordered elements was seen to be contingent upon and confined by the disordered elements. The wayward, the spontaneous, the unpredictable limit and constrict the precisely governed operations of the remaining organized elements. The efficient functioning of organization thus depends upon the unhampered orderliness, the exact and predictable course not only of all elements within the related whole but equally of all contiguous elements. Thus organization, by virtue of its inherent morphological relationships, was seen to exert always an implicit pressure in favor of further organization. This dynamic principle, it is clear, reaches its highest potential and its greatest effectiveness in the degree in which the nuclear organization attains internal perfection. But nowhere, it is significant to note, has man achieved an articulation in this respect comparable to that attained in the organization of the machine. Herein, then, we may perceive the source of the overwhelming potentialities of the machine in transforming the *structural* relationships of society.

In the far-flung panorama of human affairs the principle of organization, historically considered, appears at best only in disconnected and intermittent aspects—indeed, in the guise often enough of opposed and contradictory trends. The achievements of intelligence in marshaling into orderly patterns the chaotic world of men and events, of all the diverse trends and forces of life, are necessarily partial, detached, and isolated in time and place. Yet the internal, structural pressure of organization acts unceasingly toward the harmonious unification of this patchwork quilt of disparate elements into ever wider and more inclusive patterns. For behind the apparently haphazard appearance of the historic scene, a persistent, converging, and inclusive principle operates toward the achievement of ever greater unity and coherence. Under the impact of intelligence events are seen to move in converging trends and correlated patterns; under the impact of the machine this drift has become at once conscious, immeasurably intensified, and overwhelming.

A world-picture of orderly relations is thus seen to be implicit in the historic process. Its final realization is doubtless unattainable, like a mathematical limit, however closely human affairs may come to approach such a state of affairs. Long before the possibility of such a world-pattern had ever emerged, however, it lay implicit within the framework of historic forces; and man must have gradually prepared himself for this eventuality by an "inner accommodation," in the phrase of Lewis Mumford, before he finally came to an explicit and conscious recognition of its imminence. It is this very period of accommodation that calls for study and analysis in order to comprehend the unique role of the machine and its extraordinary effects upon the course of human history.

For this period presages the crucial stages in the conflict between the forces of instinct and intelligence. When at length, in this battle of historic influences, the dynamic power of intelligence balanced the static force of instinct, man found himself in a condition of strained uncertainty and ambivalence. Drawn first in one direction and then in another, he must have wished above all for the resolution of this pressing conflict; and, despite his zealous efforts to achieve an ideal fusion of these discordant trends, he must have surmised that the mounting influence and dynamic ascendancy of intelligence were assured in an ultimate and irrevocable decision. For the triumph of intelligence was implicit from the beginning, if only because, as we have seen, it was based upon an immemorial advantage in which the faculties of speech, of consciousness, of memory, and, above all, the cumulative nature of knowledge were destined to overwhelm, sooner or later, the slowly receding influence of the instincts. In that moment, historically speaking, man arrived at the threshold of a truly crucial turning point. If he did not at once comprehend its character, he found himself nonetheless compelled to accept an indefinable challenge in all his well-established values. The trend of events rather than his critical faculties made him question his habits and customs, his beliefs and dogmas, all his approved patterns and norms of behavior. The entire orientation of his being demanded to be revised, transposed, revaluated; and not only his concrete attainments but the whole fabric of his faiths and assumptions called for re-examination in the light of this pervasive and profound change. In this all-embracing revolution man altered not so much his distant goals and basic desires as his method of approach to these ends. But in effecting this change, he changed all else. This universal transition—in so far as we may say that it has in some degree been accepted and realized—was unwittingly accomplished; it came about unheralded and unpremeditated. Man did not prepare himself for its emergence as though he had contrived its occurence: it stole upon him. For it was not his choice but rather his fate that intelligence should in time supersede the instincts as the dominant directive force in his affairs. And this change, by virtue of its comprehensive scope, its inherent necessity, and its irreversible drift, must be acknowledged as evidence of an inescapable *historic determinism*.

If precise dates cannot well be established in the annals of history for this crucial epoch, it is nonetheless clear that our own period falls within its range. The immensely accelerated trend toward organization, it is now apparent, is related on the one hand to the growing dominance of intelligence as a guiding principle of social procedure and on the other to the profoundly sweeping effects of a correlated machine technology in the establishment of world order. For the more efficient functioning of the machine— in itself the most perfect, as it is the most dynamic, embodiment of the principle of organization —is directly and inherently contingent upon the ever more complete organization of the world at large. This dictum rests upon the principle elaborated above that organization inevitably demands further organization; and that the machine, as the most highly crystallized form of organization achieved by man, demands a degree of co-ordination in the societal relationships of man corresponding to its own high functional development. The pressure of this demand will have far-reaching and profoundly significant consequences: in time it will necessarily transform society from an organic into an organizational entity.

IV

HISTORIC DETERMINISM

Does it make sense to talk about a flow of entropy? This is an example of what happens when we carry familiar patterns of verbalizing into new situations: we have at first no guarantee at all that the old verbalizing will even have meaning, but we do at least in this way provide ourselves with a program of exploration.

—P. W. BRIDGMAN in *The Nature of Thermodynamics*

I

THE GREAT COMPLEXITIES and vast systems of modern life have called into being a technique of dealing with mass phenomena by means of statistical averages and probabilities. Behind the maze of modern civilization we come upon rigorous scientific predictions and rigidly established expectations. But in these very terms we may detect the presence likewise of chance, of inherent exceptions and uncertainties. In view of these circumstances it is proper to inquire in what sense we may speak of a principle of historic determinism. Has the phrase a legitimate meaning, and how, exactly, can it be defined in a world that seems partly conditioned and partly free? Is history subject to an unswerving drift like a river that moves ever onward despite its changing directions? Is history an irreversible process moving, like time itself, always in one direction?

These problems have their counterpart in the world of science. Thus physicists have been much exercised over the implications of Heisenberg's famous principle of indeterminacy and the causal basis of physico-chemical phenomena; while biologists have long been at odds over the problem of mechanism versus vitalism, or emergent evolution and organicism, as the more recent trends are termed. If the classic principle of causality has been deemed in certain quarters an inadequate if not wholly unnecessary postulate in the structure of science, it is all the more surprising that in the case of history the shoe is on the other foot: here the affirmation of determinism is quite as revolutionary a doctrine as its denial in the realm of physics. Actually many of the laws of nature are now interpreted in terms of statistical formulations; and it is not inconceivable that in the future such laws as historians may be able to enunciate will have a like statistical nature on the plane of human affairs. Thus the apparent contradiction between the trend of science and that of history may in the end be bridged by a common recourse to statistical analysis. In this connection it is not improbable that the future may bring about a deeper *rapprochement* between the sciences of organic and inorganic systems, and such a basic and comprehensive approach will doubtless embrace the specific domain of man and his affairs as well.*

Historians, it is true, have paid little attention to the task of applying mathematical or scientific procedures to the interpretation of historic events, and, despite the influence in their time of such men as Comte or Spencer, they have generally eschewed the logic and the methods of science. Nevertheless,

* Referring to the "apparent contradiction" between the trends of science and of history here noted, Dr. Richard Hanau of the Physics Department of the University of Kentucky has kindly made the following comment:

At present science is beginning to break away from strict determinism, and to think more and more in terms of averages and probabilities. History, on the other hand, having ventured into generalizations, is beginning to cast about for more rigorous laws on which to build a "science of history." Now the apparent contradiction between them is due, not to a divergence in direction, so much as to a comparison between two trends at different periods of their development. Science began—at about the time of Aristotle—to make generalizations and sweeping statements. As men became more cautious, they saw that progress could only be made by means of more rigorous laws. The phase science is now in has been forced upon it by the attempt to push the applicability of rigorous laws into the microscopic field, where it broke down as shown by the principle of limited measurability. Unable to study the individual, science, against its inclination, perhaps, had to evolve the method of statistical mechanics to deal with the bulk effects of large numbers of random, individual effects.

Now history, it would appear, though apparently tugging away from the path science is taking, is merely following science—having arrived at the point science had attained when Galileo and Newton took over. Perhaps history, like science, has to go through its own period of rigorous laws and attempts at the last decimal place, until it evolves its own principles of indeterminism.

the situation is changing. As man himself becomes more deeply entrenched in his scientific approach to life, so does his approach to history, and even his expectations and prognostications of the future appear more rational in temper and technique. Sociologists and historians, in increasing numbers, are asserting the need of a science of society, if not of history—a science that, in the words of Henry Adams, "... must be absolute, like other sciences, and must fix with mathematical certainty the path which human society has got to follow." * In this pronouncement we perceive that Adams is thinking of humanity as a unified whole, composed doubtless of individuals whose existence, in terms of a scientific approach to the historic process, is comparable to that of molecules in a physico-chemical system. That is to say, just as the characteristics of molecular structure and the laws of molecular behavior are reflected in the identity of things on a macroscopic level, so too will the mass of individuals in their common properties and average qualifications define the character of the collective whole. Such an analogy provides for relatively fixed laws on the historic plane; in a word, it implies some form of historic determinism. Certainly the trend of historians in their interpretations of society has veered ever more insistently toward the mass conception of man and his activities; and this point of view cannot be looked upon as merely a reflex to scientific thinking and to a scientific approach to the problem: it must likewise be viewed in terms of an emerging crystallization of mankind as a collective whole.

Thus the question of whether mankind is subject to some principle of historic determinism takes on an unexpected and even dramatic aspect. Such a conception would lead us to anticipate some sharply emerging change of status or phase as a result of a persistent clash of forces that had in the past obscured rather than revealed the intrinsic trend of events. Perhaps a further analogy from the physico-chemical world may

* Henry Adams, "The Tendency of History" (A Communication to the American Historical Association, 1894) in *The Degradation of the Democratic Dogma* (New York: The Macmillan Company, 1919), p. 129.

help to elucidate the point: though water, for example, turns into a solid state of ice under changes of temperature at constant pressure, it does so only at a definite point and without forewarning. History, viewed as a transitional movement in the development of man, may likewise have its unrevealed critical eras, its morphologically significant turning points. It will be apparent from preceding chapters that the groundwork has been prepared for enlarging upon this analogy in terms of the crucial relationship between instinct and intelligence along with all its correlated implications. Thus it is tenable that the emergence of a principle of historic determinism is compatible with a particular level and degree of development in the grand perspective of man's historic course. Such a conclusion is not surprising in view of the overwhelming changes demanded by our relatively recent machine technology, for example. Actually the impact of the machine, as we have seen, is rooted in a general principle of organization that in turn is deeply correlated with the dominance of intelligence over instinct. But here, plainly, we come upon a whole cluster of concepts and relationships—the eclipse of the individual and the rise of collectivism; the obligatory nature of the process; the structural implications of a principle of organization—all of which, seen in their proper historic context, point to a crucial change of direction in the social development of mankind. They point toward some form of historic determinism arising out of the inherent functioning of statistical averages, in which the individual in all his vagaries may be equated, if only by analogy, with the random motion of the molecule. Viewed from such a standpoint they constitute a definite problem and suggest not only specific analogies but a tangible "program of exploration" as well.

In this way and from this point of view we may at least anticipate certain pregnant analogies that may bear fruit some day in those precise social laws demanded by Henry Adams. But the certainty of such laws, in any event, will be of a statistical order not unlike that which sustains the formulations of statistical mechanics, whose rigidity is no less final for being relative rather than formal. Such is the character of all our statistical laws of nature. They represent formulations whose finality comes to depend upon probabilities, it is true, but of an order that in the macroscopic world is tantamount to certainty. In this sense there are indeed no "laws of nature"; only probabilities of such unimaginable magnitude as to confirm our sense of absolute order, of utter determinism. In the sphere of human relationships, likewise, we may perceive the operation of social mandates that represent the workings of averages and probabilities, and that constitute in their massive effectiveness and inexorable pressure evidence of an inherent morphological determinism.

Man today is aware of living in a grave period of transition. Having attained in the long course of his development a sense of individual freedom and responsibility—a sense of the "infinite worth of the individual"—he now finds himself in the grip of contrary centripetal forces that draw him, irresistibly, into ever more rigorous orbits of collective procedure. The traditional freedom of the individual, thus narrowed by the organized patterns of collectivized society, no longer sustains a sense of inward autonomy: as the wells of inward values are drained, the nuclear sense of the person as the source of free choice and of values must likewise vanish. It is as though man had achieved for a brief moment, as a transitional being, a perspective of far-off values—a vision of spiritual freedom—only to be swept under by the force of his own numbers, like the molecules spoken of above, whose individual freedom of action gives rise in the aggregate to the most precise laws and the most rigid conformity. For the common denominator of human actions, crystallized in the norms of organized social patterns, expresses only the implicit and attainable averages of human hopes, wishes, endeavors, and capacities. It is the very force of these averages that constitutes the sense of an emerging historical determinism—the sense of man as a collective entity molded and crystallized into organized forms by the overwhelming momentum of his numbers. The dominance of the collective aspects of man is inherently assured; and with it the gradual conversion of the individual into a frictionless and depersonalized member of the community. For the individual as such will be absorbed in the shadow of his collectivized self. The process, as we shall see, is irreversible and implicit: history moves in only one direction—"inert and unerring, she flows toward her goal."

The awareness of historic fatality is deeply connected with the problem of time and of irreversibility. But these ideas, no less than those notions of statistical averages and probabilities mentioned above, are concepts that belong primarily to the field of thermodynamics, where they possess greater scope, precision, and universality. It is therefore not surprising that a kinship of some kind has been suspected between their bearing in the domain of history and even more so in that of biology —particularly in relation to the theory of evolution—and their meaning in the field of thermodynamics. The exact nature of this relationship has been a matter of growing interest to scientists if not to historians. Yet the challenge of the problem has not altogether escaped their attention: thus Professor Carl Becker, for instance, found occasion to use the symbol of increasing entropy—"ds/dt is always positive"—as a suggestive subheading to the last chapter of his fascinating book *Progress and Power*. But certainly among historians no one has been as insistent as Henry Adams in attempting to establish a relationship between the historic process and the Phase Rule of Willard Gibbs in an effort to achieve that science of history which he believed to be firmly implied in the universal formulae of thermodynamics. The subject invites speculation. History itself seems at long last to have given us a hint of some as yet unrevealed pattern—a portent of order, direction, or design in the affairs of man that demands recognition and definition. Such portents are, it is true, perhaps only vaguely apparent, but their emerging form suffices to place the search for a science of history beyond a mere intuitive exercise or a remote if diverting possibility. World trends are converging into an unmistakable picture; and world forces are shaping themselves according to compelling and predetermined principles whose exact formulation remains to be achieved, but whose inexorable

operation is everywhere increasingly patent. The acceptance of
the thesis indicated above seems thus not too improbable in
some form; and we shall have occasion to note the qualified
assent which scientists have granted at least to the validity of
the problem if not to any of its proposed solutions.

II

A half century ago Henry Adams voiced the belief that historians were obligated to attempt the formulation of a science
of history, even though, he added characteristically, their efforts might well come to naught. In his communication to the
American Historical Association referred to above, he expresses
himself as follows: "No one who has watched the course of
history during the last generation can have felt doubt of its
tendency. Those of us who read Buckle's first volume when it
appeared in 1857, and almost immediately afterwards, in 1859,
read the Origin of Species and felt the violent impulse which
Darwin gave to the study of natural laws, never doubted that
historians would follow until they had exhausted every possible
hypothesis to create a science of history. Year after year
passed, and little progress had been made. Perhaps the mass
of students are more skeptical now than they were thirty years
ago of the possibility that such a science can be created. Yet
almost every successful historian has been busy with it, adding
here a new analysis, a new generalization there; a clear and
definite connection where before the rupture of idea was absolute; and, above all, extending the field of study until it shall
include all races, all countries, and all times. Like other
branches of science, history is now encumbered and hampered
by its own mass, but its tendency is always the same, and cannot be other than what it is. That the effort to make history a
science may fail is possible, and perhaps probable; but that it
should cease, unless for reasons that would cause all science
to cease, is not within the range of experience. Historians will
not, and even if they would they can not, abandon the attempt.
Science itself would admit its own failure if it admitted that

man, the most important of all its subjects, could not be brought within its range." *

In substantiation of this prediction it is interesting to observe that since his pronouncement was first issued, and perhaps particularly since the first World War, a number of new attempts have been made on an expansive scale to encompass the story of human history in terms of general principles if not explicit laws. The shattering effect of a world war, one might readily believe, would dishearten the most ardent advocate of an underlying world trend in history. On the contrary, however, the most cursory analysis shows that the first World War, like the second, is but an integral act or movement in a titanic upheaval of world-wide, universal order. Hence it is not surprising to find that at least three major contributions to a world picture of human history have seen the light of day in the interval between them: namely, the works of Spengler, Pareto, and Toynbee. Nor can we doubt that a wholly new series of such attempts will arise out of the profound ferment of the last conflict.

Adams returned to the attack in the year 1910 with a proposal, or rather a challenge, entitled "A Letter to American Teachers of History"—a document that raised so far-reaching an issue in the fields of physics, biology, and history that he whimsically excused historians from answering it. "If I call this volume a letter," he wrote, "it is because that literary form affects to be more colloquial or more familiar than the usual scientific treatise; but such letters never require a response, even when they invite one; and in the present case, the subject of the letter involves a problem which will certainly exceed the limits of a life already far advanced, so that its solution, if a solution is possible, will have to be reached by a new generation." † This famous "letter" concludes with the following words: "If the physicists and the physico-chemists can at last find their way to an arrangement that would satisfy the sociologists and historians, the problem would be wholly

---

* Henry Adams, "The Tendency of History," in *The Degradation of the Democratic Dogma* (New York: The Macmillan Company, 1919), p. 126.

† Henry Adams, "A Letter to American Teachers of History," in *The Degradation of the Democratic Dogma,* pp. 138, 139.

solved. Such a complete solution seems not impossible; but at present,—for the moment,—as the stream runs, it also seems, to an impartial bystander, to call for the aid of another Newton." *

The problem Henry Adams thus gently placed in the hands of historians concerned itself with the applications of the laws of thermodynamics to the processes of history. Recognizing the universal sway of the laws of thermodynamics, Adams logically enough accepted their challenge in his own field of history. More particularly he was concerned with the apparent contradictions involved in the doctrine of human perfectibility inherent in the theory of progress, on the one hand, and, on the other hand, the degradation of energy, whatever its form, implicit in the formidable second law of thermodynamics—the threatening law of the ultimate unavailability of all energy.

The running down of the universe is a heroic theme. Yet its relation to our immediate lives, and even to the whole course of human history, appears sufficiently remote, inducing us to enjoy its lurid, far-off vistas with philosophic composure. The problem presses upon us only after we come to realize that it is not concerned with a sudden, single event, like Judgment Day at the end of time, but with a continuous and ineluctable process coloring in some manner every aspect and phase of life. Exactly in what manner it thus impinges upon us is the question Henry Adams addressed not only to historians but to biologists and physicists as well. It was their task to cross this bridge, if only because they had arrived there. The historians, however, seemed not inclined to venture over, being content to look backward, as was doubtless their privilege, thereby leaving the question to the physicists and biologists, who could answer it only in the most general terms and without convincing accord, at least as far as a philosopher of society was concerned. Nor has the problem been much advanced since, though its challenge, to be sure, has invited an increasing volume of discussion and speculation. The end is not yet.

The laws of thermodynamics, clothed in mathematical regalia, are among the more abstruse formulations of physical

* *Ibid.,* p. 263.

science. But their meaning is readily apparent, and the analogies and examples illustrating them endless, since the laws are universally applicable. The first law is known as the principle of the conservation of energy; the second, like a diabolical afterthought, conditioning the universe in its sweep, is the law of the degradation of energy. It states simply that "we grow old instead of young"; that energy tends always to become dissipated, that is to say, unavailable. Authoritative scientists assure us in respect to the question that the known universe is running down in unarguable unison to a kind of ultimate perdition. This position, however, has been open to some counterarguments on the basis of modern statistical interpretations of the second law. A further problem has arisen in regard to consciousness and indeed in respect to all organic systems in their relations to the workings of the law of increasing entropy. We shall have to postpone for the moment the significant complications to which these reservations give rise. The essential meaning of the law remains—that law which states unequivocally that the entropy of the universe tends toward a maximum; in other words, that ultimately all energy will be equalized and unavailable in a final state of universal stability or "heat death." For though this final conclusion of the law is open to question on theoretic grounds, its operation, its meaning and significance remain untouched for us: its unfailing pressure will characterize the future of man, as it has his past, beyond any assignable time within the cosmos we inhabit.

Henry Adams approached the problem of its significance with a touch of morbid joy, seeing that it all led to extinction; and certainly something of this subjective acceptance of the conclusions to which physics pointed led him to treat the question with more poetic license than scientific caution. He was well aware of this. In his essay on "The Rule of Phase Applied to History," he is clearly making a tentative gesture toward a solution of the problem more by way of suggesting a method than a solution. Indeed, he seems in some measure to absolve the historian of any obligation in this connection when he says: "... The task of framing the formula and assigning the values belongs to the physicist, not the historian; and if one such arrangement fails to accord with the facts, it is for him to try another, to assign new values to his variables, and to verify the results." * This somewhat cavalier suggestion, however, did not, it appears, induce physicists to undertake the problem; and historians, for their part, have been inundated with such a flood of contemporary drama ever since Adams propounded his problem that they have had little time, and doubtless less inclination, to meddle with the recondite formulae of thermodynamics while the world was being annihilated before their very eyes—at least in terms of structures and values with which they were familiar, if not according to the law of increasing entropy as well.

Adams, however, was not content merely to state the problem; he essayed to indicate an approach to its solution. Since 1910, when he wrote his challenging thesis, history has passed before us with unbelievable rapidity; change following change with appalling speed. In view of this profound and rapid shift of events it is questionable whether Adams might not have been led to assign other values to his variables and to his basic dates had he written his essay more recently, though in some respects his predictions—startling as they were—have been fulfilled in an amazing manner, as has been pointed out by James Truslow Adams.† But Adams worked with large concepts, and even a world war might not have seemed to him an event of staggering importance beside, for example, the doubt that physics cast upon the principle of causality. The point is that history is an accommodating field, and the philosopher of history need have no fear that his theories will fail for want of facts; indeed, he need fear only a surplus of facts! Adams based his predictions upon a bold analogy between the three variables of temperature, pressure, and volume involved in a change of phase in physico-chemical systems, and his own transposed values for these factors in the sphere of history. With this wholly arbitrary framework as a basis of calculation he took the period of three hundred years from 1600 to 1900 as constituting a dis-

---

* *Ibid.*, p. 310.
† James Truslow Adams, "Henry Adams and the New Physics," *Yale Review*, Vol. XIX, No. 2, pp. 283, 302.

tinct historical *phase,* and, calculating by a "rule of squares," he arrived at a period of some 90,000 years which he designated the religious era, preceded by an almost infinitely remote instinctive phase. Following upon the mechanical phase represented roughly by the period between 1600 and 1900, the rule of squares took Adams rapidly through two more phases: the electrical, as he chose to call it, lasting till 1917, followed by a brief period of about four years, bringing "thought to the limit of its possibilities in the year 1921." Fantastic as these predictions doubtless seemed to Adams, they appear even more fantastic to us because of the measure of truth they chanced to embody. In a sense the amazing and wholly unexpected developments in the doctrine of relativity, and later the new quantum theory and Heisenberg's principle of indeterminacy, seemed to come extraordinarily close to fulfilling Henry Adams' formula. The point is nonetheless acceptable, even if, among other doubtful matters, the principle of causality was not in fact taken from under the feet of physicists, as certain members of the fraternity would have us believe. Indeed, sober reflection will certainly show, as regards this aspect of his work (and Adams would be the first to acknowledge it) that neither the particular formulae he chose to use nor—an even more serious matter—the transposed values which he assumed, almost casually, to represent in the field of history the three variables that determine a change of phase in the material world, were anything but wild guesses.

Of course Henry Adams did not directly presume to establish a science of history by the questions he asked or the solutions he offered. On the contrary, he wished merely to see in what manner the law of increasing entropy, with which physicists had apparently lassoed the universe, applied to the processes of history. That the precise course of history involved quite other factors he would have been the last to deny, and if his question was thus limited it was nevertheless profoundly stimulating in the immense and unexpected vistas which it revealed. If his quest was unsuccessful, largely because the concepts that science develops in one field of research or one aspect of the world do not apply directly to another, the matter need hardly surprise us. The bridges by means of which scientists penetrate the unknown are often enough awe-inspiring in their spans but so narrow that even the expert cannot be sure of a safe crossing. Moreover, a question that could not, in the nature of the case, be answered by experiment might go begging a long time, and Adams asked just such a question. But perhaps the basic difficulty with the contribution of Henry Adams was the fact that he approached the problem from the wrong end. Accepting the conclusions of physicists in regard to the universal validity of the laws of thermodynamics, he accepted the whole paraphernalia of their concepts and their mathematical formulations as well, and, thus equipped, he proceeded to look at history. Scientists as well as philosophers are loath to admit the frail intuitions upon which they set to work, and Adams doubtless wished to come upon the scene as formidably prepared as possible. Hence he started from the camp of the physicists, and, squeezing history somehow into their formulae, he achieved very dubious results with the explanation that even the wrong answer might illustrate the right method. But, just as in a game of chess it is well to analyze the opponent's position before venturing a reply, it would seem as though a firmer insistence upon the intrinsic meaning of the historic process as a whole, upon its underlying significance as a unified trend, might have led, if not to a decisive answer, at any rate to a far more conclusive approach.

III

In his essay Adams speaks of the "physicist-historian" whose task it will be to establish a precise dynamics of history; but the emphasis clearly is upon the physicist, since it is he who furnished the groundwork of the problem in the first place by enunciating the challenging and universal principles of thermodynamics. Adams, one suspects, may have been indulging in a sly gibe at his fellow historians in intimating that, while physicists might well master history, historians could hardly be expected to feel at home in the rarefied atmosphere of physics and higher mathematics. Nevertheless he took it upon himself to invite the historians to the table of the physicists, and in this gesture he was only acting in consonance with the trend of modern science in general. Meanwhile physics and along with it chemistry, as well as other sciences, have been moving steadily in the direction of the precise but abstract symbolism of mathematics—the ultimate language of science. Today psychology and biology, for example, are rapidly following suit and are deeply influenced by the penetrating instrument of mathematical analysis. The work of such men as Alfred J. Lotka has gone far toward establishing a wholly new field of "physical biology," as distinguished from biophysics, in which we come upon "the application of physical principles and methods in the contemplation of biological *systems*." * Significantly, the emphasis here is not upon the *individual* organism but upon *systems* of organisms, the dynamics of which are analyzed in mathematical terms. Whether the interpretation of history with its incredible and inscrutable complexity of detail will ever be subject to mathematical analysis on the basis of its collective aspects, or will ever reveal itself in terms of precise thermodynamic principles or a rule of phase such as that entertained by Adams, must in the present state of our knowledge remain unanswered; but perhaps we need have no reason to despair because the problem seems at first glance altogether insurmountable. Not a few of the established laws of science, and the second law of thermodynamics among them, were perceived and understood in their essential meaning long before their exact interpretation in mathematical symbols and precise numerical relationships seemed to anyone feasible or even possible. The irreversibility of natural processes was known to us of old, according to Eddington, in the sad fate of Humpty Dumpty. For

"All the king's horses and all the king's men
Cannot put Humpty Dumpty together again."

Thanks to the work of Boltzmann and others this tale of woe has received mathematical interpretation in the formulae de-

* Alfred J. Lotka, *Elements of Physical Biology* (Baltimore: The Williams and Wilkins Company, 1925), p. viii.

fining increasing entropy. Similarly, the problem proposed by Adams may yet receive an absolute and crystalline answer; but meanwhile the lesson to be drawn from his effort lies in the fact that the business of assigning the term "phase" to specific historic periods can at best have value only as a suggestive analogy.

Yet such analogies are often far less fortuitous than they seem. The structure Henry Adams erected may have been nothing more than an *"ignis fatuus,"* as James Truslow Adams maintains, built upon the "pitfall of a transfer of concepts"; but the problem he raised concerning the relationship between the historic process and the principle of increasing entropy is in fact but the acceptance, in the sphere of human affairs, of a challenge inherent in all the sciences dealing with "irreversible phenomena." His analogy, faulty as it may have been, had the minimum virtue, at least, of calling attention to the problem long before its general implications were widely appreciated. Curiously enough this vital problem is only now receiving the critical study it merits from biologists and biochemists, as witness for example a symposium held before the Society for Experimental Biology in London, in 1937, on the subject of "Reversibility in Evolution," or, more recently, in 1941, the critical essay by Joseph Needham on "Evolution and Thermodynamics." But the virtue of Adams' analogy extends beyond its undeniable heuristic value. While the sequence of a number of historic phases seems at best arbitrary, it is nonetheless true that human society has undergone decisive changes of form and structure, whereas the individual, as a biologic entity, has remained relatively stationary. In the irreversible course of human development we may thus see a possible analogy with changes of phase in purely physico-chemical systems. The question which Adams raised in the domain of history has its analogues in the field of biology, and must be accepted as valid, if unanswered. In this situation his thesis may turn out to be the starting point, not of a direct advance but of a retreat from which ultimately a new approach may present itself. For obviously the problem must be stated in a more basic and generalized form in order to fathom, if possible, the relation of

thermodynamic principles to the whole development of man
and of organic systems in general, before concentrating upon
the historic aspect of man in particular.

History, on the one hand, and the development of man considered as a whole, on the other, are separate aspects of his
basic deviation from the biologic domain, the one falling within the other as a chapter within a book. The apparent burden
of the story, as we have seen, sustains a distinct interpretation
of the process on the basis of a vast conflict between the forces
of instinct and intelligence. Adams himself, it is interesting to
note, though he had no such conception in mind, dwells upon
an "instinctual phase" at the beginning of his series of phases
and winds up with his famous pronouncement about thought
reaching the limits of its possibilities in the first quarter of the
century, or in the year 1921 by way of making his guess precise! In other terms, and in the accents of literature, Adams
spoke of the Virgin and the Dynamo—the opposite polarity
of man's deepest feelings and highest intelligence furnishing
the datum points from which he would survey the historic
process and establish his phases. Adams devoted his *Mont-
Saint-Michel and Chartres* and *The Education of Henry Adams*
to an elaborate analysis of these datum points. Too much the
historian to discard history, Adams escaped beyond its confines only through the accident of a formula that carried him
backward into the remote depths of man's past, even though,
in the other direction, it left him staggering and bewildered
with little or no visible future ahead of him beyond the year
1921! But the nature of history—or rather of the historic
process—is not to be surmised apart from its position within
the larger picture of man's entire development. Only thus is it
possible to see that history may be merely a transitional period
between two far more extensive eras; and on the basis of such
an interpretation, it is plain, the analogy of a rule of phase may
well carry an entirely different complexion. The limiting periods or phases of instinct and thought, within which Adams
saw the historic process unfold, lead one to believe that he was
intuitively drawn to some such conclusion, though his formulae and his dates, at once casual and arbitrary, took unfortu-

nate precedence over his acute sensibilities. The problem must therefore be restated, as it were, in perhaps less ambitious but more generalized terms; and discarding the superstructure that Henry Adams reared, along with his transposed concepts, we may yet entertain the more basic implications of his analogy.

In restating the problem it will be necessary in the first place to reduce the mass of historic material to its simplest and most comprehensive aspects. This process of abstraction is common to all the sciences; phenomena must be studied in their generalized aspects in order to perceive their operation unencumbered. If society has experienced changes of form comparable to those with which physics deals under the term phase, they should be apparent to us, as Adams pointed out, in fundamental changes of structure or direction. But, as we have seen, in attempting to define such changes we must forego, contrary to Adams, the search for significant historic dates as far too limited and localized in comparison with the vast theater of operation which the basic forces of history, or rather of man's whole development, will certainly demand. We must forego the conventional historic epochs if these can be subsumed under more comprehensive terms; and similarly we must pass by individual cultures, contrary to Spengler, as the branches and twigs into which the trunk of history divides itself. The point deserves emphasis.

In his monumental work on *The Decline of the West*, Oswald Spengler developed, preliminary to his more specific purpose, a "morphology of world history" in which he elaborated a theory of the cyclical nature of all historic cultures. In his introduction he asks: "Is it possible to find in life itself...a series of stages which must be traversed, and traversed moreover in an ordered and obligatory sequence? For everything organic the notions of birth, death, youth, age, lifetime are fundamentals—may not these notions, in this sphere also, [i.e., of history] possess a rigorous meaning which no one has yet extracted?" * Spengler, speaking here as though he were about to illumine for us the "obligatory" character of the his-

* Oswald Spengler, *The Decline of the West* (New York: Alfred A. Knopf, Inc., 1926), p. 3.

toric process by some explicit reference to thermodynamic ir-reversibility, passes on to apply his conception of a distinct life-cycle to individual cultures only, contemptuously ignoring "mankind" as an "empty word" or at best a "zoological ex-pression." "I see in place of that empty figment of *one* linear history," he continues, "...the drama of *a number* of mighty Cultures, each springing with primitive strength from the soil of a mother region to which it remains firmly bound throughout its whole life circle; each stamping its material, its mankind, in *its own* image; each having *its own* ideas, *its own* passions, *its own* life, will and feeling, *its own* death." And, further on in the same passage: "...There is no aging 'Mankind.' Each cul-ture has its own possibilities of self-expression which arise, ripen, decay, and never return." *

Clearly, an acceptance of this view would imply that the path of history could be represented only by a series of discrete circles, so to speak; and our search for changes of direction would be doomed from the start to an aimless wandering among the diverse cultures of the world. Spengler, whose profound "feeling" for history led him to perceive the morphological similarities beneath all cultures, failed to take adequate ac-count of their differences or their cumulative relations. Thus, for example, the expansive policies of ancient Rome had a quite different morphological meaning from the contemporary urge on the part of a number of nations to establish some form of international suzerainty. The complexion of this trend is pro-foundly different from that of an earlier imperialism if only because science has unified the world through the impact of its abstract validity. Thus, totally new elements disrupt the anal-ogy; and the present must be counted a poor moment in which to discard mankind as a proper historic entity when the destiny of the human race is visibly shaping itself in terms of a world picture. If the diverse cultures of the past are giving way to a world-wide system of converging trends, it is the business of the historian to acknowledge the fact and to explain as best he can its morphological implications and significance. Thus it is precisely because, in the past, there have been at once cul-

* *Ibid.,* p. 21.

tural differences as well as cultural similarities, that the search for more general terms, commensurate with the historic process in the widest possible sense and taken as a whole, is amply justified.

Once established, such concepts may well reveal a biological rather than a historic flavor, particularly if the interpretation of history is not arbitrarily confined to specific epochs, peoples, and cultures, set within an equally arbitrary geographic and chronological framework. That Spengler disregarded the wider concepts of world history along with the term "mankind" is not surprising—though he hurled decimating epithets at historians who were content to confine themselves to the traditional ancient, medieval, and modern epochs of Western civilization—since he envisaged history as a "...second Cosmos different in structure and complexion" from mere nature. He believed, intuitively, in an "...opposition of History and Nature through which alone it is possible to grasp the essence of the former." In thus setting himself adrift, however, he failed to allow for the basic generality of such physiologic terms as birth, youth, age, and death, which in turn may have a far deeper and more revealing thermodynamic significance. In so far as man is a member, in the words of Spengler, not only of the cosmos of history but also of nature, it is plainly necessary to square the account with nature before venturing to discover in what manner man escapes beyond nature, or contravenes her principles, or transcends her domain and the laws that govern it. Spengler himself speaks of the true problem of history as a *destiny-problem,* by which he means the "problem of time." But our sense of the irrevocable flow of events, hounding us with absolute, mechanic finality, is deeply embedded in the idea of increasing entropy—of the irreversible flow of energy in the economy of organic no less than inorganic systems. We grow old instead of young; and whether it is man or nature, the universe hurries on. The forces that cause the tree to grow and flourish and die doubtless affect the life span of the species as well; and the dynamics that govern separate cultures may conceivably govern mankind. Thus neither physics nor biology may be brushed aside in the casual and a priori manner of Spengler until their contributions to an understanding of the historic process in its full and widest sense have been explored and absorbed. And even if, finally, they should afford us no more than obscure intuitions and remote analogies based on the behavior of biologic organisms or the physical structure of "rigid being," they will have served in some measure to illumine that sense of historic destiny which we feel but do not fully comprehend.

Once more, then, we must return to the task of establishing, beneath the cyclical growth and decline of individual cultures and civilizations, the changes that pertain to the development of man as a whole. The doctrine that history is subject to causal laws, to some manner of underlying drift and conditioning, to some principle of development, whether progressive or not—in short, to general laws—is a relatively modern thought and, like the theory of evolution, constitutes in itself an aspect of modern history. But this conception, if ever it can be crystallized into explicit and concrete terms, will certainly not only be concerned with forces that animated the whole of our historic course; it will embrace, necessarily, these same forces in their incipient, prehistoric stages. And here anthropologists, taking perhaps a wider view of the matter, point to a single, basic, and extraordinary change in the development of man: namely that, whereas in his earliest stages he was at the mercy of his environment, he has ever since increased his mastery over it. It is interesting in this connection to note that biologists consider the degree of active independence attained by an organism over its environment as an indication of its degree of development; and certainly, carrying this conception to extremes, it would imply in one direction a virtual merging of organic and inorganic forms or systems; in the other, a level of freedom from the environment attained only by man, and perhaps, in the logic of the case, to be surpassed by him in some emergent level of even higher independence. From a purely human and historical point of view, however, it might be more illuminating to state this principle on the basis of the thesis previously developed: namely, that by virtue of man's unfolding intelligence he was enabled to respond to his environment in ever more pragmatic and fruitful terms than those his instincts alone envisaged. History is thus seen as the arena within which the conflict between these forces emerged in significant and dramatic forms: through intelligence man has quickened and widened the scope of his activities into a rising flux of events, concepts, and achievements, against the steady undertow of his instinctive urges toward a primal state. But in the course of his development, as he diverged ever further from his erstwhile relation to nature and to his environment, he discovered, as we have seen, that he came to constitute in his own collective body a new, self-created environment. This astonishing inversion explains why history seems to him somehow a "cosmos" different from nature; in this relationship man intensified his awareness of his values into all the infinite reaches of his searching mind and fertile imagination. Thus arose the cumulative structure of his civilizations.

We may, then, summarize the search for the basic change that encompasses all other changes, that accompanies, envelops, and interpenetrates the whole course of the historic development of man, in the ever changing relationship, indicated in an earlier chapter, between the forces of instinct and intelligence. There we saw that by virtue of an inescapable time-principle the impress of intelligence grows upon us as that of the instincts declines, molding the forms of life to its demands. But for the changing emphasis in this relationship, our development might have been static, and our history but an unbroken and stable equilibrium. Indeed, our development, in all likelihood, would have been no more significant or challenging than that of any other form of life but for the ferment of this basic and unique dichotomy in our approach to the problems of existence.

Accepting the overwhelming transition from the dominance of the instincts to that of intelligence as the most comprehensive, basic, and significant change in the whole development of man, we may return to the logic of Henry Adams and inquire in what sense this dramatic change can be interpreted in the light of the universally applicable principles of thermodynamics.

IV

It is conceivable, of course, that the problem here entertained is not susceptible of a solution, at least in the form in which the question has been asked, and in the terms of a science that, however universal its implications, has developed its concepts, its formulae, and its principles in the domain of physicochemical systems. In a somewhat similar predicament the early Greek mathematicians, wishing by means of their traditionally limited geometry to trisect an angle and to square the circle, discovered unexpected realms of mathematical riches without, however, finding the answer to their original questions. "In the effort to solve these problems," writes Tobias Dantzig in his fascinating treatise on *Number*, "the Greek geometers discovered the conic sections and a number of higher curves. They never suspected that a solution such as they sought did not exist, and the difficult and recalcitrant nature of the problem only spurred their efforts and drew into the arena of geometry their greatest minds from Archimedes to Appollonius of Perga." * It is safe to say that the problem of establishing precise laws of historic development and, more particularly, the relation of the historic process to thermodynamic principles —whether under the Rule of Phase or otherwise—will reverberate through the critical literature of the century. And it will haunt the mind of the scientist even more than that of the historian to the point where a new dynamics of life will be evolved, should it prove necessary, to facilitate the work of establishing its solution. For the challenge of the problem is inescapable, while the instruments of thought, the necessary conceptions and formulations for its solution, seem, in reality, not too forbidding. Meanwhile, we may indulge in intuitive explorations, while awaiting with Adams the coming of a Newton whose mission it will be to supplant tentative analogies and fleeting surmises with orderly and predictable relationships.

At the outset it will be apparent that history, conceived as the impress of intelligence upon instinctive behavior, may be a

* Tobias Dantzig, *Number—The Language of Science* (New York: The Macmillan Company, 1930), p. 114.

valid approach to man's past without being either final or exhaustive. It serves our present purpose, however, in being the simplest and most comprehensive approach to the infinite complexities of man's changing world, a kind of lowest common denominator of the whole historic process. In previous chapters we have seen that the relationship between instinct and intelligence in their bearing upon the development of man reaches a decisive turning point—a moment of equilibrium after which their power and influence are relatively reversed. This turning point in the affairs of man has a distinct morphological significance: it was the moment, however extended, during which man enjoyed the mirage of individualism, that critical moment between an earlier, fundamentally instinctual development of communal society and a later, rationally oriented collectivism—a moment of transition between two periods, the one running backward into the remote era of preconscious times, the other stretching forward into the future under the increasing dominance of man's conscious guidance. That transitional moment, however defined in terms of historic epochs, is the occasion of man's deepest travail, of his highest illusions and his boldest dreams. It is the moment of greatest strain and intensity, of profound and contrary impulses that herald an imminent crisis. For man is aware of a vast and fateful metamorphosis; and in this painful moment of suspense he is torn between heroic hopes and grim fears. Marching always between the past and the future, man has never before been as conscious of the immense impact of these vistas; today he sees the pageant of history as a premonition of a change transcending history itself.

In tracing to its source the cumulative trend toward increased organization in every phase and aspect of modern life, we came upon the basic dichotomy of instinct and intelligence. The drift toward organization was seen to register the triumph of intelligence over instinct with the unfailing precision of an inherent modulus. And correlated with this drift the form of society itself changed slowly in a structural sense from organic to organizational patterns, from preconscious to ever more conscious formulations. Under the impact of science and a machine technology, together with the stark and sudden increase in world population, we came at length to a crucial epoch in the affairs of man—to a series of deeply interrelated social changes whose impact, taken in its totality, constitutes a change of direction, a change of historic phase. For the structure of society is undergoing not merely slow, cumulative changes but a sudden, drastic, morphological change, at once all-inclusive and irreversible, the full significance of which we can only surmise, but the meaning of which, even now in its formative stage, indicates a change of phase under an all-pervasive historic determinism.

Caught in the midst of this change, we are at a loss to account for its suddenness. Nor are we aware of its more basic and ulterior significance in the future development of man. Yet we have not lacked sharp and penetrating glimpses into our probable future; nor have we been wholly without intuitive premonitions of the transient character of history itself, as though, in truth, it were but a period of "inner accommodation" to a future essentially different in nature and character from our past. If history is indeed but a transitional era culminating in a change of historic phase under the compulsion of some sweeping historic determinism, we ought to be able, certainly, to discern the outlines of this constellation of factors in some unique and outstanding phenomenon of our development. And here, obviously, it would seem as though the emergence of the machine constituted that revealing phenomenon. But its precise role in this vast transition remains to be established and defined, and its significance in relation to the historic process as a whole to be more clearly indicated and interpreted.

The meaning of the machine, its deep structural implications in the development of human society, and its drastic bearing upon the future of man, have too often been underestimated or misinterpreted because the machine has been conceived of as an isolated if startling phenomenon. It is true the development of the machine can be traced backward to the tenth century, as Lewis Mumford has shown, and even further to examples in ancient Greek and Roman times. Doubtless an unbroken descent could be established between the machine and the humblest tools and implements of primitive man. But this chronological procedure throws no light upon the sudden rise and impact of the machine in modern times, on the one hand, or upon its profound integration with certain basic aspects in the development of man, on the other hand. The machine remains an isolated and incongruous fact unless both of these apparently unrelated if not antithetical aspects can be subsumed and explained by a single, comprehensive principle. It is not surprising that the machine in its first demonstrations of higher power was looked upon as the work of the devil. Even today it is often viewed as an alien and inimical intrusion; and indeed, it must be granted, the machine is a curious and even unique concatenation of inorganic elements in the service of life. Its emergence as a source of unimagined power added to its mysterious and alien character; and though the machine has been developed in an altogether phenomenal manner since, let us say the middle of the eighteenth century, and though certainly it has been universally accepted, profoundly affecting the forms of societal relations everywhere, it remains nonetheless a kind of separate cosmos, a realm apart, an exact, mechanical order capable of endless development, following indeed the laws of nature, yet distinct alike from the organic and the inorganic world.

There is of course a bridge between ourselves and the world of the machine, and that bridge is the faculty of intelligence. The challenging nature of the machine, its sudden emergence, its power and universal triumph, are seen in focus and clarified for us in the light of this instrument of adjustment. As we have noted previously, it was not until the dominance of intelligence was assured that man attained the necessary intellectual freedom to plunge deeply and fearlessly into the remotest recesses of the mechanical world and to return laden with gifts of unimagined power. In this case man had to unburden himself before he could proceed; disengage himself from a profound entwinement in which his instincts and his intelligence were mortised awkwardly into a precarious and impermanent bond. Nor was his will concerned in dissolving

this transient amalgam: he did not *will* the triumph of his intelligence; he suffered it, under the cumulative impact of his
experience and his knowledge. In the final dominance of intelligence over instinct we come thus readily upon an explanation of the comparatively sudden emergence of the machine as
a wholly new and immensely potent force in the affairs of man.
For the machine is the gift of pure intelligence, unimpeded.

Therein, too, lies the secret of its further anomaly as a new
but deeply integrated phenomenon in the totality of man's experience. If the machine seems indeed alien to man, it is only
on the basis of qualities and attributes other than intelligence.
And only as intelligence itself rose clear and free into its dominant position could the machine arise in all the promise of its
full potency. The machine was thus a long-delayed offspring
of intelligence, once that faculty achieved a kind of creative
self-assertion, as it were; a divorce from the entangling and
dissipative bonds of instinct. And penetrating more deeply into this approach to an understanding of the problem we can
perceive that the machine, product of pure intelligence, reflects
in its essential nature the character of its heritage. For the
machine is, above all, an organization. In this fact we come
upon the kernel of its historic role, upon its deepest significance
for the future of man. Moreover, the machine represents the
highest degree of organization—the perfect adaptation of
means to the achievement of specific and attainable ends. The
true power of the machine in its eventual effects upon the
structure of society will come to depend not only on the fact
that it is a magical lever between man and nature, enriching
life beyond our dreams, but that, following an inherent principle of organization, it will demand an ever greater degree of
integration and co-ordination in the social aspects of life commensurate with its own perfection. That is the essential and
primary meaning of the machine in respect to man's future.

But this fact has perhaps an even more dramatic bearing
upon his present estate. For it is in our modern era, taken in a
wide sense, that we have witnessed three profoundly significant
deviations from the past course of history: namely, the emergence of the machine, the sudden correlated quadrupling of the

earth's population, and the coincident rise of an ever more inclusive trend toward organization. It is not necessary to disentangle cause and effect in this congeries of related events. Nor is it surprising that the machine, which is at once the most deliberate, dynamic, and exact organization that man has yet perfected, should be correlated with man's own profound social readjustments in terms of organized patterns. The cumulative drift toward organization in every aspect of modern life is not due to some conscious desire to convert the complexity of society into the likeness of a smooth-functioning machine; it follows, on the contrary, from an inherent necessity, a principle of organization itself, which demands, imperatively and implicitly, an ever increasing extension of organization in the name of its higher functioning and perfected development. For the principle of organization, as we have seen, carries with it a kind of extroverted necessity to expand: organization breeds organization as a crystal breeds crystals. Such is the inherent law of organization—a principle that we have not yet apprehended clearly, but which, nonetheless, is transmuting the world of yesterday into that of the future.

Neither in nature nor in society do we come upon "isolated systems." The conception is a convenient fiction possessing only relative validity. Certainly the history of man shows plainly enough that we are drifting from whatever degree of isolation we may have originally exhibited to a state of ever closer integration. The idea of "One World" only epitomizes this trend; it has been in process from the beginning. Moreover, it is intensive as well as extensive in its operation; it combines integration with consolidation in one principle of organization. But what, we may well ask, hastened this principle with all the startling transformation the modern world is witnessing? And the answer, as indicated above, points clearly to the transmuting influence of the machine. But before the machine could ever have been conceived and perfected, and long before its effects could possibly have transmuted the whole panorama of society and the world, a preparatory process was in action establishing and extending that state of "inner accommodation" without which the whole vast movement might never have come to a climax—in short, to a change of historic phase or direction. The long travail of man's past in which his instincts and his intelligence reacted upon one another in all the diverse facets of his history, of his rising cultures and dying civilizations—the summation of that past must be looked upon as a kind of prologue of clashing forces tending toward an inherent but wholly unsuspected climax. The dynamic protagonist in this drama of human history is man's intelligence, through whose agency he established, slowly and by uncertain stages, a condition of inner accommodation, of mounting compliance with the rational elements in his nature.

This state of inner accommodation, becoming ever more intensified, might be compared to the slow concentration of a solution. To outward appearances no perceptible change seems to be taking place. As the solution becomes supersaturated, however, it approaches a state of incipient change. And if at this stage, as is well known, a crystal of the same substance is introduced into the solution, an immediate change of state takes place, and all the excess salt crystallizes forthwith. Similarly, a subcooled liquid may be induced to crystallize; and in the domain of physico-chemical systems such transformations are known as "changes of phase." Returning to the field of history, it is plain, on the basis of this analogy, that the incipient and diffused trend toward organization has been hastened into a universal movement by the sudden introduction of a pure crystal—the machine. In consequence the world is becoming rapidly organized, intensively and extensively, in every phase and aspect, as though indeed a universal process of crystallization were at work: through the machine the incipient drift toward organization has been broadened into an obligatory and all-pervasive principle, encompassing in its sweep the whole of life.

V

Quite apart from any value that there may be in the analogy between a crystal and the machine, on the one hand, and between a supersaturated solution and a slowly intensified state of "inner accommodation," on the other, it is clear that the

vast transformations which have been going on in the modern
world are in fact due to the machine and to that state of inner
accommodation which includes in its widest implications the
whole development of science itself. The analysis stands; but
what of the analogy?

Now the value of an analogy may be merely verbal or perhaps literary, opening up for us momentary vistas of the mind
like weather-lightning, without enabling us to advance one
step in the ensuing darkness. Or again, as Professor Bridgman suggests, a way of speaking may afford us a program of
exploration. Perhaps the merit and validity of an analogy can
be assessed only on the basis of its pragmatic carrying-power.
What inferences, what manner of superstructure will it bear?
And this question in turn will come to depend not upon the
momentum of some apt phrase but upon some inherent morphological similarity, or some implicit identity of operational
principles. The device is not without its grave risks; to follow
the path of an analogy is to enter upon one of those speculative bridges that narrow as their spans widen, ending abruptly,
often enough, in midair, like a surrealist dream. Nor can one
gain comfort and encouragement from the spectacle of Henry
Adams, whose logic, spurred on by supporting analogies and
spurious formulae, led him to a kind of glorious disaster. Adams
took a flyer and came a cropper! Since his time, however, the
analogies which he pursued have been taken over by eminently
respectable biochemists and theoretical biologists in terms
suitable to their own domain; and if, ignorant of his efforts
and his particular statement of the problem, they have attempted to fathom the relation between evolution and thermodynamic principles, as he wished to do in regard to history, it
is because some relationship is seen to exist, some binding and
common principle deeper than the verbal analogies and intuitive comparisons that may have suggested their existence in
the first instance. The sweeping applicability of the second
law of thermodynamics constitutes an inviting terrain in which
to build analogies: its meaning, at once self-evident and mysterious, invites speculation, and perhaps nowhere more so than

in the relationship between organic and inorganic systems. But the high point in any such analysis must always be the unique problem of man himself.

If the analogy between the machine and a crystal is to be granted value beyond that of a mere literary device, it will be necessary to establish a significant parallelism or equivalence in the thermodynamic meaning of their mutual roles. A supersaturated solution or a subcooled liquid will undergo a change of phase upon the introduction of a suitable crystal. May we speak of the change that the machine is bringing about in the transformation of society as a comparable change of *historic phase?* Both processes represent structural changes. Both exhibit changes of order: the one in causing the formation of a crystal lattice; the other in an ever wider and more penetrating extension of organized patterns of procedure. Both exhibit the same "spontaneous" development characteristic of irreversible processes; that is to say, the process of crystallization, once started, continues spontaneously, just as the trend toward increased organization follows an obligatory course in the development of that historic determinism associated with the dominance of intelligence. There is, moreover, a condition, known in the terminology of thermodynamics as a "metastable state," which describes precisely the condition of incipient change between two phases of a system that would seem to serve as the perfect analogue to that state of "inner accommodation" spoken of above. We have thus, in view of these analogous characteristics, at least an intimation of a significant parallelism, inviting us to further exploration.

The sharpness of the analogy at best, however, is at the mercy of certain unhappy anomalies that have yet to be resolved in the relation between thermodynamic principles and organic systems. Nor is the field of thermodynamics itself, as we shall see, free of ambiguities. The difficulties are technical and abstruse, and even experts seem perplexed and bedeviled by their forbidding subtleties. Certainly it will prove instructive where possible to familiarize ourselves with these hurdles even at respectful distances. Meanwhile, the analogy may serve to give us a greater insight into the operation of certain challenging aspects of our emerging world picture. We may, for example, note a possible relationship between the eclipse of the individual together with the rise of collectivization in the modern world, and the operation of the laws of statistical mechanics. Thus, historic determinism may prove to have a statistical basis not unlike that upon which the interpretation of many thermodynamic concepts rests. Such forays into unknown territory must, in the present state of our knowledge, remain purely speculative, but they may nonetheless prove rewarding.

From this angle it is instructive, for example, to observe how certain aspects of this picture were already recognized in the eighteenth century, according to J. B. Bury, by such men as Condorcet, who interpreted them, however, in a highly sanguine manner because of his faith in the prevailing doctrine of progress. He emphasized the historic significance of the mass of men in distinction to the role of the individual; and though this was doubtless a far step from comprehending the philosophic implications of collectivism as we are beginning to sense it under the converging pressure of modern civilization, it was nevertheless a step in that direction. The fact that Condorcet, who was a mathematician as well as a social philosopher, was known to have worked with the theory of probabilities is particularly interesting in view of the modern approach to the study of large numbers by means of statistical analysis. The possibility of applying laws to large aggregates comes to depend often enough upon a statistical approach involving probabilities; and though it is unlikely that Condorcet had such an approach in mind in his sociological thinking, he nevertheless came to view the conception of the mass of men as the necessary basis for an understanding of their development according to general laws. "Though Condorcet had no idea of evolution," wrote J. B. Bury, "the predominant importance of the masses was the assumption which made it possible to apply evolutional principles to history. And it enabled Condorcet himself to maintain that the history of civilization, a progress still far from being complete, was a development

conditioned by general laws." * If Condorcet was innocent of
the laws of evolution, he was even more so of the modern conceptions of thermodynamics. Yet, in perceiving that the historic process could only be formulated in terms of the mass of
men, he anticipated the direction deemed most likely to afford
a solution of the problem as to whether history is subject to
scientific generalizations. Today, when the collectivization of
society has progressed beyond its early, incipient stages, such
an approach seems axiomatic; but in his day the position he
took may well have seemed highly speculative. We may take
courage from such instances in carrying further the speculative implications which the statistical approach to a study of
aggregates suggests; and though doubtless the concepts obtaining in the dynamics of society will differ from those of other
aggregates in character, scope, and significance, according to
the inherent structure of each domain, that is a far cry from
denying the possibility and abandoning the effort to establish
their underlying similarities.

Among such basic analogies one of the first that will strike
the mind is concerned with the statistical interpretation of the
second law of thermodynamics in its possible bearing upon the
concept of society as a mass of individuals, and history as
the evolution of that mass. Hazardous as the idea may appear
at first glance, it is suggested by the very depth and sweep of
the second law of thermodynamics itself; and the literature of
thermodynamics is not without distinct and explicit references
to some such possible applications. In a volume by J. F. Klein
dealing with the *Physical Significance of Entropy,* a work
based directly upon the interpretations of two outstanding authorities in the field of thermodynamics, Boltzmann and Planck,
we may read the following pertinent passage: "The Second
Law ... has no *independent* significance, for its roots go down
deep into the Theory of Probability. It is therefore conceivable
that it is applicable to some purely human and animate events
as well as to inanimate, natural events; provided, of course,

* J. B. Bury, "Darwinism and History," an essay in *Evolution of Modern
Thought,* by Haeckel, Thomson, Weisman, and Others (New York: Boni and
Liveright, Inc., 1917), p. 250.

that the former possess like and uncontrolled constituents which may be properly characterized as *'elementar-ungeordnet,'* in other words, provided the variable elements present constitute adequate haphazard for the Calculus of Probabilities."* This handsome gesture is an invitation to sociologists to avail themselves of the statistical techniques applicable to thermodynamics. Torn from its context it requires elucidation. For, though the statement seems to afford a hopeful vista, it also confronts us with certain contingent and disheartening conditions. To begin with, the term *"elementar-ungeordnet"* means simply a state of elementary disorder or molecular chaos, i.e., the random, haphazard motion of molecules assumed as a basic postulate of thermodynamic theory. This concept is fundamental in the statistical approach to the second law; it is this random movement together with the staggeringly incredible number of molecules involved that constitutes an "adequate haphazard" for the Calculus of Probabilities. Taken in a very literal sense, these conditions seem forbidding indeed for any possible analogous formulations in the domain of social relations! The meager figures involved in the whole world population, running to something above two billions, shrink into insignificance beside the molecules in a sphere of air the size of a very big pea which come to a number of the order of 6×10^{18}—a magnitude belonging to another realm or level in the categories of nature. The numerical discrepancies alone would thus seem to present an unbridgeable chasm, for statistical laws and averages based on the order of numbers involved in one case can hardly be expected to apply to those of the other. But curiously enough this particular obstacle upon further scrutiny strengthens rather than weakens the argument in hand.

To understand the logic of this contention it will be necessary to delve somewhat deeper into the statistical interpretation of the second law of thermodynamics. The dissipative processes of energy are said to be due to the fact that nature tends always toward more probable states. This is but another way of

* J. F. Klein, *Physical Significance of Entropy* (New York: D. Van Nostrand Company, Inc., 1919), p. 90.

stating the law of increasing entropy. There is nothing abstruse in this conception: it says merely that, in a well-shuffled deck of cards, a random arrangement is more likely to appear than an ordered series. The larger the number of cards the greater this likelihood. Granted numbers of sufficiently great magnitude, the likelihood will correspondingly approach certainty. The classic illustration of this matter is usually given by picturing a vessel containing two gases separated by a partition. Upon removing the partition the molecules of the gases mutually interpenetrate, tending thus toward a mixed or "nondescript" state; and the entropy of the system is said to increase accordingly. Will the molecules, in the course of their random gyrations, return unaided to their original positions? Curiously enough the proper answer was given in an aphorism of Herodotus: "If one is sufficiently lavish with time everything possible happens." * They will, in short; but the likelihood of the event happening is comparable to that of a stone falling upward—a miracle that may possibly take place, according to Perrin,† in some $10^{10^{10}}$ years, or about 1950 with some 10 billions of zeros added! Physicists designate occasions when events occur under such altogether improbable possibilities as "fluctuations." The rarity of such occurrences, it is well to remember, however, is related to the magnitude of the numbers involved. The larger the aggregate or ensemble of elements, the fewer the number of significant fluctuations; and conversely, the smaller the ensemble, the greater the probability of such fluctuations. We may thus see directly that "fluctuations" are likely to occur more frequently in the ensemble of humanity, considered as an aggregate, than in the molecular structure of physico-chemical systems. ‡

* Quoted by C. E. Guye, *Physico-Chemical Evolution*, translated by J. R. Clarke (London: Methuen and Company Ltd., 1925), p. 136.

† Quoted by Ludwig von Bertalanffy, *Modern Theories of Development*, translated by J. H. Woodger (London: Oxford University Press, 1933), p. 59.

‡ The fact that, according to statistical mechanics, "fluctuations" occur with increasing rarity as the number of discrete particles involved increases has led Lecomte du Noüy to argue that life on this planet could not have appeared spontaneously. See his book *Human Destiny* (New York: Longmans, Green and Company, 1947), pp. 33 ff. This contention, in turn, is held to support a philosophy of religious finalism according to which evolution, and particularly

This conclusion, while adding to the difficulties of formulating general laws for the dynamics of society, undoubtedly accounts in some measure for the apparent lack of behavior patterns readily susceptible of explicit formulation. In a sense, at least on this basis and in terms of this hypothesis, there would be every reason to expect the wayward and the haphazard to play a role in history denied to them in the domain of physics. And on this basis also we may perhaps find an explanation of that curious ambivalence which moves historians to accept with equal certainty the doctrine that a law or principle of historic development must ultimately be attainable or, on the other hand, that it can never be achieved! Such conclusions go contrary to the grain of statistical laws; and the answer to this enigmatic situation may conceivably reside in the greater incidence of "fluctuations" in the field of historic events than in that of physico-chemical systems. For it is upon the latter, in the last analysis, that our sense of the finality of natural laws is based. And even here we must bear in mind that, at least as regards the statistical interpretation of the second law of thermodynamics, such fluctuations are specifically indicated. This fact was emphasized in the famous definition of the law offered by Willard Gibbs: "The impossibility of an uncompensated decrease in entropy seems to be reduced to an improbability." The phraseology has a New England accent; but the statement says clearly enough that natural phenomena involve in their operations a final increase in entropy, though this conclusion is only a probability of high order, rather than an a priori necessity. Behind the blind workings of chance we perceive the operation of law. Certainty is due to a cumulative sense of increasing probabilities; and the spontaneous unfold-

the evolution of man, is interpreted teleologically. It is interesting to note, however, that even Du Noüy acknowledges that his reasoning cannot amount to proof since chance is always present and may cause a fluctuation at any point in the immense range of improbabilities involved in the huge aggregates he employs. Actually a more important consideration is the likelihood that other physico-chemical factors may have been present, drastically reducing the sum total of such improbabilities. This likelihood has been explored in some detail and lends support to a contrary conclusion not only with respect to our planet, but to others in similar physico-chemical states. See "Some Physico-Chemical Aspects of Life and Evolution in Relation to the Living State," by J. Lee Kavanau, in *American Naturalist*, LXXXI (May-June, 1947), 161, 184.

ing of natural processes, referred to above, the unidirectional flow and irreversibility of natural events, is now seen to follow the principle laid down by Boltzmann: "The driving motive (or impelling cause) in all natural events is the difference between the existing entropy and its maximum value." * Here indeed we come upon that deep-seated feeling of *direction* associated with all evolutionary processes, upon which, basically, our very sense of time itself is thought to depend.†

Broadly interpreted, these abstract considerations sustain the possibility of such a conception as that of an inherent historic drift, of a form of historic determinism punctuated, as it were, by historic fluctuations. In the domain of physics fluctuations are not to be mistaken for uncaused events, or in the field of history for undetermined or miraculous interventions. On the contrary, they merely signify those exceptions in the law of averages revealed by statistical analysis itself; and in the case of history they imply trends divergent from the main course of events, momentary reversals or movements tangential to the dominant direction of an encompassing determinism. Thus an element of elasticity must enter into our historic conceptions and definitions; and in this connection it is well to bear in mind the significant point emphasized by Gibbs: that the whole edifice of this interpretation has a statistical foundation and expresses, accordingly, probabilities—however great—in distinction to an inescapable finality.

Returning to the conditions upon which the Theory of Probabilities was deemed applicable alike to the second law of thermodynamics and to "purely human and animate events," in the words of Klein, we may recall that he demanded of these events that they "possess like and uncontrolled constituents which may be properly characterized as *'elementar-ungeordnet.'* " Now it will not be readily apparent how such a condition can be fulfilled in the field of history in consonance with the relatively direct concepts of thermodynamics. Human beings and their actions possess a random element insofar as their

* Quoted by J. F. Klein, *Physical Significance of Entropy* (New York: D. Van Nostrand and Company, Inc., 1919), p. 98.

† See A. S. Eddington, *The Nature of the Physical World* (New York: The Macmillan Company, 1929), Chap. IV.

direction, so to speak, is inwardly determined and orientated. It would seem here as though only the personalized and introverted concept of the individual, or, in broader terms, the centralized ego-concept of the individual could possibly answer to a "like and uncontrolled" quality in the mass elements of a physico-chemical system. Indeed, it may be necessary to go even further and seek this analogous but necessary requirement in the basic biologic drives that Freud has conceived as fixed points in the psychic structure of the individual. Here we come upon the like and anarchic elements of individual behavior which, in their totality and interplay on the plane of societal relations, give rise to our cultural developments. The relation of the individual to society has undergone profound changes correlated with the varying pressure and relative dominance of instinct and intelligence upon his behavior. Certainly at no time in his history has the anarchic self of man risen to such an arresting and autonomous position as in the passing moment of balance between them. Such a moment, however, has no precise chronological center; it has moved uneasily throughout history, coming to a climax and turning point in our own era. But beneath this revealing moment the primordial center of man's ego exerts always an individual, if disguised, pressure. We may thus say that the conditions for sustaining an analogy between the fundamental processes of history and those of physico-chemical systems may be entertained at least on the broad basis of the second law of thermodynamics. Hence we may provisionally equate, for purposes of our analogy, the individual with the random molecule; the machine with the crystal; society as an organized entity with a physico-chemical system having a crystal structure; and, finally, a basic change of historic direction with a thermodynamic change of phase.

VI

In these matters it is easier, it must be confessed, to run into a bramblebush of difficulties and objections than to find a ready path between a universe of frozen procedure and the apparently willful activities of man. According to an unvoiced thesis of science, nature has traversed this path though man has thus far admittedly been unable to retrace the stages. The attempt has not infrequently been altogether abandoned or perhaps eluded, as for instance when biologists, seeking support from "entelechies" and other vitalist mechanisms, have faltered on the way; while even today certain physicists, confronted by this dilemma, are inclined to find refuge in the principle of indeterminacy. Actually biologists have long since returned to the attack and are seeking, even more ardently than the physicists, to trace the path, step by step, between organic and inorganic systems. In this situation the fact that certain basic and universal laws were seen to have a statistical rather than an absolute meaning appeared like a ray of light in an otherwise enclosed and impenetrable darkness. For here was a procedure that allowed for laws and exceptions to those laws; for averages and fluctuations; for regularity and chance; indeed, for uniformity that grows directly out of chance—a resolution of an age-old anomaly.

In particular it seemed that the running down of the universe might not be as final as it was originally thought to be. The great law of Clausius to the effect that "the entropy of the world tends toward a maximum" was questioned as thus stated, and by no less an authority than Professor Gilbert N. Lewis, to mention but one among many distinguished names. The dissipative processes of nature were not necessarily absolute, and irreversibility not necessarily final. Fluctuations, it was seen, not only affirmed the impossibility of absolutism in statistical laws; they ultimately undermined the concept of irreversibility—at least in finite systems. In his illuminating book *The Anatomy of Science*, Lewis has analyzed this situation in the following words: "We then find not even a shred of truth left in the statement that an isolated system moves toward a state of equilibrium. It will move toward it and move away from it, and in the long run as often in one direction as in the other. It is only when we start far away from the state of equilibrium, that is, when we start with some state of unusual distinction, and when we follow the system a little way along its path, that we can state that it will, as a rule, proceed toward more *nondescript* states." * He would amend the statement of Clausius to read: "An isolated system always proceeds in the direction of greater entropy, provided that it be so far removed from the state of equilibrium that the chance fluctuations in that state may be ignored." In compliance with this view, Lewis feels there is no evidence for the hypothesis of continual degradation of energy. How then can we reconcile this point of view with the fact that "all things are supposed to be moving toward a final state of equilibrium where all happenings cease?"

The matter is of moment since it throws light upon the essential nature of irreversible processes, upon the scope and meaning of determinism, and upon the role of fluctuations in relation to the problem of organic and inorganic systems. Thus it has been maintained, for example, that life itself, in its embryonic beginnings, may conceivably have been nothing but a fluctuation in an otherwise inanimate universe. And beyond the question of the origin of life, there remains the great challenge of the development of life—a principle that constitutes in certain aspects an apparent contradiction of the second law of thermodynamics itself. It was already indicated in connection with the aphorism of Herodotus that fluctuations, however unusual, will come to pass given sufficient time. The logic insisted upon by Lewis and others in this contention is unassailable; yet the problem we are concerned with must be set within our vista of the universe, within the humanly significant perspective of cosmic events and processes. Their logic says nothing about the scale of the data involved; yet this turns out to be the crucial and determining factor for us. Projected against the illimitable possibilities of an abstract number system, our finite world loses its identity, as it were; it becomes distinct only in terms of actual probabilities, and its reality must be explored on the basis of relative certainties rather than on that of abstract contingencies. The problem, it will be seen, devolves ultimately upon the emphasis we choose to ascribe to the fact of fluctuations. In this emphasis we reveal

* Gilbert N. Lewis, *The Anatomy of Science* (New Haven: Yale University Press, 1926), p. 153.

a psychological approach to the problem of world-destiny; but whether a theory of eternal recurrence is more or less preferable to an ultimate end in the Nirvana of immobility must remain a matter of subjective choice. If natural processes are in fact not absolutely irreversible, at least in isolated systems and possibly for the universe as a whole, it is necessary for us to glance at the *measure* of their relative certainty.

In the interpretative literature of the subject one is certain, sooner or later, to come upon two illuminating fantasies: the Maxwell demon and Borel's monkeys. We will have occasion to become acquainted with the demon; for the moment it is the monkeys that merit our attention. Lewis describes their quaint activities in the following passage, though he draws a somewhat different conclusion, on the basis of their efforts, from the one here emphasized. "Borel makes the amusing supposition of a million monkeys allowed to play upon the keys of a million typewriters. What is the chance that this wanton activity should reproduce exactly all of the volumes which are contained in the library of the British Museum? It certainly is not a large chance, but it may be roughly calculated, and proves in fact to be considerably larger than the chance that a mixture of oxygen and nitrogen will separate into the two pure constituents." *

From this statement we know very little about the time consumed by these literary monkeys, or about the volume of gas involved; but it is plain that this mathematical fable is intended to impress upon us the inconceivably minute chance of a reversal in the spontaneous, dissipative processes of nature. Our respect for the law of entropy, at least as regards large aggregates, is considerably restored; and we are hardly in a mood to seek for the fountain of youth in the formulae of thermodynamics! In any humanly significant perspective of the world-picture we must accept the frigid certainty of the laws of statistical mechanics as virtually final. This situation is well summarized by Alfred J. Lotka as follows: "The actual process of isothermal gaseous diffusion is, in fact, periodic, but with a period so long that, humanly speaking, the return to

* *Ibid.*, p. 158.

the initial state never occurs at all. For all stretches of time that can have any real significance in human thought (and this includes the vast historical ranges of all geology and astronomy), it may therefore be said in a certain sense that evolution proceeds, in all but a vanishingly small class of exceptional cases, from less probable states . . . to more probable states, tending ultimately toward a most probable state. This statement cannot, however, be allowed to pass without a word of caution. It is meaningless unless the characteristic with regard to which probability is reckoned is explicitly or implicitly indicated." * This latter part of the statement can perhaps be best understood in terms of the deck of cards previously referred to. Judged purely on the basis of the back of the cards, no amount of shuffling will ever change the significance of their arrangement. Such significance is dependent upon the characteristics that give identity and meaning to the face of the cards. We may say, in conclusion, that natural spontaneous processes may therefore be counted irreversible, despite the logic of probabilities, insofar as our human perspective is concerned. This conclusion rests at bottom upon the immeasurable magnitude of the aggregates involved in physico-chemical systems.

But that is not to say that those biologists who believe life to have sprung from fluctuations in the operations of physicochemical systems are necessarily mistaken. Such a point of view rests upon the fact that "life" may conceivably have arisen in submicroscopic entities where the decrease, numerically, of the particles involved is such, according to statistical principles, as to favor fluctuations. It is interesting in this connection to bear in mind that organic and inorganic forms converge in the submicroscopic realm. In his stimulating essay "Evolution and Thermodynamics," Joseph Needham speaks of this matter as follows: "We cannot make any sharp line of distinction between the living and the non-living. At the level of the submicroscopic viruses, they overlap. Some particles show some of the properties of life but not others. Some 'dead' protein molecules are much bigger than the particles of some

---

* Alfred J. Lotka, *Elements of Physical Biology* (Baltimore: The Williams and Wilkins Company, 1925), p. 33.

'living' viruses. Particles which show the properties of life can be had in paracrystalline, and even in crystalline, form. There are many similarities between the morphology and behaviour of crystals and living organisms." *

If organic and inorganic phenomena seem in some respects to converge as we approach the submicroscopic, they diverge if seen in an opposite perspective, and perhaps nowhere more significantly from a thermodynamic point of view than in the problem of "order." It is this problem specifically that Joseph Needham set out to solve in the essay mentioned above. Here indeed we come upon certain basic difficulties and anomalies not only in regard to the relation of evolution and thermodynamics but within the field of thermodynamics itself. Now it may seem at first glance that these recondite and technical matters are irrelevant to the main thesis in hand. But such is not the case: in order to appreciate the relevance of the problem we need only remember that the term "order" as used in thermodynamic discussions has certain universal implications that apparently contradict equivalent concepts in the field of organic evolution. And it is only in so far as these difficulties can be absorbed and resolved that we may finally pass upon the validity of such analogies as those proposed in the course of the argument.

Entropy is a measure of the unavailability of energy. It is historically noteworthy that man, sensing always the inherent discrepancy between his dreams and his reality, postponing indeed until the hereafter his hope of paradise, should at length, in our own era, have given precise and explicit expression to the universal and inescapable fatality of increasing entropy. In an age of optimism and fulfillment, when man had sought to escape the tragic undertones of life, he discovered the measure of this ever increasing deficit. It is therefore hardly surprising that he should have struggled against the implications of the second law of thermodynamics; against the threat of ultimate extinction in a dying universe. The door to that

* Joseph Needham, *Time: The Refreshing River* (New York: The Macmillan Company, 1943), a collection of essays including "Evolution and Thermodynamics," p. 224.

escape was furnished by the logic of statistical analysis itself, as we have seen, in the saving role assigned by certain scientists and philosophers to the idea of fluctuations. Here man's own sense of the tragic, his intuitive awareness of an overwhelming finality in the passage of time, have combined, however, to refute this abstract escape. Life is irreversible. But in this irreversibility organic and inorganic systems appear at one: the same law seems to embrace both spheres. Where then is the disharmony; the anomaly of contrary trends?

That organic processes are in fact irreversible is not merely an intuitive perception: biologists have analyzed the concept from various angles and have come always to the same conclusion. Thus, for example, in support of his argument, Henry Adams referred to the fact that evolution was considered an irreversible process according to the views of Louis Dollo (1893). Nor has this view lacked support from biologists since, as witness the findings of Professor Hermann J. Muller set forth in an article on "Reversibility in Evolution Considered from the Standpoint of Genetics" (1939). "In addition to the sheer statistical improbability, amounting to an impossibility, of evolution ever arriving at the same complex genic end-result twice, whether by reverse, parallel, or convergent evolution, there is the point raised in the discussion concerning relaxation of selection, that a given gene or genetic differentiation, once established, tends to become necessary in other ways than it may have been in the beginning." * And further: "In the ultimate sense, then, a reversal of evolution is an impossibility, although much phenotypic reversal (even on the deeper living plane of partially analysed ontogenetic and physiological processes) may take place, and although the individual genes often undergo reversion in a much more exact, possibly even in an accurate chemical sense. But collectively there cannot be a real reversion of the genes, unless selection were not natural but guided by biologists far more intelligent than ourselves." †
This view has been amply substantiated by other biologists.

* Hermann J. Muller, "Reversibility in Evolution Considered from the Standpoint of Genetics," *Biological Reviews of the Cambridge Philosophical Society*, XIV (1939), 271.
† *Ibid.*, p. 276.

Needham, for instance, in an article on reversibility in evolution (1938), expresses the matter as follows: "The gene-pattern allowing of a new adaptation would thus be formed by chance, and preserved by natural selection once formed, but not likely to be formed again. In this way we may envisage Dollo's Law as the consequence of the genetic equivalent of the second law of thermodynamics." * A final quotation on this subject from Dr. Harold F. Blum in a provocative article on "Evolution from a Thermodynamic View-Point" must suffice. "The concept of a changing environment is a necessary postulate for the theory of evolution by natural selection, and it would seem quite reasonable to consider the organism and the environment as mutually fitted to each other. This leads to the search for a common directive factor in the evolution of both the environment and the organism. To the writer it appears that we do not have far to seek to discover a possible directive factor, since it would seem to be provided by the second law of thermodynamics. The principle of irreversibility involved in this concept supplies the necessary irreversibility which has been shown to be required for the evolutionary process, the direction of development being such as would always be accompanied by an increase of entropy, the return over the same pathway being prohibited by the fact that it would involve a decrease in entropy." †

Thus we perceive in evolution a certain drive, an inherent direction, which is not to be identified on the basis here indicated with any teleological end. On the contrary, the principle merely states that evolution proceeds in an irreversible manner; that evolution, and along with it our own development in its widest sense, passes through ever changing forms, slowly or rapidly, or remains stationary; but that, unlike the theoretic conception of a reversible cycle in the physico-chemical domain, it can never recover an earlier state or return *in toto* to an earlier condition.

* Joseph Needham, "Contributions of Chemical Physiology to the Problem of Reversibility in Evolution," *Biological Reviews of the Cambridge Philosophical Society*, XII (1938), 248.
† Harold F. Blum, "Evolution from a Thermodynamic View-Point," *American Naturalist*, LXIX (1935), 354.

Resuming the discussion of the problem of "order," we may note that statistical irreversibility is synonymous with the spontaneous trend toward more random or nondescript states—toward "mixed-up-ness," in the awkward but more precise phrase of Willard Gibbs. The degradation of energy thus signifies a drift or movement in which molecular particles, shifting from more or less "ordered" states to more or less "disordered" states, leave the sum-total of energy correspondingly unavailable. This spontaneous drift has been described as a movement from less probable to more probable states. And by the same logic the trend moves toward a *most* probable state: entropy (the measure of mixed-up-ness) tends toward a maximum. These notions can be readily understood in terms of such haphazard, shuffling processes as the stirring of two liquids or the mixing of two gases: the longer the process continues the greater the probability that the ingredients will be more stirred or more mixed until at length they have reached a maximum or equilibrium in respect to their random mixed-up-ness. Here spontaneous processes come to rest, though the actual realization of this condition, as in the equalization of temperature differences, may be achieved absolutely only in a virtual infinity of time.* But this refinement in an understanding of the principle of the second law of thermodynamics, like a number of other obscure points, need not detain us in regard to the major question at issue.

Thus it may be said in general that the universe seems to be passing from an ordered to a comparatively disordered state. What is the meaning of this sweeping condemnation? In the irreversible drift of all natural processes is the universe rushing toward a nondescript, chaotic "dead level" of inactivity? Thermodynamics appears to give an unequivocal answer, at least as regards the direction if not the final condition of this drift. But if this is the case, what of the apparently contrary direction of organic phenomena which manifest in the evolutionary series a diversifying trend that encompasses an increasing rise in the parts of the organism and their relations—

* Cf. Planck, *Where Is Science Going?* (New York: W. W. Norton and Company, Inc., 1932), p. 189.

in a word, a rise in complexity and organization? Is the question itself due merely to a verbal bridge, as it were, through which the terms *order* and *organization* have become identified though they belong to diverse aspects of the world? Or is the organic realm but a minor sphere within the larger scope of the inorganic, and its manifestation of order but a postponed debit paid ultimately in terms of the entropy of the system as a whole? Or does life in fact somehow "cheat" in the game of entropy, as G. N. Lewis maintains? Whatever the answer, the problem not only embraces the organic realm of biology, it includes equally the whole range of man's development: for ourselves also we may ask, do the problems of form and structure, of organization, obey the universal dicta of thermodynamic principles?

VII

In view of the multiplicity of opinions which this problem has elicited, all sustained by ample and impressive authority, it would seem as though a new approach to the question were called for. Alfred J. Lotka in his book *Elements of Physical Biology*, already quoted, attempted to establish a new dynamics of living systems without, however, resolving this particular problem, as Joseph Needham remarked. Nevertheless he wrote: "We may have little doubt that the principles of thermodynamics or of statistical mechanics do actually control the processes occurring in systems in the course of organic evolution." * He felt that the methods and concepts developed in thermodynamics and statistical mechanics did not directly yield fruitful results when applied to particular problems in the domain of organic systems. He therefore conceived the notion of developing an analogous discipline suitable to the problem, and he expressed this idea in the following manner: "It would seem, then, that what is needed is an altogether new instrument; one that shall envisage the units of a biological population as the established statistical mechanics envisage molecules, atoms and electrons; that shall deal with such average effects as

* Alfred J. Lotka, *Elements of Physical Biology* (Baltimore: The Williams and Wilkins Company, 1925), p. 39.

population density, population pressure, and the like, after the manner in which thermodynamics deals with the average effects of gas concentration, gas pressure, etc.; that shall accept its problems in terms of common biological data, as thermodynamics accepts problems stated in terms of physical data; and that shall give the answer to the problem in the terms in which it was presented. What is needed, in brief, is something of the nature of what has been termed 'Allgemeine Zustandslehre,' a general method or Theory of State." *

Pending the elaboration of this Theory of State, toward the development of which Lotka's labors must be counted, according to Needham, as among the three or four greatest contributions in the whole field of biological inquiry during the present century, we may take refuge in the thought that there must be a kind of ensemble architecture valid alike in the realms of the organic and the inorganic. Moreover, there are two further factors that would seem to indicate a basic thermodynamic unity: on the one hand, the organic and inorganic realms converge toward an indistinguishable point; on the other, they both follow irreversible courses. It is true that they seem to point in opposite directions, as it were, but in this inherent and obligatory quality we may observe at least a kind of inverted parallelism, the meaning of which has not yet been clarified. For in the one case irreversibility is directly synonymous with a leveling process resulting in greater disorder; in the other with an ascending trend toward increased complexity and higher organizational levels, in a word toward higher order.

One might hazard the guess that irreversibility in the organic domain is the necessary tribute paid to the inorganic realm, in that life is always the longest possible route to death; that only on pain of ever further developments can the forms of living matter escape from an ultimate denouement, from a final return to the world of inert matter. Should such a speculative guess be substantiated and translated into some explicit formulation, it would go far toward explaining the point of view of vitalism, with its sense of a mysterious urge, on a causal and even a mechanistic basis. Here the death of the individual or-

* *Ibid.*

ganism is incidental, like the falling of the leaves of a tree, for the immortal span of life is carried on by the unbroken continuity of the germ plasm through all its evolutionary transformations. Such an approach would reveal the inverted connection between the two realms, and thus establish a relationship between them. It would go far toward explaining the apparent anomaly engendered by seeing irreversibility synonymous with the trend toward disorder in the inorganic realm and, conversely, synonymous with an inherent trend toward higher order in the organic domain. Such a point of view is perhaps in principle only a variation of the thesis that organization "can be drained from contiguous systems," in the phrase of Eddington, according to the basic law which demands that the entropy of the systems *in toto* be increased accordingly. Thus water may be made to rise in the form of a fountain on its way to the sea, but such is not the spontaneous nature of water; and the same problem remains to haunt us in regard to the first leap of the organic from the inorganic system. Only if life is conceived as a kind of self-perpetuating fluctuation can we reconcile these apparently contradictory conceptions. Our impasse has given rise only to a verbal escape.

Professor Ralph S. Lillie comes close to accepting some such self-perpetuating fluctuations at the base of living forms, for he speaks of a pre-existing set of conditions that must be assumed which "counteracts the tendency of chemical and structural symmetry which is the typical result of forces distributed at random. In the living system randomness is replaced by some kind of directive influence, originating intra-atomically and acting on the atomic or molecular scale." * In his essay on "Directive Action and Life" he develops the thought that the fine scale of protoplasmic activity, encompassed within a small and highly diversified volume, "represents a device (so to speak) by which local processes are removed (at least temporarily) from the interfering influence of mass effects." † That is to say, protoplasmic activity, arising in some intra-atomic

* R. S. Lillie, "The Problem of Vital Organization," *Philosophy of Science*, Vol. I, No. 3, p. 304.

† R. S. Lillie, "Directive Action and Life," *Philosophy of Science*, Vol. IV, No. 2 (April, 1937).

action, escapes the rigors of the second law by virtue of its fine scale and its minute action; it constitutes in effect a field for fluctuations.

The derivation of organic process on the basis of fluctuations has appealed not only to biologists but to physicists as well. One further quotation may be of interest, this time by a biochemist, Joseph Needham:

"From the description of the second law already given it must have been quite clear that this generalization has a statistical basis, and hence that if we had to deal with vessels so small that individual 'complexions' could be separated, the statistical law valid for swarms of them might not in all cases hold good. Disentropic, 'unusual,' fluctuations might then, if amplified (and amplification is a process at which living matter is very efficient), account for such phenomena of high organizational level as 'free will.' Such a point of view has been ably put by Ralph Lillie and discussed by Donnan. It would be related to the standpoint of A. H. Compton, and of G. N. Lewis, who describes living organisms as 'cheats in the game of entropy.'

" 'They alone,' he wrote, 'seem able to breast the great stream of apparently irreversible processes. These processes tear down, living things build up. While the rest of the world seems to move toward a dead level of uniformity, the living organism is evolving new substances and more and more intricate forms.' " *

Here the forbidding perspective of the second law of thermodynamics is sharply challenged. Not only are organic forms viewed as possible fluctuations in the overwhelming averages of inorganic existence; on the basis of a theory of organizational levels, free will † itself may be looked upon as the final

---

* Joseph Needham, "Evolution and Thermodynamics," *Time: The Refreshing River* (New York: The Macmillan Company, 1943), p. 215.

† Though incidental, it is important that this hypothesis of the derivation of free will be sharply distinguished from that based on the principle of indeterminacy. Both belong to the domain of modern physics, but beyond that they are distinct and unrelated. Indeed, the latter notion has been emphatically disavowed. In a review of Sir James Jeans's *Physics and Philosophy*, Professor P. W. Bridgman leaves no doubt on that score. "There is no connec-

and highest development of such fluctuations. The main theme of the essay on "Evolution and Thermodynamics," however, concerns itself with the anomaly noted above: namely, the relation of the thermodynamic trend, in the inorganic realm, toward increased entropy and increased "disorder," and the contrary biologic evolution toward increased organization.

Two possible explanations present themselves, according to Needham: either "The concepts of organization as held by physicists and biologists are the same; but all biological, and hence social, organization is kept going at the expense of an over-compensating degradation of energy in metabolic upkeep"; or "The two concepts are quite different and incommensurable. We should distinguish between *Order* and *Organization*." * In this latter alternative, favored by Needham, order is associated with the thermodynamic concept of entropy; organization with the evolutionary trend of biological phenomena. In supporting the second explanation, he does not deny the sovereignty of thermodynamic principles in respect to the law of increasing entropy in physical processes, including indeed all metabolic reactions. He drives more deeply into the concept of "order," insisting upon a basic distinction between what he terms "patterned mixed-up-ness" and "chaotic mixed-up-ness." This distinction is based on another notion: namely, that the opposite of mixed-up-ness is not organization but *separateness*. While the logic of this seems to rest on verbal distinctions, it may be said that they are intended to undo verbal confusions. And here it is instructive to compare two passages bearing on this aspect of the matter. "When crystals form spontaneously," writes Joseph Needham in the essay under consideration, "they do so in processes which involve decreases in free energy. The physicist must therefore say that disorder has increased, but the biologist, as a student of patterns, cannot but say that there

tion," he writes (*New Republic,* April 26, 1943), "between the details of physical theory and philosophy; Heisenberg's principle of indeterminism, for example, has absolutely no bearing on the problem of free will. As H. N. Russell recently remarked, what an enormous amount of grief would have been spared if the principle had been named in the first place 'the principle of limited measurability,' as Max Born proposed too late."

* Joseph Needham, "Evolution and Thermodynamics," *Time: The Refreshing River* (New York: The Macmillan Company, 1943), p. 220.

is more order and organization in the well-arranged crystal than in its homogeneous mother-liquor or corresponding gas." * Speaking, curiously enough, of precisely the same difficulty, Professor P. W. Bridgman voices the discomfiture of the physicist. "Even in the domain of situations which would be unanimously described as primarily 'thermodynamic,'" he writes, "it would appear that there is a rather large verbal element in the coupling of 'disorder' with entropy, and that this coupling is not always felicitous. Consider, for example, a quantity of sub-cooled liquid, which presently solidifies irreversibly, with increase of entropy and temperature, into a crystal with perhaps a regular external crystal form and certainly a regular internal arrangement as disclosed by X-rays. Statistically, of course, the extra 'disorder' associated with the higher temperature of the crystal more than compensates for the effect of the regularity of the crystal lattice. But I think, nevertheless, we do not feel altogether comfortable at being forced to say that the crystal is the seat of greater disorder than the parent liquid." † Plainly, the nomenclature is suspect. This corroborates, in a sense, the position affirmed by Needham.

Language developed in the macroscopic world of common experience is perhaps at best inadequate as a vehicle of expression for the precise description of molecular relationships. Words are likely to have a momentum that readily carries us into false conceptions. Although the passage by Professor Bridgman quoted above seems to sustain the objections voiced by Needham in respect to the verbal confusion involved, it does not necessarily support his resolution of the difficulty. According to Professor Bridgman, the disorder "associated with the higher temperature of the crystal more than compensates for the effect of the regularity of the crystal lattice." In other words, though the entire transaction involves an increase of entropy, the incidental and apparently contradictory emergence of higher organization in the crystal structure has been amply and duly paid for in a correlated temperature

---

* *Ibid.*, p. 225.
† P. W. Bridgman, *The Nature of Thermodynamics* (Cambridge, Mass.: Harvard University Press, 1941), p. 174.

change. Here the evidence of increased order is acknowledged, but only upon the payment of the price in the total of increased entropy. The logic of this position, carried over into the domain of biology, would seem to sustain the first alternative rather than the second proposed by Needham. Thus we may behold, in the domain of thermodynamic reactions, an apparent increase in order coupled with an increase in total entropy! If life-forms in their most elementary examples are held to be morphologically akin, at least in certain aspects, to crystalline structures, as Needham maintains, is it not probable that their development involves no other interpretation in respect to thermodynamic principles than that accorded to crystals proper? An affirmative answer would be tantamount to a preference for the first rather than the second alternative.

Like Lotka, Needham draws no sharp line, as we have noted, between the living and the non-living. "Now although biologic organization," he writes, "depends everywhere on a continuing metabolic upkeep, energy entering the plant as light or the animal as chemical energy in the foodstuffs, and being degraded in combustions and dissipated as heat; biological organization is only the extrapolation of patterns already to be found in the non-living world." * If, finally, quoting from the same passage, there are many "similarities between the morphology and behaviour of crystals and living organisms," how can we reconcile ourselves to a wholly different conception of their thermodynamic interpretation? In the natural course of events both are the products of irreversible processes; yet Needham identifies the crystal with "chaotic" mixed-up-ness, and the living organism with a contrasting "patterned" mixed-up-ness. To sustain this conception in a consistent structure he would equate the condition opposed to that of mixed-up-ness not with an ordered or organized state but with one that may be characterized as "separateness." This may point to a solution of the difficulty presented within the realm of thermodynamics itself—the anomaly hidden in the term "order" as discussed above by Bridgman. But now to sustain the distinc-

* Joseph Needham, "Evolution and Thermodynamics," *Time: The Refreshing River* (New York: The Macmillan Company, 1943), p. 224.

tion, indeed the opposition, between organic and inorganic processes in respect to their divergent trends, Needham would have the original, primal condition of universal separateness break down into "one of general chaotic mixed-up-ness (thermodynamic disorder) plus local organization (patterned mixed-up-ness)"—a term intended to cover the evolution of biologic organization. Thus, in conclusion, it is clear that to speak of evolution as the unfolding of a "patterned mixed-up-ness" may indeed solve the dilemna, but only, it would seem, at the cost of injecting into the discussion a peculiarly difficult and antithetical concept.*

We are reduced, it would appear, to the position indicated by Lotka at the beginning of this section—of awaiting the development of a general "Theory of State" or "*Allgemeine Zustandslehre.*" Yet it is to be observed that Lotka himself, though avoiding the particular problem with which we are here concerned, voiced an opinion that would seem to sustain the first of the two alternatives mentioned by Needham: namely, that all biologic and social organization is duly compensated by an adequate degradation of energy in metabolic upkeep, and that accordingly the organization of the physicists and that of the biologists are akin if not identical. It is true enough that he refrains from drawing any such conclusions—or any others, since

* To clarify this conception, Needham here introduces an analogy based upon the idea of children's building blocks separated in the cupboard according to their colors and shapes. Tumbled out upon the nursery floor they represent "the highly probable universe of the thermodynamician"—that is, a state of chaotic mixed-up-ness. Assembled into the form of buildings, on the other hand, they represent a condition of "patterned mixed-up-ness." The distinction is sufficiently clear, but the analogy fails to provide for the irreversibility of the process. Here, possibly, a box of water-color paints would serve better. As the process of painting proceeds, two kinds of mixing processes ensue: a patterned mixed-up-ness, resulting in the painting, and a chaotic, nondescript mixed-up-ness on the palette, ending up finally in a state of complete disorder, of ultimate mixed-up-ness. In both processes the manipulator has been omitted as a *deus ex machina:* it is plain, however, that he is essential in the first instance and not in the second; only the artist can bring about, within the restrictions of the analogy, a "patterned mixed-up-ness." The point is not without significance and may possibly have a bearing upon the meaning of instinct and intelligence. A further point worth mentioning in the latter analogy is that the *process* of producing a painting, if continued long enough, will eventually result in a condition of chaotic mixed-up-ness. Are we to suppose that the arc of organic evolution, reaching an unimaginable diversity, is but a vast digression in an ultimate descent into inert matter?

he does not concern himself with the problem directly; but in speaking of the *direction* of evolution he comes close to such a conclusion. "Having analysed the submerged implications of the term evolution as commonly used, so as to bring them into the focus of our consciousness, and having recognized that evolution, so understood, is the history of a system in the course of irreversible transformation; we at once recognize also that the law of evolution is the law of irreversible transformations; that the *direction* of evolution (which, we saw, had baffled description in ordinary biologic terms) is the direction of irreversible transformations. And this direction the physicist can define or describe in exact terms. For an isolated system, it is the direction of increasing entropy. The law of evolution is, in this sense, the second law of thermodynamics." * This passage did not escape the scrutiny of Needham, who emphatically denies the idea that the direction of evolution defies description. He implies that biologists, if not physicists, are prepared to give the answer in pointing to the rise in level of organization inherent in biologic evolution, and in social evolution as well. The defense Lotka prepared for just such an attack, it must be confessed, is not impregnable: he maintains that such phrases as "the passage from lower to higher forms" are vague and, moreover, often suggest anthropomorphic interpretations. He objects, likewise, to the notion that evolution proceeds from less specialized to more specialized forms, since the rule is one with many exceptions. He wishes to define the direction of evolution as a whole, and this leads him to arrive at his definition of evolution as the history of a system undergoing irreversible changes. Perhaps the most arresting and significant point about this definition is the fact that it does not distinguish between the living and the non-living: irreversibility embraces both.

If Needham rejects the notion that the *direction* of evolution cannot be defined apart from its irreversible course, he is moved to do so by the overwhelming strength of the evidence. But it is likewise plain that he welcomes this position for the support it gives, as well as the support it receives, from his sweeping

* Alfred J. Lotka, *Elements of Physical Biology* (Baltimore: The Williams and Wilkins Company, 1925), p. 26.

conception of "Integrative Levels" *—a conception of successive forms of order or organization, each distinct and self-contained, yet interrelated in the hierarchy of nature. This powerful and comprehensive conception cannot be used as a fulcrum for arriving at a decision in the matter here under discussion, but it must be acknowledged that the choice favored by Needham strengthens and extends the conception. The biologic "order," as it is often referred to, seems indeed a more complex and specialized level than that of the non-living domain, however defined; hence, far from accepting organization as a basic postulate of biology, Needham insists that it constitutes one of its central problems. For nature, he asserts, presents itself to us as a continuous rise in level of organization: a point of view closely related to the organicism of Whitehead and others. In this approach to nature, however, organization is not a conception confined to biology or the organic realm; on the contrary, it is held to be universally characteristic, in its own particular framework, at every stage and level of nature from the subatomic to the sociological and psychological levels of man.

Underlying all these forms of organization there must exist some manner of ensemble architecture—to return to a phrase previously used. The residue of abstract relationships caught in the web of these generalizations may well constitute the substance of a new type of basic morphology—a kind of dynamics of organizational relations. Such a study may conceivably substantiate for us those wholly imaginative or intuitive insights that precede formulation and exact definition, using analogy and similitude as instruments of thought and analysis. Speaking of the categories of Organization and Energy as replacing the more ancient concepts of Form and Matter, Needham writes: "From this point of view there can no longer be any barrier between morphology and chemistry. We may hope that the future will show us, not only what laws the form of living organisms exhibits at its own level, but also how these laws are

* Joseph Needham, "Integrative Levels: A Revaluation of the Idea of Progress," *Time: The Refreshing River* (New York: The Macmillan Company, 1943), pp. 233 ff. The conception of Integrative Levels is related to the emergent evolutionism of Lloyd Morgan and S. Alexander.

integrated with those which appear at lower levels of organization." * There is here the acknowledgment of a relationship of natural laws at all levels of integration; a kind of structural unification without which, indeed, the universe would be a disjointed and meaningless medley. Obviously some new approach to the problem of the relationship of organic and inorganic forms is imminent. For however differentiated the diverse integrative levels of nature may be, they are meshed into one another like cogs and wheels, each with its own gear ratio, its own scale and structure. The search for the terms of a more basic unity must proceed, as Henry Adams insisted; and we are not surprised to find Lotka searching eagerly for a comprehensive "Theory of State"—a more generalized instrument of analysis; while Needham, despite his insistence upon separate and distinct integrative levels, regards Organization and Energy as universal factors—"the two fundamental problems which all science has to solve," biology no less than physics, psychology equally with sociology. Energy and Organization: the animating principle and its inherent relationships; if these obtain in every level and aspect of the world, they must reveal also its unifying structural continuity.

VIII

Science has not yet produced the Vignola of its ensemble architecture—the Newton called for by Adams. His formulations would clarify for us the basic relation between evolution and thermodynamics; between the historic process and man's development as part of the evolutionary picture, within the encompassing sweep of the organic realm and the universal strictures of statistical mechanics. They would afford us an insight into the framework of each integrative level, since they would reveal to us also the inherent similarities and relationships of these diverse levels. They would establish a common denominator for the diversified scale of natural phenomena, a basic modulus enabling us to measure order in evolution as

* Joseph Needham, "A Biologist's View of Whitehead's Philosophy," *Time: The Refreshing River* (New York: The Macmillan Company, 1943), p. 206.

entropy measures disorder in thermodynamic procedure, the positive counterpart of this negative "ghost" quantity. However far removed from realization, the conception of such a modulus has been entertained and even prophesied. "The nature of holistic organization is certainly not susceptible of the same kind of measurement as thermodynamic mixed-up-ness," writes Needham, "but we have no reason whatever for supposing that its measurement is impossible. When such a measurement has been achieved, it would be feasible to apply it also to human social evolution. I see no reason for doubting the possibility of this." * Here indeed are words that echo the faith of Adams: three decades after his speculative mind entertained the problem, science has come to concede its cogency; to sharpen its statement, if not to forge its solution.

Statistical analysis might be said to constitute the grammar of an ensemble architecture such as that here conceived; but the special methods by which we are to express the relationships of organic and inorganic processes in harmony with this grammar remain to be developed. An oblique side light into the nature of the problem may possibly be gained by a consideration of the meaning of Maxwell's demon. The role of this creature as conceived by Clerk Maxwell was simple: it was his duty to guard a trap door in a partition dividing into two compartments a vessel containing a quantity of gas. By passing all molecules of high velocity into one compartment, and conversely all molecules of relatively slower velocity into the other, he could readily raise the temperature of one side and lower that of the other in defiance of the spontaneous equalization called for under the second law of thermodynamics. By his adroitness the demon could perform other wonders of a like heretical nature. Here in effect a principle of choice counteracts the law of chance: the demon would undo the trend toward mixed-up-ness, restoring the system to a condition described by Needham as "separateness." He would reverse the course of entropy and restore to energy that had been degraded its original availability.

* Joseph Needham, "Evolution and Thermodynamics," in *Time: The Refreshing River*, p. 230.

The Maxwell demon, dealing with individual molecules, is a purely imaginary construct. This phantom creature does not exist, though Hans Driesch in support of his vitalist philosophy thought that we ourselves were such demons! But there is a fatal difference, for whereas the demon can reverse the course of entropy, we can do so only by means of a deferred payment. All living organisms partake of this quality which in some mysterious manner permits them to pursue a contrary course to that of the inorganic realm. It was this fact which prompted the hope that, as entropy is a measure of disorder in the inorganic realm, so too there might be a measure of evolving order in the organic domain. But how are we to account in the first place for the capacity to make deferred payments—a faculty that enables organic forms to diverge ever further, it would seem, from their origin in the molecular level? In the economics of energy the organic realm appears to create by means of deferred payments an ever larger pool of available energy. For there is not only a universal trend toward mixed-up-ness, embracing the entire world; there is, likewise, not so much a contrary trend as a subsidiary drift toward deferred disorder which characterizes the entire organic domain. How are we to account for this contrary direction; how measure its inevitability? Inevitable indeed, for evolution, as we saw previously, is an irreversible process.

In a sense the demon is but a figure of speech representing the faculty of discrimination. He substitutes, as we observed above, choice for chance. But here the argument swings back suddenly to the very beginning of the discussion; for what are instinct and intelligence but *guiding principles*—devices, more or less perfected, for the cumulative exercise of choice in the manifold possibilities of the world? Or perhaps, indeed, instinct and intelligence are but the names we ascribe to the faculty of making deferred payments. In life the demon plays his role; in death he vanishes before the engulfing sweep of darker forces.

Clearly, as the forms of life develop, they exhibit in ever higher degree this faculty of discrimination. Or conversely, it might be said that the action of this faculty measures the development of the organism from those elementary functions that guide plant life through the gates of chance to the conscious and systematic techniques of man. We have seen that instinct and intelligence are different modes of achieving the same end result: namely, the guidance of the organism through the haphazard possibilities of life. In a passage bearing on this question Lotka implies that the distinction is one of degree, not of kind; and this is true as far as the ultimate success of instinct and intelligence is concerned, but not as regards their mode of operation. "Though man does far excel the other creatures in this respect," Lotka writes, "the difference is, after all, one in degree and not in kind. Many, if not all organisms, possess in some degree the power of selection, are in some measure independent of pure haphazard. This introduces an altogether peculiar complication into the dynamics of systems comprising living organisms, a complication of which the statistical dynamics of molecular physics are free. Not only is the living organism capable of performing, on a macroscopic scale, exploits analogous to those which in the world of molecules are permitted only to such figments of the imagination as Maxwell's demon; but this power of 'cheating chance,' as it were, is possessed in different degree by the several living organisms, and a dynamics of systems comprising living matter must necessarily take account not only of this faculty, but of the gradations in this faculty which have a large part in assigning to the several biological species their place in the scale of evolution." *

The distinction between instinct and intelligence in respect to this faculty may be perceived in the following incident. A valuable watch was lost in a large field of alfalfa that had just been mowed. The farmhands, the guests, and members of the family spread out over the field in all directions looking everywhere without avail. Their movements bore a humorous resemblance to the random and haphazard trails followed by insects in search of food. Finally, after long and fruitless effort, it was proposed that the entire company join hands in a single line. Advancing methodically up and down the field in this

* Alfred J. Lotka, *Elements of Physical Biology* (Baltimore: The Williams and Wilkins Company, 1925), p. 121.

formation, they soon recovered the watch. The incident was not without certain sociological implications concerning individual and collective effort; it suffices for us, however, in illustrating the essential difference between the operation of instinct and that of intelligence as discriminating agencies, as instruments of guidance. Chance is plainly present in both procedures, but it is lessened as systematic and deliberate action supplants the random movements of a haphazard procedure co-ordinated only by virtue of its objective. Thus the operations of instinct and intelligence are alike analogous in function to the role of the Maxwell demon; but intelligence, clearly, is not only the superior faculty because of its conscious attack upon the problem, it also introduces a wholly new and different technique with which to achieve its purpose.*

The obligatory character of evolution, implicit in its irreversible nature, colors the meaning of the term choice as here used in conjunction with the notion of chance. "Pattern mixed-up-ness," to use the phrase of Needham, is no less inevitable, it should be noted, than the descent toward maximum entropy —toward "chaotic" mixed-up-ness. Yet it is clear how the notions of purpose and drive, direction and design, have entered the picture. In fact, the more remote the organism is from those ambiguous manifestations that cause the line between organic and inorganic forms to waver and vanish, the more convincing these teleological conceptions become. That is why, doubtless, we must invert our usual understanding of instinct and intelligence in thinking of them as mere designations of different techniques for extending to the utmost the span of life and postponing the ultimate satisfaction of thermodynamic indebtedness. If we meet with ever higher levels of integration in the course of these transactions—as Needham and others maintain—it is nonetheless clear that this organic progression

* Incidentally, while intelligence appears to call for a deliberate tempo, instinct seems to diverge toward the opposites of intense activity or extreme placidity and patience, merging, indeed, into the immobility of plant life. The extremely rapid activities of some organic forms may be due to their random, haphazard mode of search; the placidity of others to a contrary technique involving a kind of faith in the stream of chance, so to speak. The food of plant life being virtually universally available, movement in this sphere would obviously be meaningless.

has the same ineluctable and necessary character that marks the reverse direction toward increased disorder in the inorganic realm. In the higher reaches of the evolutionary span we are likely to forget this fact and to interpret intelligence in particular as an autonomous faculty—a free agency as well as an agency of freedom. But life and life processes are inevitable no less than death: we must concede that the emerging levels of integration, the vast panorama of living forms whether of evolution or devolution, issue forth from the lap of nature in an irreversible stream, in a sequence no less determined than that of inorganic forms.

Necessity pervades the inorganic realm, permitting us to formulate its laws. But the closer our scrutiny the more we must accede that necessity hounds the organic domain no less, even though the complexities of living matter defy definition and formulation. And even in the highest reaches of human action we come to see that free will is perhaps merely a kind of accompanying consciousness to necessary choice. To say that we choose to do that which we must do, is merely to permit the demon of intelligence to function on pain of a greater or lesser triumph in the art of achieving deferred payments! Thus intelligence exerts an inescapable pressure; it partakes of the character of an irreversible determinism. We do what we must, if only because each action has its specific consequences: our freedom is but the high functioning of our intelligence. But in this sense, also, it must be granted that intelligence, marshaling the means of life, is animated and bounded by the primal instincts that are to be identified with the core of life itself.

These reflections afford us a somewhat deeper insight into the universality of necessity. For even if we equate instinct, and even more so intelligence, with the Maxwellian demon, we must still grant that we are concerned not with the opposition of freedom and necessity but with obligatory, if opposed, trends. The function of the demon, as far as life processes are concerned, must be thought of as one not of caprice but of principle—the principle, in short, of deferred payments. In the end, as the world of chance overwhelms the world of choice, the demon himself is overthrown. Meanwhile, in man, the

demon may be said to be aware of his function: this still recent, youthful consciousness of power has led man to believe
in the possibility of an eternity of bliss in some utopian paradise. But a maturer reality principle reveals these dreams to
be as futile as the hope of perpetual motion; and this is true
essentially, as we have seen, for like thermodynamic reasons.
That is why, perhaps, the wisest of men have stated in one
form or another the principle of freedom in terms of necessity:
to be free is to make a virtue of necessity.

Though heading the procession of living forms, we can no
more escape the drive of evolution than the humblest creature.
In attaining our eminence we have only gained consciousness
and insight into the obligatory aspect of our course. If nature
does indeed reveal itself to us in terms of emerging levels of
integration, it is plain that each stage in this cosmic evolution
pays homage, as it were, to those preceding it: the higher the
strata the more circumscribed and constrained within the mesh
of increasingly complex laws. For nature sculptures its forms
and makes itself manifest through ever more intricate reservations, ever more subtle strictures. And by the same token we
may perceive, in a reverse sense, that all manifestations of nature, however high in the scale of integration, must yet obey
the more basic laws of lower levels; and, indeed, that the whole
organic realm is thus anchored in the wider, universal domain
of the inorganic.

This inherent unity, embracing all phenomena, justifies the
notion of a universally applicable approach—a kind of *"Allgemeine Zustandslehre,"* as mentioned above—in the analysis
of nature. More particularly in relation to the argument in
hand, it justifies the concept of historic determinism in the
sense of a vast obligatory course inherent in the evolution of
man's development. For though, as we have seen, both instinct
and intelligence as guiding principles partake of the character
of the Maxwellian demon, yet their function itself is set and
predetermined; and the course of evolution, whether in man or
animal, is an irreversible procedure as definitely obligatory as
the irreversible course of entropy in the inorganic world. Or,
to state the matter more simply, neither instinct nor intelligence

has anything to do with caprice.* Under their sweeping direction man finds himself thrust forward and pulled backward in the awkward and contradictory gyrations of history; like a betwitched dancer, man follows the bewildering rhythms of his course. And thus, looking upon the matter from a wide perspective, we may come to ask whether man has not indeed changed his direction as intelligence, triumphing over instinct, became the dominant principle of guidance; and whether under these circumstances man has not entered a new phase in his development, comparable, in the very sense Henry Adams sought, to a change of phase in physico-chemical systems. And perceiving, moreover, the nature of the machine as an example of pure organization, acting inevitably as an agency of organization in all contiguous fields—like a crystal in a supersaturated solution—have we not here the analogous situation to a change of phase in the thermodynamic sense? For here also there is a morphological realignment comparable to the structural transformations that accompany a change of phase: the drift toward organization embraces the individual in a new arrangement precisely as the individual elements of a physical ensemble undergo structural transpositions in a phase change. The impending, inevitable, conscious collectivization of man, under a universal system of organization, will constitute, it is clear, a basic change of direction for humanity—a new phase.

Conceivably, then, man has entered upon a crucial turning point in his evolution. Such relatively sudden transformations are not unknown in either the organic or inorganic sphere, and the only question that remains is the problem of a possible relationship between the two spheres. Here we must await not only the coming of a Newton but the development of a science not yet begun! Yet, as we observed earlier, Alfred Lotka, among others, has broken ground in this direction; and in that amalgam of disciplines described as physical biology and conceived as "a branch of the greater discipline of the *General Mechanics of Evolution*," we may hope in the future to receive

---

* In the very young, it is true, a play instinct appears which seems charming to us largely because it seems pointless: in fact, however, it is a rehearsal of more mature maneuvers.

explicit answers to the questions here entertained. In a highly significant passage following this definition, Lotka gives us a further glimpse into the scope of such a science. "It so happens that many of the components that play an important rôle in nature, both organic and inorganic, are built up of large numbers of individuals, themselves very small as compared with the aggregations which they form. Accordingly the study of systems of this kind can be taken up in two separate aspects, namely, first with the attention centered upon the phenomena displayed by the component aggregates in bulk; we may speak of this as the *Bulk Mechanics* or *Macro-Mechanics* of the evolving system. And, secondly, the study of such systems may be conducted with the attention centered primarily upon the phenomena displayed by the individuals of which the aggregates are composed. This branch of the subject may suitably be termed the *Micro-Mechanics* of the evolving system. It is evident that between these two branches or aspects of the general discipline there is an inherent relation, arising from the fact that the bulk effects observed are of the nature of a statistical manifestation or resultant of the detail working of the micro-individuals. The study of this inherent connection is, accordingly, the special concern of a separate branch which we may speak of as *Statistical Mechanics*. This terminology is in part coincident with accepted usage, but in part must be understood to refer to an expansion of the subjects beyond the bounds hitherto covered, whereby its scope shall be extended so as to include the statistical treatment of the dynamical problems presented by aggregates of living organisms; that is to say, aggregates of energy transformers possessing certain significant special properties." *

Nothing is said in this passage directly concerning the *relationship* between organic and inorganic systems: only the relationship between the macro- and micro-mechanical aspects of individual systems—whether organic or inorganic— is under consideration. But it will be apparent that, in so far as the macro-phenomena of both spheres are subject to a com-

---

* Alfred J. Lotka, *Elements of Physical Biology* (Baltimore: The Williams and Wilkins Company, 1925), p. 50.

mon statistical approach, they exhibit certain parallel characteristics. Statistical analysis may in fact be said to constitute a
kind of mathematical bridge between organic and inorganic
systems or ensembles of large aggregates—an abstract instrument of analysis revealing similarities of a purely structural
type. This structural parallelism, pointing to an underlying
unity in the ensemble architecture of nature, is not to be interpreted, however, as affording directly an identity of structural meaning; rather it sustains and warrants significant analogies, far richer in implications than the mere harnessing of
phenomena under a vague verbal collar of intuitive extraction.
It is indeed the signal and basis for a wider generalization: for
that science of macro-dynamics of all irreversible systems that
will embrace organic and inorganic phenomena alike.

That science will embrace the social dynamics of man. It
will deal with the patterns, techniques, and structure of collectivization under the comprehensive principle of organization
set in motion on a universal scale by the machine; it will interpret this dynamic drift as a vast and sweeping phenomenon
of integration under the compulsion and ascendancy of the
principle of intelligence. It will recognize and delineate the
dynamics of this basic transformation in terms of a historic
change of phase, analogous in its structural meaning to a
change of phase in the physico-chemical world. And in general
it will establish the laws and structure and principles of an inescapable historic determinism.

V

VALUES AND VISTAS

Many of us will also find it hard to abandon our belief that in man himself there dwells an impulse toward perfection, which has brought him to his present heights of intellectual prowess and ethical sublimation, and from which it might be expected that his development into superman will be insured. But I do not believe in the existence of such an impulse, and I see no way of preserving this pleasing illusion.

—SIGMUND FREUD

I

LOOKING BACKWARD, it is interesting to observe that nothing could have been more extravagantly weird than some of the flying devices that anticipated the airplane. At once strangely prophetic and absurd, they range from Leonardo da Vinci's not inept flying machine to such grotesqueries as Sir George Cayley's birdlike baby carriage with its medley of attached umbrellas, kites, and propellers, intended to serve as helicopter and airplane in the year 1809. Yet they affirmed a purpose that has been accomplished, however far wide of the mark in visualizing its attainment they may have been. The future, we are always discovering, bears only a faint and superficial resemblance to the bold prophecies ventured on its behalf. For the future as well as the past changes as our own values change; and we seem consigned somehow to a warped field of operations in which only the immediate present appears firmly established. If our prophecies and predictions in respect to an exact mechanical problem were for the most part woefully incongruous, they have been no less awry concerning our own estate. Our guesses have on occasion, it is true, served to point out the direction in which the processes of history did in fact unfold themselves, as though guided by an intuition of the inevitable course of events. More often, however, in the turmoil of history, amidst the contrary winds of action and re-action, it has proved impossible to foretell which nascent trend would emerge ascendant, and which, dominant today, would fade and vanish from the picture tomorrow. Our vision of the future is subject at once to overemphasis and undervaluation; at best we perceive only a distorted image glimpsed through the opacity of time.

In the shifting panorama of history, the doubts, problems, and antinomies of one age are not so much resolved as sup-planted by those of another age. Man moves not from solution to solution but from problem to problem; that is why, essen-tially, he learns nothing from history and repeats the error of his ways with discouraging persistence. And always the prob-lem, reflecting some characteristic situation of the period, ar-ticulated in terms of contemporary events, belongs uniquely to its age. It has been said that the fundamental question of our era is the problem of integrating freedom with planning; but long before this stubborn challenge will have been re-solved, we shall have lost our contemporary sense of its mean-ing and be immersed in new and more pressing difficulties. And if man moves through history as through so much unfinished business, leaving behind him at each stage a residue of incon-clusive struggles and unsettled conflicts, it would seem as though he was being harried, in reality, by the same problem under different guises; and that indeed his solutions, at once fleeting and partial, only precipitated the selfsame difficulties in new forms. A central theme dominates man's history. Each age in turn touches upon that theme; and it is only in so far as our predictions concern themselves with some inherent and eventual climax in this shifting challenge that we approach the core of the historic problem.

The belief that man is in fact approaching a historic climax in our own age is well-nigh universal. The evidence is suffi-ciently clear and overwhelming; what is lacking is any common understanding or generally accepted interpretation of its significance. For the most part predictions concerning the nature of this change are followed by dire warnings of failure and collapse, chaos and corruption, unless mankind accepts the challenge of events and chooses wisely between the forces of darkness and light. Behind these warnings there is a fatalistic optimism—not indeed as to the issues involved, which are followed always by a dark coda of fateful forebodings, but rather a pious optimism about man's freedom to choose, to accept or reject his fate, according to some inviolable technique of the spirit, aloof from all contingencies. This limitless freedom is an act of faith. The problems of freedom and necessity are here resolved by recourse to a kind of arid, higher wisdom, above the battle, which conveniently charges us to accept the right and reject the wrong path. But this essentially moral and religious approach to the eventualities of life is at best but a spiritual exhortation—a counsel of perfection issued in a void. It is the compass needle of men of good will; it is neither a program of action nor a chart of exploration. And though it may be dangerous to embark upon a voyage without a compass, of what avail is the compass without a vessel? Granting the limitations imposed upon us by our conditioned nature, by our encirclement within a setting of impinging forces, we cannot in the nature of the case devise our course, or foretell our future, without taking into account these set circumstances and these fixed conditions. That is the meaning precisely of our conditioned estate; and if, in the past, man has seemed like a shuttlecock thrown back and forth by opposed historic forces, it may simply be that he has thus far achieved no final solution to the half-free and half-bound situation in which he has always envisaged himself. Nor will he escape this fancied dilemma until the problem itself shall have evaporated. Certainly, in any possible future solution of this persistent antinomy, man will find himself swept past his immemorial dichotomic status; and he will find his future course fixed and set, like a resolution of forces, in the silent elimination of his past condition. The problems of freedom and necessity will no longer remain poised in midair, subject to the winds of moral exhortation; they will be resolved, slowly and inevitably, in the

wholly new terms of an all-pervasive structural reorientation
of man and his affairs.

In attempting to fathom the future state of man, we are
brought up sharply by certain limiting conditions and trends
that promise to become more urgent and more decisive than
they have been in the past. And if, as we have seen, the basic
form and structure of human society are destined to be
changed, inherently and inescapably, it will be necessary to
adjust our vision of the future accordingly, and to interpret
the spiritual conditions of man's estate against the background
of his morphological status. For the mesh of his societal relationships will be drawn ever finer and more firmly, reducing
the individual to an ever minuter atom within the expanding
patterns of his social aggregates. Nor will this process take
shape under some overt edict or planned policy: it will occur
spontaneously and silently, like a chemical transformation,
without effort, without design, in conformity with the decisive
laws of future social necessity. Indeed, all the deliberations of
contrived policy, all the conscious adjustments of social organization, will be merely the instruments of this necessary
procedure. Yet, that is not to say that man lacks within his
rich and volatile nature elements presaging another destiny,
loftier, perhaps, more spiritual and humane: it is merely to
affirm that the future will evolve within the mold of certain
structural conformations that will unavoidably transmute the
basis of his person and his values as he now conceives and un-
derstands them. But before we can envisage such a change we
must attempt to fathom the abstract implications of that *morphological determinism* under which the future must necessarily emerge, whatever its particular characteristics or its
eventual constitution.

And here we must bear in mind the hazardous nature of venturing into the future; for how are we to interpret the events
and values of tomorrow except in our own terms of today?
The highest reaches of the past—the eternal verities of our
moral cosmos—melt away as the very light by which we perceive them changes, bringing ever new facets of reality into
prominence. Thus, both our hopes and our fears for the future

are merely the highlights and shadows of our immediate responses and reveal more about ourselves than about some remote
state to come. Even the ingenious zeal with which, in *Brave New
World,* Aldous Huxley explored the barren wasteland of his
prematurely precipitated, rationalistic society is seen to be
but a method of arriving at the present by a sham detour into
the future. We must content ourselves, it would seem, with less
vivid portrayals.

It is not by a projection of our latest scientific discoveries,
or our most recent spiritual orientation, that we are likely to
envisage the future course of man. Our guiding principles must
be more deeply rooted, more comprehensive and abstract. Only
on the basis of the widest possible summation of the past can
we hope to discern the drift into the future. Nor may we linger
too long before even the great syntheses achieved by the human
spirit in the past: only the dynamic antinomies that have
marked the entire development of man from prehistoric times
onward will reveal the vital factors of his future course. For
here we come upon the intrinsic principles of the historic process, the innermost sources and mechanism of change. The most
basic and universal terms under which these fecund antinomies
could be subsumed was seen to be the profound dichotomy between the instincts and intelligence—a conflict that has animated the entire course of human development, and that
promises to prevail in some form throughout equally extensive
periods into the future. For this struggle encompasses the history of consciousness; and though today we are passing
through a crucial epoch in this struggle, insuring an imbalance
in favor of intelligence as previous ages exhibited an imbalance
in favor of the instincts, the conflict will have entered merely
upon a new phase, opening up in turn new vistas in the development of man. There is little reason to doubt that, however
far-reaching the triumph of intelligence may be, it will always
represent a triumph over the instincts, and that man's future
development must thus be looked upon as an asymptotic progression in which the roots of his being will still draw nourish-
ment from the soil of his instincts. But, as the scales of the
balance shift ever more definitely in this direction, man will

have entered upon an entirely new domain, differing in both its vistas and its values from that of the past. And thus even his intelligence, which today is looked upon as the gift of the individual, may in time be accepted instead as an ingrained attribute of society as a whole, displacing our common impulses by an equally common rationality.

A change in emphasis as radical as this will necessarily give a wholly different hue and complexion to all the conditions and affairs of man. Above all, the coherence of society will be established on a new basis and maintained by a new technique. Even now a different approach to the problem of social forms is in fact emerging, however unacknowledged and unforeseen, in the vast and cumulative trend toward increased organization in every phase and aspect of human existence. This ubiquitous transformation, as we have seen, is destined to encompass the farthest reaches of life in an ultimate crystallization of its structural patterns. In place of the immanent values that arose, in the incipient stages of their development, out of the primal instincts, man will come to depend, under this new dispensation, upon increasingly rational and wholly extrinsic solutions of his problems. In short, a new manner of approach in the very perception and appraisement of phenomena, social no less than natural, is fashioning the world. How far we are justified in attempting to establish the consequences of this trend in shaping the edifice of the future, it would be difficult to say; certainly our own contemporary judgment of its essential character will in all probability not be shared by those destined to inhabit it. For the individual of the future will indubitably be as different from us in his basic orientation to life as his society and his world are certain to be different from ours. And though he will of necessity be more fully integrated and profoundly adjusted to his world than we, living in a transitional era, are to ours, we dare hardly peer beyond this generalization in our attempt to portray him. For our efforts in this direction will doubtless prove even more questionable and difficult, more arbitrary and unrewarding, than our attempts to comprehend the mental and emotional responses of our remote ancestors in early prehistoric times. If we are, perhaps, too rational to understand primitive man, we are still too emotionally and instinctually conditioned to envisage our successors in a remote future.

The extent to which the formulations of intelligence may come to supplant the directive guidance of the instincts is virtually unlimited, from our point of view; and however different life may come to be in the far future from what it is today, the integration of society will be effected, we may be sure, on the basis of conscious procedures and organized efforts. And just as the answer to a question is implicit in the statement of the problem, so the values and aims and conditions of man, the character and quality of life, are set in the very modes of its procedure and the forms of its operation. The organization of society will unquestionably proceed until its final crystallization shall have been achieved ecumenically, because of the relationship of this trend with the inherent dominance of the principle of intelligence. But the process, once dominant, implies in turn a steady decrease and retardation of social change—the gradual slowing down of the momentum of history until, indeed, we shall be confronted by the inverse of our historic ascent in ever more delayed sequences of stability and permanence in the conditions of life. And thus, in a period devoid of change, we may truly say that man will enter upon a *posthistoric age* in which, perhaps, he will remain encased in an endless routine and sequence of events, not unlike that of the ants, the bees, and the termites. Their essentially unchanged survival during some sixty million years testifies to the perfection of their adjustment, internally and externally, to the conditions of life: man may likewise find himself entombed in a perpetual round of perfectly adjusted responses.

Curiously, we seem to have returned, via the route of intelligence, to the very status from which man departed, aeons ago, under the undivided dominance of the instincts. For here, too, in the conditions of the future, the organism appears suspended within set responses, following interminably the selfsame patterns until altered by the slow processes of biologic mutations. These extremes of instinct and intelligence throw light upon the nature of consciousness; for, obviously, it is only in the strained field of their mutual interactions that consciousness itself can arise. Consciousness depends upon a state of imbalance, a condition of tension. It is an awareness, in its widest and most intensified aspects, of that unstable equilibrium whose passing phases in the development of man we call history. Thus we are led to perceive that history itself, however inclusive we may conceive its sway, must be counted in reality as a high transitional era of relatively short duration in comparison with the slumbering eternity that preceded it, or the ever more static ages that will follow upon it. Consciousness will gradually evaporate and disappear in this posthistoric period, very much as it condensed step by step into ever sharper focus during man's prehistoric era. In the ultimate state of crystallization to which the principle of organization leads, consciousness will have accomplished its task, leaving mankind sealed, as it were, within patterns of frigid and unalterable perfection. In this consummation we perceive the essential meaning of the posthistoric period of man's development.

II

Visions of the perfected mechanization of man and all his institutions seem to us harsh and forbidding; yet, in the words of Alexander Goldenweiser, they possess "a certain icy grandeur." * For all that, like many other prophets of the future, he recoils from these intimations of perpetual and static perfection as from some unending and inhuman ritual. For the scene presents itself to us not only as the death of the spirit of man but as a ceaseless movement of rigid and inanimate parts like the recurrent motions of a dancing marionette, or the precise gyrations of a machine. We are reminded of Descartes' automatism: of an involved complex of movements so precisely determined as to seem somehow uncaused, like the intricate behavior of a swarm of insects. Spectacles of mechanical finality at once fascinate and terrify us; and perfection of adjustment, whether

* Alexander Goldenweiser, *Robots or Gods* (New York: Alfred A. Knopf, Inc., 1931), pp. 126 ff.

attained through the agency of the instincts or through that of intelligence, appears to us always slightly incomprehensible in its finality. Our sense of incongruity is due, doubtless, to the fact that we are naturally incapable of effecting an ultimate separation in the routine of our lives between instinct and intelligence, feeling and thought. We flounder, involuntarily, as we approach these extreme positions, perceiving that, in their unqualified dominance of the field, these forces, acting independently, threaten not only the operation but the very existence and possibility of consciousness as we know it. Our intelligence informs us that instinct, in its pure essence, possesses a quality of automatism; and our instincts warn us equally that intelligence, left to its own devices, is wholly arbitrary and inflexible.

Each faculty may thus be said to give rise in its own characteristic manner to a state of absolute and uncompromising finality. The distinction between these basic techniques in this respect is perhaps, in a manner of speaking, merely one of introversion and extroversion. A hand puppet, operated invisibly from within, presents to us a no less mechanical aspect than the marionette, animated by strings from without. Thus the instincts, in their smooth and inevitable functioning, bear an external resemblance to intelligence in its ultimate perfection, operating with all the mechanical finality of the law of cause and effect. And, as we move from the farthest extremity of our primal state under the instincts toward our ultimate destiny under the sway of intelligence, it is plain that the unconscious functioning of the *organism,* in its strikingly fixed and inflexible operations, is not unlike the frictionless functioning of a perfected *social organization.* But this is only to say that opposites meet; and possibly it was this curious and misleading similarity, like that of poles lying on the same line though pointing in contrary directions, that gave rise to an erroneous and now discarded theory to the effect that the instincts are, in fact, merely ingrained habits originally fashioned by intelligence. Biologically, the priority of the instincts is not open to question, and the thesis in consequence is altogether untenable.* It is only in the case of man, moreover, that intelligence is sufficiently developed to reveal its operation apart from the enveloping penumbra of the instincts; and it is only in the case of certain insects that social life has been developed to an ultimate degree on the basis of pure instinct. The apparent parallelism between instinct in its primal sovereignty and intelligence in its inherent and final dominance, as exemplified by the social insects, on the one hand, and implicit in the ultimate social structure of man, on the other, is due to the virtual identity of their objectives: namely, an ever finer, subtler, and more enduring adjustment of the organism to the demands of life through a collective rather than an individual technique of adaptations.

In the highly evolved habits of bees, ants, and termites we may observe the extraordinary development which the instincts

---

* There are, to be sure, "automatized acts" of intelligence which bear a striking resemblance to instinctive behavior; and it is precisely on the basis of such acts, conceived on a universal scale as the sole mode of operation of society, that the similarities between instinct and intelligence in their independent functioning were here developed. But that is not to say that instinct and intelligence are interchangeable modes of operation, or that intelligence may have preceded instinct in some instances of biologic behavior, since the reverse is uniformly true.

The faculty of intelligence is indeed inheritable, but not the behavior patterns developed by that faculty. Those of instinct, however, are so transmitted; to assume a similar genetic transmissibility for the patterns of intelligence is to revive again the discredited theory of the inheritance of acquired characteristics. Hence it is misleading to speak of these patterns as becoming *ingrained* in a biologic sense, however *fixed* they may become in a social sense.

Nevertheless Arnold J. Toynbee (*A Study of History*, London: Oxford University Press, 1935-1939, III, 108 ff.) leans heavily upon the theory enunciated by R. W. G. Hingston in his book *Instinct and Intelligence* (*The Book League Monthly*, Vol. I, No. 6, April, 1929, pp. 281, 285) that instinct in the case of the social insects may be but a residue of patterns, developed originally by intelligence, that have become ingrained through their inflexible repetition. Hingston believes, moreover, that "we are not justified in making barriers between insect and human mentality" (p. 285) since their minds operate in the same way "in their main essential characteristics." This thesis is flatly denied by Julian Huxley, who assures us that the insects have no vehicle for the operation of intelligence. See his essay "The Uniqueness of Man," already referred to. A certain retrogression accompanied the development of insect societies, according to William Morton Wheeler, but this is not to be interpreted in the sense indicated above. Thus, in his book *Emergent Evolution and the Development of Societies* (New York: W. W. Norton and Company, 1928, p. 44), he says: "Many more examples might be cited but these will suffice to show that evolution by atrophy certainly accompanies an advance in social integration in the insects.... Turning to man we notice a similar regressive development of the individual as civilization proceeds."

are capable of achieving in respect to social order. A significant explanation of the high degree of social behavior attained by these insects has been advanced on the basis of certain genetic principles by Professor Hermann J. Muller, which it would be well to quote at length. "There are certain genetic considerations which allow us to conclude that, in most species of animals, the process of biologic evolution in respect to traits that make primarily for widespread mutual aid is a slower one than the evolution in respect to ... traits that help the individual and his immediate descendants as much as they do the group. For the former, the social traits, must in a state of nature become selected biologically mainly by means of inter-group competition, while the individually useful traits become selected both by inter-group and also by inter-individual competition.... We must make an exception here of the ants, bees, and some other social insects, since in them the group as a whole, consisting of workers that are all the off-spring of a single individual, shares the variations of that parent individual and virtually *is* that individual in an expanded condition, inter-group and inter-individual selection here being practically the same thing. In correspondence with this we find social instincts and behaviour and social characteristics in general developed to a far higher level among those insects than in man or any other social mammals or birds." *

It would seem as though intelligence, having reached a position of dominance in the case of man, could at best only attain more quickly perhaps what the instincts had achieved, in the case of certain social insects, many aeons ago. For the organization of human society depends of course upon the operation of relatively far more rapid modes of social and cultural inheritance than the excessively slow mutations of purely biologic techniques. It is important to bear in mind, moreover, that intelligence can implement these gains by a conscious manipulation of the evolutionary process itself. And here, indeed, intelligence achieves a new phase and opens up a new aspect in the entire panorama of organic existence. Thanks to the science

* Hermann J. Muller, *Out of the Night: A Biologist's View of the Future* (New York: Vanguard Press, Inc., 1935), pp. 99, 100.

of genetics, which belongs almost wholly to this century, we have been granted at least a glimpse of unimagined potentialities in this direction. Through deliberate and conscious genetic control, man may lift himself by his bootstraps, biologically speaking: he may henceforth improve his stock in a manner beyond that of his earlier plant and animal husbandry, according to his highest scientific judgment. Here, if anywhere, it would seem as though man could breach the trend of events and retard, perhaps for a long time, the final crystallization of society in a universally organized condition of "invincible equilibrium." The very novelty of the technique defies comparison and silences doubt: man's divergence from the biologic series amounts here almost to a severance in which, henceforth, he will steer his own course and be the master of his own fate. There is a peculiarly baffling logic in this position. Who is to say that man might not escape his present destiny, seeing that what appears inevitable for him today may bear little or no relation to the creature he may become, by a magic of his own, in some distant future stage? Nor has nature itself established any precedents by which to gauge the plasticity of life in its genetic potentialities, and more particularly under the guidance of man's intelligence. To deny these possibilities, even in their farthest reaches, would be altogether dogmatic; to accept them without question or scrutiny would be a meaningless gesture of pure faith. For there are, obviously enough, contingent conditions and implicit reasons for supposing that this approach to the future of humanity possesses, like all else in nature, its own inherent and unique limitations; and though man may likely enough alter his genetic constitution and therewith his faculties and his abilities—even his psychic and mental capacities—it is nonetheless doubtful whether he will eventually contravene his long-established innate drift, or whether, indeed, he may not in reality accentuate it—reinforcing and sealing his fate as far as may be by harmonizing his genetic manipulations with the conscious acceptance of his predestined course.

The possibilities of this approach to the future condition of man have nowhere been more ably or fearlessly explored than by Professor Hermann J. Muller in his book, previously men-

tioned, *Out of the Night: A Biologist's View of the Future*.
Combining the critical knowledge of the scientist with the
fervor and imagination of the humanist, he envisages for us a
well-nigh limitless development—contingent, it is true, upon
man's acceptance of the challenge before his sun will have set,
irretrievably, in the inherent biological deterioration that is
otherwise in store for him. Summing up his position, he writes:
"And so we foresee the history of life divided into three main
phases. In the long preparatory phase it was the helpless
creature of its environment, and natural selection gradually
ground it into human shape. In the second—our own very short
transitional phase—it reaches out at the immediate environment, shaking, shaping, and grinding it to suit the form, the
requirements, the wishes, and the whims of man. And in the
long third phase it will reach down into the secret places of the
great universe of its own nature and, by aid of its ever-growing
intelligence and coöperation, shape itself into an increasingly
sublime creation—a being beside which the mythical divinities
of the past will seem more and more ridiculous, and which,
setting its own marvelous inner powers against the brute
Goliath of the suns and the planets, challenges them to
contest." *

The involved technical reasons for believing such a transformation possible, and the numerous steps required to bring
it about, need not detain us here. It depends in the first instance
upon a more equitable distribution of the means of life not
only to establish a kind of laboratory equalitarianism the better
to judge the natural endowments of the individual but also to
create the necessary social basis for the entire co-operative
enterprise. It involves, in its consummation, the necessity for
defining those social ideals toward which mankind should be
directed, and includes in its technique the artificial insemination of women with the seed of the truly great and notable men
of the race—a procedure that would parallel on a higher level
the unique genetic traits of bees and ants with a like trend
toward uniformity and collectivization—coupled, moreover,
with the sterilization of the defective and deficient. And it

* *Ibid.*, p. 125.

depends, finally, upon a sustained program of action over a period of innnumerable generations. All these factors, taken singly or in their totality, imply a highly scientific and wholly rationalistic approach to the future. But in thus harmonizing their technique with the deliberate and conscious procedures demanded by intelligence, it is plain that our genetic explorations and achievements will far more likely implement the trend toward social crystallization than contravene it: man will hasten along his predestined way under the illusion of attaining his freedom on ever higher levels of existence, while actually sealing his fate by all the devices his dominant intelligence can command.

The controlled procedures demanded by a eugenic program based upon the scientific tenets of genetics are contingent in the final analysis upon a degree of social organization, of collective order, unity, and conformity, beyond anything dreamed of by man, unless it is in the satiric novels of frightened antirationalists, or the visions of utopia which, as Toynbee has admirably shown, are so often the projections of a wish for inflexible stability, rather than happiness or progress, in the affairs of man. Plainly, in reaching a sufficiently high level of corporate and collectivized existence to insure the effective operation of genetically desirable procedures, mankind will already have gone far toward a reorientation of its basic values, its ultimate aims and ideals; and we may thus confidently predict that the direction of its genetic aims will coincide and reinforce its now deeply established trends. In this redoubled adjustment man may achieve a supreme fitness as his self-willed goal merges imperceptibly with his predestined condition. If freedom is indeed an acceptance of necessity, he will surely approach his fate with a bland sense of divine accomplishment. Unerringly, his drive toward conformity will guide him into an ever more static condition of fixity and permanence; and the perfection of his adjustment will come to be synonymous with a slow but ultimate fading out of his consciousness. His triumph will be complete, and by that very token his awareness, no longer necessary, will evaporate, leaving only a fixed routine of actions whose perfect suitability will erase all memory of thought. Man will have attained a crystallized phase of complete and universal organization.

Man's social progress was due not to some sudden increment in his intellectual endowment but to the cumulative nature of his experience. The intelligence of contemporary man, according to a consensus of opinion among qualified authorities, is essentially the same as that of primitive man in the Stone Age. We may perceive in this fact the immense absorptive capacity of society: all progress is due to the accretions of individual experiences harmonized and welded into the vast edifices of civilization. And though, doubtless, genetically favorable selection, exercised over a long period of consistent effort, would raise the average intelligence of man beyond even that of our own exceptional men of genius, the momentum of society would have outstripped this slowly moving average and established its norms and standards indelibly upon the texture of life. But this is not to deny the certainty of genetic manipulation in the future history of man: on the contrary, the drift of the argument is to emphasize the unity of direction which such a program would inevitably share with the implicit drift of man under the compulsion of his intelligence. The convergent trends of life under the dominance of intelligence will inevitably accelerate the coming of universal organization; and the future condition of man, as we have seen, gives evidence of ever greater stability and fixity, approaching in an asymptotic sense an ultimate state of final crystallization. Nor can we doubt, under this equation of change, that man will in time direct his psychology in extrovert harmony with the established drift of life, eliminating ever more ruthlessly the friction of divergent personalities and tangential philosophies under the plea of social efficiency and social health. Thus, the meshes of the social sieve are being constantly tightened, so to speak; and the acceleration toward an ever more highly organized condition of man's affairs must in itself become the dominant directive force of society. Under these circumstances the meaning of the individual, and the moral, ethical, and religious relationships arising out of the conception of the person as the fountainhead of spiritual values, will gradually lose definition and become dissipated under the impact of a purely collectivist dispensation. But even more basic, perhaps, in the final long-range perspective of this aspect of man's future estate, is the fact that human consciousness itself will slowly relax its tension and become dissipated.

The general trend toward greater unification in the social systems of man and the consequent reabsorption of the individual into the mass patterns from which he originally emerged —this extraordinary return on a universal basis under the influence of intelligence to a status essentially similar to that evolved on the basis of small local groups under the guidance of the instincts—will be accepted, by and large, as a token of liberation in the natural course of our evolutionary development. Man will accept the centripetal pull of organization as a kind of social gravitation, at once universal, inescapable, and beneficent. And, as he lifts himself out of the confusion of his transitional turmoil, he will come to accept, as though it were indeed his choice, that which is inevitable.* Dr. R. W. Gerard, in an interesting discussion of successive levels of biologic and social integration, expresses himself on this point as follows. Designating society on the human plane as an "epiorganism," he writes: "The individuals are imperceptibly conditioned to the social milieu, the internal environment of the epiorganism, and overwhelmingly they behave as they do with no feeling of coercion but rather with the feeling of free and voluntary action." † He recognizes, moreover, the different ratios of advance on the part of the social whole and the individual, and

---

* In sharp antithesis to this implicit acceptance of the future, Friedrich A. Hayek, in his book *The Road to Serfdom,* warns us against the dangers of centralized planning, collectivization, and the entire contemporary trend toward a deepening of unified controls and internationally organized procedures. Aware of the direction of events, Hayek would have man reject what he deems a hazardous and unfeasible drift, in favor of a deliberate return to a less articulated scheme of things. But this *"reculer pour mieux sauter"* (p. 241), this return to nineteenth-century liberalism, however alluring, constitutes in fact a historic self-contradiction: man cannot return upon himself by calling the inevitable unwise, or by a deliberate attempt to circumscribe the inherent momentum of historic forces beyond his control. Samuel Butler, perceiving the deeper trends of history, allowed his wise Erewhonians to accomplish a retreat, the better to advance, by a ruthless elimination of all machinery!

† R. W. Gerard, "Higher Levels of Integration," *Biological Symposia,* edited by Jaques Cattell (New York: The Ronald Press Company, 1942), VIII, p. 83.

he ascribes the drift toward ever higher levels of integration in the social systems of man to an ever changing emphasis upon intellectual in place of emotional attributes.*

The disparity between the advancement of society and the development of the individual *per se* will be apparent in an ever more decisive manner, until at length the individual will no longer retain his supreme status as the focal point of the multitudinous values of life. That is to say, the person as the source and citadel of spiritual realities, as the ultimate center of being and the nucleus of creative thought and activity, will ultimately come to seem a remote myth, a vague historic concept devoid of all contemporary relevance, like the divine right of kings. In so distant a perspective, human society may conceivably have become stratified into distinct functional orders —a condition anticipated in Plato's *Republic*—under which, nonetheless, the individual as such will be wholly submerged in the common group characteristics of the mass. Indeed, his present amorphous potentialities will have become crystallized in terms of distinct functional capacities that will reduce him to merely an indistinguishable member of one or another highly articulated group. The increased use of emblems, uniforms, and other specialized apparel, quite apart from military and political activities, is a symbol of the growing specialization of man's affairs and at the same time a subtle indication of the immersion of the individual in his functional capacities. Whether or not society will eventually be separated into morphologically specific orders and classes, it would be rash to say: it is significant, however, that in most utopian projections of man's future, society is envisaged as an orderly ensemble of functionally specialized classes that seem, in some sense, analogous to the highly differentiated caste systems of the social insects. But whatever the particular nature and structure of future society, it is amply clear that human individuality must necessarily become more and more blurred as man finds himself increasingly absorbed in his functional capacities within an all-

* In respect to certain of its biologic and social implications, however, this essay has been called into question. See Dr. Alex B. Novikoff, "The Concept of Integrative Levels and Biology," *Science,* Vol. 101, No. 2618 (March 2, 1945).

embracing collective entity. And under this dispensation his acute consciousness, his individual psyche, must likewise fade and vanish, to be supplanted in time by a compensatory sense of fitness and adjustment in the scheme of things—a bland acceptance of his status within the rigidly crystallized patterns of life which alone will afford a set measure of expression for the awareness of his long-atrophied self.

III

The idea that the triumph of intelligence over instinct as the dominant faculty in the guidance of life indicates a concomitant mental superiority on the part of the individual is not only unsupported by the evidence but constitutes a misunderstanding of the operation of intelligence in the development of society. That triumph, as we have observed, is due to the cumulative nature of social experience. As mankind establishes an ever larger bank account of relatively small accretions, the individual perforce finds himself on the edge of an ever wider circle of knowledge, inherited experience, and accumulated wisdom. The individual as such might thus remain stationary in his mental capacities and endowments while society continued to evolve; indeed, the mechanism of the process must inevitably reduce the individual to a more or less limited, vicarious, and partial share in the ever widening panorama of societal enterprises and relationships. In the long run, under these circumstances, we might conceivably advance socially while remaining stationary as individuals in quite other aspects than our innate mental capacities, until at length the progressive curve of man's development would taper off toward a condition of increased fixity in which both the individual's development and his status would become likewise fixed and static. Relatively, if not actually, the individual would appear to have suffered a degeneration; and in this respect, as William Morton Wheeler has shown, man would only be following the course pursued by the social insects. "It would seem," he writes, "that the present very imperfect state of our society may allow for not a few successive emergents in the form of greater solidarity and higher ethics. But here we touch on a consideration which even Herbert Spencer felt to be ominous. Will this prospective, more intensive socialization be analogous to that of the highest social insects, a condition in which specialization and constraint of the single organism are so extreme that its independent viability is sacrificed to a system of communal bonds, just as happens to the individual cell in the whole organism?" * Wheeler sees in man a regressive development of the individual, as civilization advances, not unlike the evolutionary atrophy which accompanies the advance in social integration among the insects, and he foresees that we may be drifting in the direction of a type of society "quite as viable and quite as stable through long periods of time as the societies of ants and termites, provided it maintained a sufficient control of the food supply." †

In emphasizing the growing disparity between individual and race, Wheeler quotes an interesting passage written by Friedrich Schiller in 1795, which, curiously enough, also serves C. G. Jung in elucidating this very point in his book *Psychological Types*. ‡ "I do not ignore," wrote Schiller, "the advantages which the present generation, regarded as a whole, and measured by reason, may boast over what was best in the bygone world; but it must enter the contest as a compact phalanx and measure itself as whole against whole. What individual modern could enter the lists, man against man, and contest the prize of manhood with an individual Athenian? Whence then arises this unfavourable individual comparison in the face of every advantage from the standpoint of the race?" § The exaggerated virtues which Schiller ascribes to the individual Greek do not invalidate his argument, as Jung points out, since the Greek, relatively speaking, was a far less differentiated person than modern man; and this distinction in fact constitutes an answer to the question Friedrich Schiller poses. Indeed, he answers

* William Morton Wheeler, *Emergent Evolution and the Development of Societies* (New York: W. W. Norton, Inc., 1928), pp. 43 ff.
† *Ibid.*
‡ C. G. Jung, *Psychological Types* (New York, Harcourt, Brace and Company, 1924), pp. 91 ff.
§ Quoted by Jung, *Psychological Types*, p. 91.

himself in a single sentence: "One-sidedness in the exercise
of his powers leads in the individual infallibly to error, but in
the race to truth." * This theme is developed by Jung at great
length; he sees that the "... great organizations of our present-
day civilization actually strive for the complete disintegration
of the individual, since their very existence depends upon a
mechanical application of the preferred individual functions of
men. It is not man that counts, but his one differentiated function. Man no longer appears as man in collective civilization:
he is merely represented by a function—nay, further, he is
even exclusively identified with this function.... Thus the modern individual sinks to the level of a mere function, because
this it is that represents a collective value and alone affords a
possibility of livelihood," † And writing in the same context he
sums up the matter as follows: "Hence we possess to-day a
highly developed collective culture, which in organization far
exceeds anything that ever existed, but which for that
very reason has become increasingly injurious to individual
culture." ‡

The position of the individual as such is thus seen to become
ever more contingent and specialized under the impact of
inevitable forces. The comparison with the status of the individual in insect societies reveals, however, a categorical difference: whereas man is conditioned socially, the types and castes
among insects are conditioned genetically. But even this basic
distinction may in time be eliminated under the triumphant
sway of intelligence; and it is not without significance that
the biologic conditioning satirically portrayed by Aldous Huxley
in *Brave New World* was soberly proposed, on a high-minded
and imaginative plane, by Hermann J. Muller, one of the fore-
most geneticists of our time, as a necessary and rational procedure in the further development of mankind. § We have

* Quoted by Jung, *Psychological Types*, p. 94.
† *Ibid.*, pp. 94-95.
‡ *Ibid.*, pp. 95-96.
§ The downward trend of evolution and the consequent need for a conscious
technique in an opposite direction is emphasized by J. B. S. Haldane in an
essay on "Man's Destiny." Fearing that science may eventually be strangled by
antirationalist forces, he says: "If so evolution will take its course. And that
course has generally been downwards. The majority of species have degenerated

already examined these proposals. Though doubt was cast upon the hope of realizing in some far-off future the vision of our own highest ideals in a co-operative commonwealth of greatly endowed individuals, there can be little question that in time man will undertake a consciously planned genetic program directed toward the development of the race and the amelioration of his condition. Not the objectives but the results, at least in one aspect of this procedure, were called into question. Here there seemed little reason to doubt that an overall drift, based precisely upon the dominance of a more rational approach to life—a drift that, as we have seen, emerges in an inescapable manner in every aspect of our existence—would necessarily embrace the genetic technique no less than other approaches in the social conditioning of mankind. A genetic program would thus only implement biologically the socially determined direction of man, and therewith complete the circle of what appears to be his predestined fate.

The social world of the insects presents, moreover, some further material for thought in connection with a socially geared program of genetic development in the world of man. It is worth noting, for example, in the words of Julian Huxley, that "...the parallelism in the social evolution of the quite unrelated ants and termites is truly astonishing; yet the termites have never produced grain-storers or slave-makers, while the ants have no system of second-grade queens in reserve." * In other words, however differently realized in the cases of ants and termites, the biological mechanics leading to socialization appear to follow certain parallel courses and to achieve certain parallel end-effects as regards the basic aspects of the social community. Are we justified in carrying over the logic

---

and become extinct, or, what is perhaps worse, gradually lost many of their functions....If scientific research is regarded as a useful adjunct to the army, the factory, or the hospital, and not as a thing of all things most supremely worth doing, both for its own sake and that of its results, it is probable that the decisive steps will never be taken. And unless he can control his own evolution as he is learning to control that of his domestic plants and animals, man and all his works will go down into oblivion and darkness." (*Possible Worlds*, New York: Harper and Brothers, 1943, pp. 303, 305.)

* Julian S. Huxley, *Man Stands Alone* (New York: Harper and Brothers, 1941), pp. 237, 238.

of this conclusion to embrace the case of man? Despite the express warnings of Huxley to the effect that analogies between man and the social insects are largely to be discounted, we are, it would seem, confronted nonetheless by a fundamental similarity in direction toward socialization in both instances. The differences between the social systems of insects and of man are due in the first place to the fact that the insects are motivated wholly by instinct while man is increasingly motivated by his intelligence, and, secondly, to the distinct principles of biologic inheritance and reproduction in the world of the social insects as distinguished from those obtaining in the case of man. As regards this latter factor, however, the artificial impregnation of women on a large scale, as suggested by Muller, would go a long way toward reducing the dissimilarities in reproductive procedures from a genetic point of view—a matter that has already been noted; while in respect to the first distinction, a like fading out of differences was indicated not between insect societies and man as he is but between the instinctually determined collectivization of insects, on the one hand, and the ultimately crystallized state of man under the final dominance of intelligence, on the other. We are thus forced to concede that man may, indeed, that man will, under the compulsion of his deepest trends, move ever closer to that condition of high socialization found pre-eminently among the insects.

That the vast drama of human history should eventually find its denouement in the sterile perspectives of a world at least analogous if not similar to that of the social insects may seem to us at once forbidding and incredible. But that, moreover, such an apparently blind and aimless state of fixity should finally crown the triumph of intelligence seems like a bitter and ironic anticlimax to all our efforts, reducing the long travail of our development to a kind of ultimate *reductio ad absurdum*. Against the high faith of man in an ever wiser and more meaningful dispensation, such a fate smacks of a contradiction in terms; and behind the confusion and doubt aroused by the contemplation of such an end, we cling desperately to our faith in another destiny. Proud and confident in our attainments, conscious of representing the very pinnacle of all living forms, we prefer to face an inscrutable future of uncharted regions and unexplored potentialities to one that at best will grant us only a final sense of security and adjustment, like a prepared niche in the scheme of things. But quite apart from our Promethean zeal, we are led to inquire whether the forces that have carried man to his high eminence will sustain him in his quest toward an ever more heroic future, or whether, reaching the zenith of their trajectory, they will deposit him, a deflated being, among the discards of evolution. All living forms appear, sooner or later, to attain a fixed status, or, having run their course, to become extinct. In his essay "Science, Natural and Social," Julian Huxley pictures mankind not only at the top rung of the evolutionary ladder but supreme in that plasticity of development which alone assures further evolutionary progress. "The human species," he tells us, "has now become the only branch of life in which and by which further substantial evolutionary progress can possibly be realized. And it has reached this enviable, but at the same time, responsible, position solely by concentrating on the brain as against other organs in its line of specialization." * For it is through "specialization" that species seal their fate, as for example many of the reptiles of the Mesozoic age, sixty million years ago, failed to forestall their doom because of an overdevelopment of sheer bulk. Will the brain of man prove an exception and permit him to enjoy an unlimited progression?

We have already surveyed in some detail the vistas which the future dominance of intelligence promises to unfold in the further development of mankind. We have noted the necessary character and the necessary consequences of this inevitable expansion of intelligence in its effects upon the structure of society. We have seen, moreover, that the triumph of intelligence will be accompanied by a relative if not an actual recession of the instincts as guiding principles in the affairs of man. And we have shown that the dominance of intelligence will necessarily result in an ever higher degree of social organization and social collectivization. Clearly, it would seem, this

* *Ibid.,* p. 244.

profound transformation of society indicates a fateful specialization in the further social evolution of man, a specific structural trend accompanied by its own inherent and fateful
consequences. Nor is the irrevocable nature of this drift affected
by the question of whether it is biologically determined or
inherent in the inescapable mechanism and set direction of our
social development: mankind is clearly fated to enter upon a
further phase in an irreversible process.

In this connection it is instructive to quote a revealing
passage from Julian Huxley's essay. For although, as noted
above, Huxley believes that man alone enjoys the prospects
of further substantial evolutionary progress, the picture he
draws of the growing integration of human society by way of
analogy with the evolutionary development of the brain is
curiously in harmony with the essential trends here indicated.
But those trends appear to lead irrevocably to a closed system
of things.

"Our brain analogy undoubtedly illuminates the social problem in an extremely valuable way. In the first place, the highest
stage of evolution in this respect which has as yet been reached
by any society is, by biological standards, extremely primitive.
It corresponds with a quite early stage in the development of
cerebral hemispheres and cortex: higher than that of a fish,
but certainly not beyond that found in reptiles. Before humanity can obtain on the collective level that degree of foresight,
control, and flexibility which on the biological level is at the
disposal of human individuals, it must multiply at least ten-
fold, perhaps fiftyfold, the proportion of individuals and
organizations devoted to obtaining information, to planning,
correlation, and the flexible control of execution. The chief
increases are needed in respect of correlation and planning and
of social self-consciousness. In these respects, wholly new social
organs must be evolved, whose nature we can only envisage in
the most general terms.

"In respect of planning and correlation, we can dimly perceive that some large single central organization must be super-
posed on the more primitive system of separate government
departments and other single-function organizations; and that

this, like the cerebral cortex, must be at one and the same time unified and functionally specialized. It will thus contain units concerned with particular social and economic functions, but the bulk of its personnel will be occupied in studying and effecting the interrelations between these various functions." *

Throughout this passage, it will be noted, the need for correlated and unified integration is sharply emphasized. The future is seen in terms of the universal co-ordination of its social facilities, and in the need of "some large single central organization" that will absorb and supersede all "single-function" organizations. But what are these stages and mechanisms for the attainment of a higher level of social integration but the correlating and converging trends implicit in the processes of universal organization? The analogy between the development of society and the evolution of the brain is arresting and instructive; but the process as here depicted carries us back to the logic of our original thesis, and strengthens the supposition that man's further social development, however extensive in scope and intensive in degree, must nevertheless take place within the *cul-de-sac* of a fateful specialization.

The question reduces itself, biologically speaking, to one of limited or unlimited progress; but quite apart from the vistas which the plasticity of the human brain or the potentialities of genetic manipulation in our further development open up to us, it is plain to be seen that progress for man will at best remain a hybrid affair of social as well as biologic factors in which, however, his values and his purposes are certain to become ever more dominant. Despite our eminence in the biologic hierarchy, it is clear in this equation that nature is innocent of human purpose and will subject man in the future, as she has in the past, to the blind workings of her forces. "Purposes in life are made, not found," † writes Huxley, which is but another way of saying that man's destiny will be of his own making. But that is not to imply a realm of unlimited possibilities, a virgin canvas upon which man may design his

---

* *Ibid.,* pp. 245, 246.
† Julian S. Huxley, *Evolution: The Modern Synthesis* (New York: Harper and Brothers, 1943), p. 576.

future with all the abandon of an unfettered imagination. On the contrary, it implies a position of somber responsibility and sober choice; but even this restricted freedom is open to question—not biologically, perhaps, but on the basis of implicit social forces and social trends. The difficulty thus reduces itself to the painful problem of whether man can explore the biologic possibilities open to him, or whether, in the very effort to reach a higher status according to his accepted values, he will not preclude his entry into these richer realms, like a chess player who has muffed his gambit. His future development, even more than that of his past, will be at the mercy, in the phrase used above, of hybrid influences; and under this dispensation not the *possibilities* but the *probabilities* of his course will come to be decisive in the very degree of their inherent likelihood.

In entering upon this question we must return, once more, to the arena of social forces, and particularly to those implicit aspects in the socialization of humanity which we have previously examined. And here it is well to reflect upon the fact that science itself, the very citadel of rationalistic enterprise, and the vehicle through which alone the biologic development of mankind could be wisely and beneficently effected, will be no less subject to the pressure of an overall socialization of life than any other aspect and expression of human activity. For though science is destined to play a dominant role in the ultimate socialization of mankind, constituting a transformation of society comparable in scale and scope only to its original formation and its subsequent evolution into civilizations, as J. D. Bernal has ably shown in his book *The Social Function of Science,* it will itself become in time subject to the all-pervasive and converging pressure of universal organization. Having passed its effective maturity, science, like the aged, can only hope to become the ward of its own offspring. Despite the promise of its infinite reaches, it will be confined by the forces that nourish it; and under the aegis of its social function it will no longer enjoy the venturesomeness of an earlier but passing millennium. For in this domain, too, as in all others, the individual as such will have become engulfed and superseded by organized groups and phalanxes whose social direction will be held adamant within the prescribed limits of established norms. The source of creative power within the individual will have become stilled; the explorer will have lost his zest, or find himself adrift in a sea of his own aspirations from which there will be no return, until at length science must inevitably approach ever closer to an asymptotic leveling-off in creative enterprise. In the cumulative circularity of cause and effect, science too will come to a status of diminishing returns; and thus we may perceive that, despite its challenging vistas, it will provide no open-sesame to a limitless future. Like other aspects of the social scene, it too will become involved in the decisive struggle between the dying ideal of the "intrinsic superiority" of the individual and his absorption and subordination within the dominant collectivity. And the final resolution of this problem, more than any other, will form the nexus between our present estate and that of our future. In that future the illimitable perspectives of science, no less than the concrete realities of everyday life, will be recast ever more finally in harmony with the intrinsic demands of a collectivized society. While science is destined to fashion that society, it will in turn be fashioned by that society: and in that consummation it will have reached the zenith of its social function.

IV

If the wide horizons of science are destined to be narrowed to a mere transit through the Scylla and Charybdis of our social conformations, a like fate is discernible in the more primary domain of man's spiritual orientation. Here, too, the drama of our entry into the future will be shaped by an inevitable conflict between our *potential possibilities* and our *actual probabilities*. A like convergence of forces will establish in time a range of values in conformity with the ideality of the community rather than with that of the individual. To say this, however, is to imply the negation of that spiritual growth of man which has been nourished from ancient times through the profound channel of individual mystics. For that higher spiritual wisdom which ever seeks a more immanent relationship to Godhead, the better to shed its radiance upon man, will have been denied by the mundane strictures of an eventually completely secularized community. And therewith the spiritual development of mankind will come to rest, as it were, upon a socially acceptable level of collective morality.

The salt will have lost its savor; and we are confronted here with the direct challenge, in the words of Arnold J. Toynbee, between the creative minority and the uncreative majority of mankind. Perhaps, indeed, this challenge embraces the very crux of the problem of our future direction: the problem of our undefined possibilities and our inherent probabilities; the problem of the mass of humanity in relation to its component individuals; of the vast, inert weight of its ever more co-ordinated and fortified averages, and the isolated, ever more futile impact of its solitary and extruded creative individuals. The problem of the one and the many encompasses the profoundest depths not only of man's relation to man but of man's relation to his universe, to the farthest reaches of that apprehensible whole of which he is a part. In the challenge of that relationship he will establish his boundaries and define, by implications that outrun his keenest vision, the future destiny of the race.

Yet the problem, in reality, will not present itself to us in the form of a deliberate choice. There is no pause in the sequence of events, permitting us to gain a leverage upon the future. Or, to be more explicit, the rational direction of man's course will effect the solution of this problem directly: that is to say, without regard to those spiritual values that might, under another dispensation, have guided man. But this is only to acknowledge the final futility of the creative minority in the face of an ever more dominant majority; to assert the ultimate triumph of overwhelming probabilities against ever more tenuous possibilities. And as the tension and conflict between the creative few and the uncreative many are certain to become increasingly weakened and be finally eliminated, the problem of the future will obviously shift its center from one of diminishing choice to one of increasing pressure, of growing compulsion, and of expanding finality in every aspect of life. And along with this development, the analysis of the problem will likewise shift ground. It will no longer take the form of a spiritual appraisement of man's course, set forth in terms of moral and idealistic exhortations; on the contrary, it will perforce become abstract and mechanistic in character, for it will seek to establish and define those structural conditions and limitations, those inherent social imperatives, that will ineluctably shape the course of man despite his fears and hopes, his ideals and aspirations. To entertain, in the face of this overwhelming movement, a belief in the active freedom of man to guide his destiny, on a scale commensurate with all mankind, is to harbor a "tragic fallacy." But that is not to deny the somber perspectives of a world of values in eclipse, or to be blind to the solemn and portentous drama of our spiritual plight, heightened indeed by the ironic certainty that man will no longer comprehend the very meaning of his lost heritage, once this fateful transformation will have been accomplished.

The movement of mankind in its course toward the future may thus be followed on two levels as it were: that of the creative minority and that of the uncreative majority. These two aspects are characteristic of man's course throughout history, as Toynbee has shown;* and the imprint of their mutual and profound interactions is apparent in all his diverse civilizations. In their reciprocal challenge these movements clarify, illumine, and define one another. But what is perhaps unique and decisive in the present historic tableau of man, from this point of view, is the fact that the dominant uncreative majority is today one of unprecedented magnitude and unparalleled scope, co-ordinated and strengthened through an ever more stringent world-drift toward universal organization. In this dynamic and unassailable external aspect, beneath which the mass of mankind remains internally unmoved and inert in its primitive acceptance of life-values, the creative minority is brought face to face with a challenge of insuperable gravity.

---

* Arnold J. Toynbee, *A Study of History*. Specific references to general topics in this monumental opus must be sought in the extensive index to the work itself. Such references occur throughout the six volumes already issued, and are indicated as subjects of further study in the volumes still to be published in completing this major work of historic analysis and interpretation.

Thus confronted, it would meet mass complacency with an individual and personal intensity of ever higher order; and it is not surprising to find this philosophy of salvation seeking expression through groups of the elite, of neo-Brahmins, of true Supermen—indeed, as Gerald Heard has indicated,* through beings of higher psychic powers than any man has heretofore exhibited! And unless man can meet the challenge in some such wholly miraculous manner, it seems certain that the creative minority will be bypassed in the tide of events, only to disintegrate and become eventually absorbed in the very suction created by the movement of the dominant majority.

Nevertheless, the position of the minority serves to throw an oblique light upon the nature of man's future course; and the very failure and futility to which its efforts seem doomed today reveal in sharp antithesis the wholly new and impregnable aspect of the forces of tomorrow. These forces, emanating from our own Western civilization, are characterized by their world-wide, universal scope: indisputably they will encompass the whole of humanity in a single, sweeping transformation. It is true, of course, as Toynbee insists, that the unification of the world under the pressure of Western economic and political penetrations is not to be confused with the unity of the world on a cultural plane.† But the problem which confronts the world today, which indeed constitutes a world-crisis for humanity as a whole, is precisely the question of whether the rationalist trends and technological conditions that threaten our cultural and spiritual development by virtue of their social and structural implications will not likewise chal-

---

* Believing that human evolution has reached its culmination in all but the further development of man's "psyche," that is to say, his consciousness, Gerald Heard submits that man can save himself from inevitable degeneration and collapse only by means of a psychological mutation. However, this is not to be effected genetically, but through a recrudescence of mystical practices such as those of contemplation and meditation followed in the Yoga discipline. In this way it is hoped a superior order of man will make his appearance in the hierarchy of human types; and through his efforts and influence humanity will achieve a new dispensation. It is interesting to note that this hope, based essentially upon the emergence of supermen, is shared by Aldous Huxley (see his *Means and Ends*), and in a somewhat less esoteric sense by not a few other contemporary writers.

† Arnold J. Toynbee, *A Study of History* (London: Oxford University Press, 1935-1939), I, 150.

lenge, in the course of their ecumenical sweep, the growth of
other civilizations in these respects as well. In effect, will not
the same conditions give rise to an essentially similar response,
colored perhaps by the idiom of each separate and homogeneous society? Doubtless the opposition to these universally
impinging forces will bear the imprint of its diverse and localized origins; but that is not to imply its triumph under one
set of circumstances or its failure and defeat under another.
The opposition to these forces has in fact nowhere attained a
more articulate, profound, and intense expression than in the
Western world, in the field of its greatest and most direct challenge; and the spiritual interpretation of the problem in the
language of contemporary Western thought is for us at least
as apposite and defined, as humanly searching and cognizant,
as the more or less idiomatic abstractions of the East. Perhaps the most telling aspect in a world-view of the situation
is the fact that, whereas the creative minority is necessarily
dispersed, the dominant forces against which it is everywhere
aligned are inherently co-ordinated into a rising movement of
universal scope and significance.

It is evident that the very basis of our spiritual structure,
which has been reared throughout our long heritage upon the
self-awareness and freedom of the individual soul, is at stake.
What was thus axiomatic, so to speak, has come to be threatened—not directly, in a frontal assault, but by an engulfing
movement that would sweep the deepest sources of our cultural and spiritual values into the limbo of things lost and for-
gotten. In meeting that challenge it is not surprising that the
more sensitive and deeply rooted minds among the creative
minority should seek strength and reinforcement from the
past, from the "Great Tradition" upon which Western society
has been nourished.* This quest of the past is not a search
for refuge among the solutions of the past: it is an effort to pre-

* In this category belong such recent works as *The Condition of Man* by
Lewis Mumford, *Man the Measure* by Erich Kahler, *The Destiny of Western
Man* by W. T. Stace, *Chart for Rough Water* by Waldo Frank—all of which
are deeply concerned with the heritage of the past in facing the challenge of
the future. Here, too, we may place in a related category such books as *Science and Wisdom* by Jacques Maritain and *The Nature and Destiny of Man* by
Reinhold Niebuhr.

serve inviolate the conception of the "infinite worth of the individual" upon which, in any final analysis, our human aspirations and our spiritual illumination are seen to rest. It is an effort to guard the vast cultural and spiritual *momentum* of mankind—not in its historical lineaments and formulated doctrines but as a flowing, living continuum of creative inspiration in all the luminous facets of the human soul. But in thus standing guard over the inmost sources of our values, this acknowledged gesture of defense testifies to a profound apprehension concerning the nature of the change that is upon us. We are, it is clear, by every sign of the times, at a crossroad in the history of man.

The central theme embodied in that august phrase "The Great Tradition" might be described as the purposeful freedom of the human soul. In a kind of lyrical affirmation, the Great Tradition has been defined in the following words: "Its birth was on the Mediterranean shores. And before it spread in Europe through Rome, and through the Spaniard and the Puritan came to the Americas, it had already many forms: Egypt, Judea, Greece. Yet its essence has never changed. *It is the knowledge that individual man partakes of the divine, which is his way of naming the universal and of naming it good and of naming it his. It is the knowledge that his life has purpose and direction because God is in him.* You can express it in a hundred different ways: religiously after Ikhnaton, Moses, Jesus, Spinoza; rationally after Plato, Philo, Plotinus; theologically after Maimonides, Aquinas, Luther, Calvin; esthetically, after every great master in Europe's art. There it is, and it has brought dignity to individual man and a strength the Hindus never had, nor the Chinese, nor the American Indian; for all these cultures, however deep, deny the basic reality of the *person*. It created Europe. It created America. It is the Great Tradition." *

The civilization of the West inherited and then enriched the Great Tradition. But it gave birth, in the course of its development, to another equally imposing, if hostile, doctrine

---

* Waldo Frank, *Chart for Rough Water* (New York: Doubleday and Company, Inc., 1940), p. 50.

in that vast externalization of its energies which was crowned by the "invention, exploitation, and proliferation of the machine." * This second doctrine, however, was not limited to the West: its inherently expansive tendencies carried it to the far corners of the world in a single, homogeneous movement. In the profoundly dualistic approach to life which these two aspects of our civilization reveal, we of the West brought to a dramatic climax the opposed categories of faith and reason, instinct and intelligence, wisdom and science. For us the issues are joined; and the future direction not only of Western civilization but of the world at large hinges upon the outcome.

It has seemed to many observers that the clash of forces, far from representing an irreconcilable conflict, will eventually be resolved in a higher synthesis, in a balanced and harmonious merging of these opposed trends. They perceive in the profound dislocations of modern life—in the dissolution of values and the concomitant dehumanizing of the personality—an extreme swing of the social pendulum toward mechanization, toward an extroverted imbalance with its emphasis upon the realm of things, of facts, of concrete realities and explicit formulations. But in time a contrary trend will assert itself. A deep, organic sense of values will infuse the growing crystallization of organized relationships with the spirit of a new social vision, imbuing our "life-sustaining" means with the springtime breath of "life-fulfilling" ends. Thus a new synthesis will emerge; a new "organic humanism," in which man will achieve a dynamic fusion of wisdom and science, a creative harmony of faith and reason, a fruitful amalgam of instinct and intelligence. Yet, admittedly, this sustaining trend will emerge from the depths of a world in chaos only if man, conscious of his present dilemma, rises to the challenge by facing his responsibilities and reforming his attitudes.†

However desperate the challenge, the problem is not new.

* *Ibid.*, p. 118.

† In the outlook of L. L. Whyte (see *The Next Development of Man,* New York: Henry Holt and Company, 1948) we come upon a significant approach to the basic problem of failure and frustration in contemporary society. According to Whyte, the integrative principle upon which the future of humanity will come to depend rests upon the recognition of a "unitary" principle of development encompassing man in all his aspects, individual no less than

The higher possibilities of humanity have ever been seized upon as the spiritual obligations of the minority; and if today, in the widening secularization of life, this conception of its function has given rise to a new humanism, to a new faith in a richer syncretism, it has but replaced the leadership of mystic and saint by that of the "balanced person," in the phrase of Lewis Mumford, as the activating agency of the masses of humanity, as the necessary keystone of the social edifice of the future. The vast hopes for a great forward movement of mankind, on the plane of a new synthesis, are thus seen to be contingent, in the last analysis, upon the heightened social awareness of the individual—upon the consciously disciplined, integrative power of the *person* as the vehicle of that lofty cultural and spiritual heritage implied in the Great Tradition. In short, the belief in a dynamic syncretism, through which alone society might attain a harmonious but mobile equilibrium, enabling it to rise from synthesis to synthesis in an ascending scale of social and cultural achievements, is seen to rest, like an inverted pyramid, upon the apex of its creative minority. But never before has this inherent imbalance of society assumed a more ominous aspect.

In the drift of Western civilization, in the dominant movement from "the organic to the inorganic, from the living to the mechanical, from the subjectively conditioned to the objectively conditioned," * we may perceive the lineaments of a Spen-

___

collective. This concept follows upon the universality of process and development—indeed, upon the recognition of the primacy of process and development in contrast to the age-old faith in the search for the permanent and the static behind the flux of events. Thus, a unitary system of thought looks toward an ever more unifying system or order in life; but this bold and imaginative approach to the problems of humanity seems destined to falter in the race between organized modes of procedure, leading ultimately to the attainment of fixity and permanence, and an organic development leading to ever wider vistas and deeper values in the process of continuing adjustment. It is not surprising that such a formulative philosophy of change and process should arise at a moment of impasse when a contrary trend leading toward universal crystallization in the forms and values of life is asserting itself.

* Lewis Mumford, *The Condition of Man* (New York: Harcourt, Brace and Company, 1944), p. 371. In the passage from which these words are quoted, Mumford takes issue with Spengler's view that the development of societies reveals always an earlier, organic culture followed by a later, more objectively conditioned civilization, on the ground that these aspects are implicitly present at all levels as cotemporaneous tendencies. On the basis of either interpretation, however, these aspects are seen as essentially divergent, if not opposed, trends.

glerian doom not only of our Western culture along with that of the world at large but, as we have seen, of the individual *per se* as well. Moreover, in the conflict between the individual and society the full disruptive influence of these trends comes to bear upon the former, while a new, compensating, wholly externalized drift of universal scope sustains the latter. If, in the past, the creative minority was faced with the task of impregnating the immobile masses with its own spiritual insight and aspirations, today it is first called upon to change the very direction of the dominant majority before attempting to secure a synthesis of wider potentialities. The power of the "medieval synthesis" lay in the harmonious acceptance of its values by saint and sinner alike. Today the widening gulf between the vision of the minority and the direction of the majority is due precisely to the lack of a common reality principle: they represent divergent aspects of experience, at once alien and incommensurate in their aims, their hopes, and their symbols. And thus, if only as a backdrop to its own lofty mission, the approach of the minority to the dilemma of contemporary society substantiates a contrary momentum in the generality of mankind. The conflict between this highly individualized, anomalous minority, on the one hand, and the vast, but ever more explicit organizational trend of the masses of humanity, on the other, is thereby acknowledged in all its fateful divergence. In that conflict our inherited faith in the *person* as the ultimate chalice of human values is being shaken—not as though by a wind in the treetops, but at its roots by an earthquake!

V

What integrative principle, under these circumstances, will sustain man in the future? History would seem to indicate that in the past man has found no ready answer to this problem: always he has gravitated from the dominance of once living traditions during a period of growth to a state of doubt and confusion in a "Time of Troubles" that presaged the eventual breakdown and dissolution of his society. In *A Study of History* Arnold J. Toynbee has undertaken to trace the parallel course of disintegration among the varied civilizations of history: sooner or later, it is clear, they have uniformly fallen under the pressure of a challenge they could no longer meet. Nor does he seem to doubt that our own Western civilization will follow, if indeed it has not already started upon, a like course and succumb to a similar fate. But the universal cataclysm which thus appears to overtake each civilization in turn, on this reckoning, is not to be interpreted, according to Toynbee, as the sign of an inescapable doom for humanity at large. On the contrary: in the very wreckage of the civilizations that comprise the story of human history to date, he sees the promise, on another plane, of a wider significance than any we may legitimately attach to their separate and ephemeral passages. The disintegration of mature civilizations is accompanied by a residue of "universal states" and "universal churches," whose meaning involves always a relation between civilizations and, by this very token, constitutes a problem apart from their individual roles. What, he asks, are we to make of these deposits? "Are they mere waste-products of the disintegration-process— a tangle of spoiled threads from a piece of tapestry which the weaver, on an impulse of his inscrutable caprice, has willed to unpick before it has been half completed? Or will these debris prove, if we pick them up, to be fresh masterpieces of the weaver's art which he has woven, by an unnoticed sleight of hand, on some more ethereal instrument than the roaring loom that has ostensibly been occupying all his attention and energies?" *

This reference to a "more ethereal instrument" implies a supramundane interpretation of the phenomenon; and in this conjecture Toynbee leaves us in little doubt. Disposing of the "universal states" with the comment that their peace is as "ephemeral as it is imposing," he concentrates upon the destiny of the universal church, "in which every higher religion seeks to embody itself," as the final field of inquiry in his monumental study of history. If the answer to this central problem has not yet been explicitly given in this still incomplete work, we

---

* Arnold J. Toynbee, *A Study of History* (London: Oxford University Press, 1935-1939), VI, 325.

have nevertheless been afforded more than a cursory glimpse of its nature: the question itself, we are assured, "holds the key to the meaning of the weaver's work." * Thus, in the residue of civilizations that have passed or are doomed to pass, Toynbee perceives a principle of salvation; and in the contrast between the ephemeral state of temporal society, which is but a "City of Destruction," and the *Civitas Dei*, which alone endures in its ecumenical sweep and its eternal verity, he sees the hope of an alternative way of life. "The only society that is capable of embracing the whole of Mankind," he writes, "is a superhuman *Civitas Dei;* and the conception of a society that embraces all Mankind and yet nothing but Mankind is an academic chimaera." † For only the fatherhood of God makes possible the brotherhood of man—"...a truth which involves the converse proposition that, if the divine father of the human family is ever left out of the reckoning, there is no possibility of forging any alternative bond of purely human texture which will avail itself to hold Mankind together." ‡ Hence the quotation on the title page of the volume containing these strictures:

" 'Except the Lord build the house,
their labor is lost that build it.
'Except the Lord keep the city,
the watchman waketh but in vain.'

Ps. cxxvii, 1-2."

Here, then, after a searching analysis of the institutions of man and the civilizations that embodied them, Toynbee affirms that no mundane state of the future will endure, however contrived, within the temporal framework of merely human devising: only the City of God can endure. But this consummation, it is granted, will rest upon the response of man to the challenge of his situation in a disintegrating society from which he can escape neither by a philosophy of detachment, nor by an act of retreat into the past, nor yet by an

* *Ibid.*, p. 326.
† *Ibid.*, p. 10.
‡ *Ibid.*, p. 9.

equally futile effort to breach the future; but only by the path
of spiritual Transfiguration. "We have seen," writes Toynbee,
"what is the goal of that movement of withdrawal-and-return
which we have called Transfiguration. The aim of Transfiguration is to give light to them that sit in darkness and to make
the darkness comprehend this light that is shining in it; and
this aim is pursued by seeking the Kingdom of God in order
to bring its life, which is 'the light of men,' into action ... in
the field of life in This World. The goal of Transfiguration is
thus the Kingdom of God." *

Of the four ways of life that constitute "alternative by-
passes" to the catastrophe of a social breakdown, according
to Toynbee, Archaism and Futurism are alike "... incompatible with growth of any kind, since they deliberately aim at
a breach in continuity.... Archaism is an attempt to take a flying leap out of the mundane Present backwards into an already
vanished Past, while Futurism is an attempt to take a similar
leap forwards into a still invisible mundane Future.... On the
other hand, Detachment and Transfiguration are both of them
reactions to the breakdown of a civilization which are still, in
themselves, ways of growth...." † But the distinction between
Archaism and Futurism, on the one side, and Detachment and
Transfiguration on the other, bears a far deeper significance.
For these latter movements "... are not attempts to escape
from the Present without abandoning the level of mundane
life, but are endeavours to act upon a belief that there can be
no salvation from that sickness of the Soul which the breakdown of a civilization brings to light through any less radical
remedy than a change of spiritual clime or dimension; and this
is another way of saying that both Detachment and Transfiguration are examples of that 'transference of the field of action'
from the Macrocosm to the Microcosm which manifests itself
qualitatively in the spiritual phenomenon of 'etherialization.'
If we are right in believing that these are symptoms of growth,
and right again in believing that every example of human
growth will always be found to have a social as well as an in-

* *Ibid.*, p. 171.
† *Ibid.*, p. 169.

dividual aspect, and if we are also bound to assume *ex hypo-thesi* that the society to whose growth the movements of De-tachment and Transfiguration thus bear witness cannot be any society of the species 'civilization'—considering that a disin-tegrating society of that species is the City of Destruction from which either movement is an endeavour to escape—then we can only conclude that the movements of Detachment and Transfiguration bear witness to the growth of a society, or so-cieties, of some other kind or kinds." *

In pursuing this inquiry further, Toynbee distinguishes not only between the mundane utopias that are the goals of Ar-chaism as well as Futurism and the *Civitas Dei* which is the goal of Transfiguration, but between the ideal of the Kingdom of God and that Nirvana which is the goal of Detachment. In aspiring toward a state of Nirvana, Detachment constitutes a movement of withdrawal from the "City of Destruction"; Transfiguration, however, completes this movement by a with-drawal-and-return through which the "City of Destruction" may be redeemed and transformed into the *Civitas Dei*. This twofold movement of withdrawal from and return to the tem-poral order thereby implies a rebirth in a "...higher spiritual dimension than the life of This World. That is the 'palingenesia' of which Jesus speaks to Nicodemus, and which He proclaims in another place in the same Gospel as the sovereign aim of His own birth in the flesh.

> " 'I am come that they might have life, and that they might have it more abundantly.' John x. 10." †

In this profound distinction between the movement of De-tachment and that of Transfiguration, in which we perceive that the latter is but a completion, on a higher spiritual plane, of the suspended action of the former, we touch upon the supra-mundane role of Christian Love, which unites the human order with that of the divine, and serves, through the mystery of Transfiguration, to dissolve the question of how the Kingdom of God can be of This World and yet not of it. "As for the

* *Ibid.*, pp. 169, 170.
† *Ibid.*, p. 174.

working of Love in human hearts as a means of access for Man to God, it is extolled as the sovereign—and sole indispensable —means to this supreme end of Man in the thirteenth chapter of the First Epistle of Paul the Apostle to the Corinthians. And if we try to take a comprehensive view of the constitution of the *Civitas Dei,* and inquire what miraculous spiritual force it is that makes it possible for its diverse members, human and divine, to dwell together in unity, we find that Love is the life-blood of this supra-mundane body social and the *arcanum imperii* of its divine king." *

In an earlier passage the aridity of Detachment as a way of escape is even more emphatically enunciated; and the matter is of particular interest to us in that Toynbee here speaks directly of that dualism of head and heart which distinguishes the halfway house of the sage in his Detachment from the full response of the Christian saint and mystic who accepts, in an act of humility and love, the burden of withdrawal-and-return to this vale of tears. "The philosophy of Detachment," writes Toynbee, "does not, after all, provide a solution for the problem which it sets out to solve; for in consulting the head and ignoring the heart it is arbitrarily putting asunder what God has joined together. This philosophy falls short of the truth by refusing to take account of the Soul's duality in unity; and therefore the philosophy of Detachment has to be eclipsed by the mystery of Transfiguration." †

In the course of our own speculative excursion we have come upon a duality in the nature of man arising out of the conflict between his instincts and his intelligence. This schism in the basic modes of his responses has characterized not only the entire period of his history but the whole of his development. And in pursuing the course of this conflict of "head and heart" we have noted that man's intelligence, by virtue of its own internal structure, is destined in time to supersede the instincts and to dominate his further social evolution. Meanwhile, in that crucial epoch of their final struggle for sovereignty, foreshadowed throughout his history, when the soul of man finds itself

* *Ibid.,* p. 165.
† *Ibid.,* p. 148.

torn apart by these contrary forces, he has sought to achieve unity in the fabric of his life through a higher synthesis of their opposing values and their divergent modes of operation. In that heroic effort man has created the tableau of his cultural heritage and fashioned, out of the depths of his travail, his deepest insight and his highest ideals. But in the critical moment of the crisis in which he now finds himself he is beset as never before by doubt and misgiving: the equation by which he sought to establish the unity and wholeness of his society seems somehow basically inadequate, if not irrelevant; and it is not surprising that he should once more seek recourse as in the past in a supramundane solution of his perplexity. The "Soul's duality in unity" is thus seen as a schism that can be reconciled, not within the province of his temporal means, but only in an otherworldly realm.

In this dispensation we may discern the possibility of one and, according to Toynbee, the sole answer to the question of how man is to achieve an integrative principle in the future: his salvation lies in seeking with a whole heart entry into the Kingdom of God. If this answer appears to carry us back to the precedent of an earlier response to the challenge of a disintegrating society—in the transcendent answer of Christianity to the breakdown and dissolution of Hellenic civilization—the return is conceived not in the spirit of Archaism but as an inner response of a supramundane order that is timeless in its eternal and inviolable verity. And though, historically speaking, this answer was given only haltingly in the past, it remains the one valid answer to the challenge of the future. Despite the apparent futility of an earlier effort, man must once more rise to the challenge of his disintegrating society by healing the schism within his soul and embracing the path of Transfiguration. For us, the hour of decision is at hand. In following the same rhythm of disintegration that has characterized other civilizations, Western society is rapidly approaching the phase of a "universal state" in a far more comprehensive sense than any heretofore attained; and if the consequences following upon this state have been fatal to past civilizations, they lie ominously upon the horizon of our own.

VI

The crisis is more complete and more compelling than ever before if only because our Western world occupies a "vastly expanded house." In the words of Toynbee, it has now "... virtually completed its stupendous feat of incorporating the whole face of the Earth and the entire living generation of Mankind into its own body material." * But the signs of approaching dissolution run deeper.

"If the analogy between our Western Civilization's modern history and other civilizations' 'Times of Troubles' does extend to points of chronology, then a Western 'Time of Troubles' which appears to have begun sometime in the sixteenth century may be expected to find its end sometime in the twentieth century; and this prospect may well make us tremble; for in other cases the grand finale that has wound up a 'Time of Troubles' and ushered in a universal state has been a self-inflicted 'knock-out blow' from which the self-stricken society has never been able to recover. Must we, too, purchase our *Pax Oecumenica* at this deadly price? The question is one which our own lips cannot answer, since the destiny of a live civilization is necessarily as obscure to its living members as the fate of a dead civilization is to scholars when their only clues are undeciphered scripts or dumb artifacts. We cannot say for certain that our doom is at hand; and yet we have no warrant for assuming that it is not; for that would be to assume that we are not as other men are; and any such assumption would be at variance with everything that we know about human nature either by looking around us or by introspection.

"This dark doubt is a challenge which we cannot evade; and our destiny depends on our response.

'I dreamed, and behold I saw a man cloathed with rags, standing in a certain place, with his face from his own house, a book in his hand, and a great burden upon his back. I looked, and saw him open the book and read therein; and as he read he wept and trembled; and, not

* *Ibid.*, p. 319.

being able longer to contain, he broke out with a lamentable cry saying "What shall I do?"'

"It was not without just cause that Christian was so greatly distressed.

> 'I am for certain informed (said he) that this our city will be burned with fire from Heaven—in which fearful overthrow both myself with thee my wife and you my sweet babes shall miserably come to ruine, except (the which yet I see not) some way of escape can be found, whereby we may be delivered.'

"What response to this challenge is Christian going to make? Is he going to look this way and that way as if he would run, yet stand still because he cannot tell which way to go—until the fire from Heaven duly descends upon the City of Destruction and the wretched hoverer perishes in a holocaust which he has so dismally foreboded without ever bringing himself to the point of fleeing from the wrath to come? Or will he begin to run—and run on crying 'Life! Life! Eternal Life!'— with his eyes set on a shining light and his feet bound for a distant wicket-gate? If the answer to this question depended on nobody but Christian himself, our knowledge of the uniformity of human nature might incline us to predict that Christian's imminent destiny was Death and not Life. But in the classic version of the myth we are told that the human protagonist was not left entirely to his own resources in the hour that was decisive for his fate. According to John Bunyan, Christian was saved by his encounter with Evangelist. And, inasmuch as it cannot be supposed that God's nature is less constant than Man's, we may and must pray that a reprieve which God has granted to our society once will not be refused if we ask for it again in a contrite spirit and with a broken heart." *

With these words, in which pious hopes float like a skiff in a maelstrom of fateful warnings, Toynbee concludes his long and searching analysis of the disintegration of human societies. What is the testimony of this far-reaching analysis? Without

* *Ibid.,* pp. 319-21.

divine guidance man's efforts are doomed to failure; and whether, with Toynbee, we interpret this conclusion in the language of Christian revelation, or accept it abstractly, in terms of symbol and direction, it represents the quintessence of Western society's spiritual heritage. Yet, undeniably, in the course of that society's long history it has lost the potency of its divine authority; with long acceptance it has become diffused, weakened, self-evident, until at length it has come to serve the generality of men as a bland phrase, an introductory prayer, a parenthesis and hollow form within which the Western world proceeds unswervingly toward its mundane goals. The *Civitas Dei,* which is to be distinguished from all temporal civilizations, past or future, seems more remote than ever; and the doom that is to follow inescapably upon our spiritual failure, according to this reckoning, more imminent and certain.

Are we to conclude that behind this stultifying vista lies that "uniformity of human nature" which seems proof, in its "invincible ignorance," against spiritual enlightenment? The truth is that spiritual genius is as rare among men as any other form of genius, and, though God's truth is accessible to all men, it has remained for the few to achieve it. Even in the days of the Church's triumphant sway, the overwhelming love of a Francis of Assisi, which but betokened the humble acceptance of Christ's teachings, warranted his elevation to sainthood. However glorious the possibility of our spiritual redemption, we are reduced to inquiring into the probabilities of salvation as seen against the backdrop of man's lengthening history. And though, doubtless, we may take courage in his unquestioned rise from a primitive status to an ever more subtle, complex, and explicit affirmation of a higher destiny, we perceive no less clearly behind this aspiring drama the slumbering mass of mankind, unenlightened and uninspired by any dream of a heavenly order.

This spiritual dilemma of mankind has been resolved in the past through the agency of its spiritual geniuses, on the one hand, and through the "principle of mimesis," by which the masses of men have been conditioned, on the other. In the crucial epoch through which mankind is admittedly passing, we must ask ourselves whether this halting procedure gives promise of renewed efficacy and growth, or whether, in view of man's dominant directions, he will not slowly loosen the bonds of this relationship, severing the dynamic tension of its spiritual import. Thus, the very notion of genius itself is already being divested of its mystery and subjected to social interpretation—as though, in its onward sweep, humanity showered forth leaders like illumined sparks whose light is engendered by nothing more esoteric than the heat of its own impact against the future. In these opposed interpretations we may perceive the eclipse of one set of values and the dawn of another. And indeed, in the very sense in which society was shaped by its geniuses in the past, it may similarly mold and condition them in the future, until they will have become immersed in the generality of men and disappear from the scene. Meanwhile, the savior without a following will mark the period of transition; and the mimesis by which mankind was held within the locus of spiritual salvation will be directed toward other and wholly mundane ends by men of another stamp.

If the thwarted, confused, vertical movement of history is at length giving way to a horizontal direction, its momentum may still inspire the illumined vanguard toward a far-off vision above, while the mass of mankind proceeds toward an attainable plateau below. In this crisis the technique of mimesis, by its very nature, will lend itself far more readily to a horizontal than to a vertical movement, if only because the very distinction between leaders and led must here ultimately tend to disappear in the harmonious acceptance of their identical direction and common goal. With penetrating acumen Toynbee has shown that the man of creative genius has arisen in a society when it is in process of disintegration no less than when it is in process of growth: the conqueror of new aspects of life gives way to the savior who would hold the gains already achieved. As long as historic processes are in an alternative phase of growth or disintegration, the emergence of exceptional men is assured: it is only when society tends toward a condition of stability, security, and eventual sterility, that exceptional men are doomed a fortiori to impotence and extinction; for in that phase of society either they will not arise or they will be suppressed. Yet the spiritual regeneration of mankind, according to Toynbee, and also to Henri Bergson, is in the last analysis dependent upon the action of the few upon the many, upon the emergence of men of spiritual genius through whose influence alone the masses of men can be inspired to move, in prosaic fashion and with pedestrian steps, toward higher goals. Speaking of the relation between individuals and societies, whether in process of growth or disintegration, Toynbee says: "If the institution which we call a society consists in the common ground between the respective fields of action of a number of individual souls, then we may take it that this is its constant and uniform consistency so long as it is in existence at all. In respect of this fundamental point it makes no difference whether the society happens to be in growth or disintegration. In either of these two possible phases of social life it is equally true that the source of action is never the society itself, but is always some individual soul; that the action which is an act of creation is always performed by a soul which is in some sense a superhuman genius; that the genius expresses himself, like every living soul, through action upon his fellows; that in any society the creative personalities are always in a minority; and that the action of the genius upon souls of common clay operates more rarely by the perfect method of direct illumination than through the second-best expedient of a kind of social drill which enlists the faculty of mimesis in the souls of the uncreative rank-and-file and thereby enables them to perform 'mechanically' an evolution which they could not have performed on their own initiative." * Earlier, in a statement as succinct as it is unequivocal, he sums up this approach to the development of society by saying: "It is human individuals and not human societies that 'make' human history." †

The high function of genius—if not the dull receptivity of the generality of mankind—is even more forcibly insisted upon by Bergson in his book *Les Deux Sources de la Morale et de*

* *Ibid.*, pp. 175-76.
† *Ibid.*, III, 231.

la Religion, some of whose passages, quoted at length by Toynbee, may with equal pertinence be given here in slightly abbreviated form.

"We do not believe in the 'unconscious' (factor) in History: the 'great subterranean currents of thought,' of which there has been so much talk, only flow in consequence of the fact that masses of men have been carried away by one or more of their own number.... It is useless to allege that this leap forward does not imply any creative effort at the back of it, and to argue that there is not here any invention comparable to the artist's. This is to ignore the fact that the majority of the great successful reforms have appeared at first unrealizable and have been so in fact. They could only be realized in a society whose spiritual condition was already that which these reforms were to induce through their realization; and there was a vicious circle here from which no issue would have been found if the circle had not been broken by one or more privileged souls which had dilated the social soul in themselves and which then drew the society after them (through the breach which they had made)...." *

"In giving to Man the moral conformation which he required in order to be a social animal, Nature has probably done all that she was able to for the Human Species. But, just as men of genius have been found to push back the bounds of human intelligence (which means that, at long intervals, individuals have been granted far more than it was originally possible to give, all at once, to the species), so there have arisen privileged souls who have felt themselves related *apparentés* to all souls, and who, instead of remaining within the limits of their group and keeping to the (restricted) solidarity that has been established by Nature, have addressed themselves to Humanity in general in an *élan* of love. The apparition of each of these souls has been like the creation of a new species composed of one unique individual—the thrust of Life arriving, at long intervals, in the person of a particular human being, at a result which could not have been attained all at once for

---

* Henri Bergson, *Les Deux Sources de la Morale et de la Religion*, pp. 73-74. 333. (Quoted by Toynbee, *A Study of History*, III, 231.)

the aggregate of Mankind. Thus each of these souls has marked the attainment of a certain point by the evolution of Life; and each of them has manifested in an original form a love which seems to be the very essence of the creative effort." *

For Bergson, as for Toynbee, it is the mystics who, more than any other types are "the superhuman creators *par excellence*." In the attainment of ever higher spiritual realms of life, they are the bridge to the future. Nor are the biologic implications of this view to be taken in any but a literal sense: the mystics are the bearers of the life force in its evolutionary movement toward higher forms.† Having come to the end of an evolutionary trend in which, according to Gerald Heard, ‡ man has turned from the development of physique to that of technique, he is now confronted by the necessity of avoiding degeneration and collapse by "a sudden and radical mutation" through the development of his psychic powers. This purely psychological "mutation" is not to be achieved by changes in the genetic constitution of man, however; nor, it is important to note, will the technique of its attainment be open to the generality of mankind. For the path of salvation demands the expansion of consciousness beyond the limited confines of the individual ego into an illumined state of absorption in the "Whole." And this prerogative, in the words of Toynbee, is

---

* *Ibid.*, pp. 96-97. (Quoted by Toynbee, *A Study of History,* III, 232.)

† This aspect of Toynbee's philosophy has been critically noted by Richard V. Chase. "We ourselves have not yet understood the force of this 'etherialization,' as Toynbee calls it, this full-blown expansion, this inspired exhilaration of the mind suddenly released from what is felt to be the dungeon of materialism and organic evolution. Nor is this recrudescence of mysticism a triviality of the weary European mind, or nothing but a literate version of charlatan religions like Theosophy and Spiritualism. For besides the work of Bergson and the considerably lesser works of Huxley, Heard, Sorokin and others, it has nurtured Toynbee's *Study of History.* And this is a work which, though still unfinished, is already one of the great philosophical visions of society, the vision of a myth-making intellect which makes other historical synthesis seem both parochial and philistine. But what image arises from Toynbee's superb mythical biology if not the psychic Superman for whose creation it is supposed to be the whole purpose of man to struggle? Like Gerald Heard, Toynbee believes that evolution is the mutation of Subman to Man followed by the mutation of Man to Superman (Toynbee's words)." (From "The Heard-Huxley Paradise," *Partisan Review,* March-April, 1943, pp. 157-8. Reference to Toynbee, *A Study of History,* III, 172.)

‡ Gerald Heard, *Pain, Sex and Time* (New York: Harper and Brothers, 1939).

limited to those "rare and superhuman souls that break the vicious circle of primitive human social life and resume the work of creation"—by means of a new factor which he characterizes by the word "Personality," as described by Jan C. Smuts: "Personality is still a growing factor in the Universe, and is merely in its infancy. Its history is marked by the thousands of years, whereas that of Organic Nature is marked by millions. Personality is as yet but an inchoate activity of the whole, but nevertheless its character is already distinct and well marked; and its future evolution is the largest ray of hope in human, if not terrestrial destiny.... The level of its power and activity is gradually rising; more and more it is gathering the unorganized centrifugal tendencies of the individual into an effective central control, and often it wins even in the most discouraging circumstances those moral victories which form the great landmarks of personal and human progress." *

Thus, our long but rewarding detour through the pages of Toynbee's *Study of History* has brought us back, once more, to the conception of the Creative Personality—to the "Person" in the mystic sense of the transfigured soul—as the unique channel through which alone the higher destiny of mankind might be realized. This philosophy of the primacy of the person, whether it is expounded in terms of a new psychic evolutionism, or an organic humanism, or again in a contrite return to divine guidance in the healing of the schism of the soul, is contingent in the last analysis upon a spiritual transcendence of the individual rather than upon a comprehensive forward movement of humanity as such. The issue is crucial in any consideration of man's future estate. If the forces that have transmuted primitive society into civilizations of higher status in the past were indeed an expression of the genius of individual "superhuman" personalities, we have still to inquire,

* J. C. Smuts, *Holism and Evolution* (New York: The Macmillan Company, 1927), pp. 306, and 308. (Quoted by Toynbee, *A Study of History*, VI, 233.)

The philosophy of "Holism," the mystic conception of the "Whole," and, in a related sense, even the "Syncretism" of Mumford, and above all the more carefully articulated philosophy of the "Person" in the works of Waldo Frank, have been anticipated, in respect to their metaphysical structure, in the rigidly logical exposition of F. H. Bradley's *Appearance and Reality* (New York: The Macmillan Company, 1902)—a neglected but significant book.

not into their continued sporadic appearance among men of "common clay," but into the probability of their sustained influence and their beneficent efficacy when the entire order of society and the basic orientation of man is undergoing an inherent and inevitable transition from the sovereignty of the instincts to that of intelligence. But quite apart from this profound challenge, in which we cannot fail to see the threat of a reversal in the relation of dominance between the individual and the masses of men, it may be well to examine the tenuous and uncertain power that "privileged" individuals of superior endowment have in fact exercised over the great body of humanity. What are the conditions under which this transmutation of society is effected? Here we may profitably return to the analysis of the matter by Toynbee, supported by allusions to the philosophy of Bergson; for, if Toynbee is perhaps less sanguine than Smuts, he nonetheless conceives the higher destiny of mankind to be ultimately contingent upon this enigmatic relationship.

Admittedly, there is no such thing as a forward movement of humanity as a whole: this is but a "...fanciful conceit; for *ex hypothesi,* a creative mutation of Human Nature is the act of an individual soul which is acting independently; and a simultaneous uniform mutation in every one of a number of individual human beings would be a sheer miracle.... There are not, of course, any authentic instances of this convenient miracle in human history." * On the contrary: Toynbee pictures for us the incidence of even an individual occurrence as limited at best; while the infrangibility of the mass remains virtually constant.

"The very fact that the growths of civilizations are the work of creative individuals or creative minorities carries the implication that the uncreative majority will be left behind unless the pioneers can contrive some means of carrying this sluggish rear-guard along with them in their eager advance.... At an earlier point in this Study, we found that the primitive societies, as we know them, are in a static condition, whereas the civili-

* Arnold J. Toynbee, *A Study of History* (London: Oxford University Press, 1935-1939), VI, 237.

zations—or, at any rate, the growing civilizations—are in
dynamic movement. We should now rather say that growing
civilizations differ from static primitive societies in virtue of
the dynamic movement, in their body social, of creative individual personalities; and we should add that these creative
personalities, at their greatest numerical strength, never amount
to more than a small minority in the society which their action
pervades and animates. In every growing civilization, even at
the times when it is growing the most lustily, the great majority of the participant individuals are in the same stagnant
quiescent condition as the members of a primitive society which
is in a state of rest. More than that, the great majority of the
participants in any civilization in any phase are men of like
passions—of identical human nature—with Primitive Mankind.

"Thus the line of spiritual demarcation between superior
personalities and ordinary human beings does not coincide with
the line of social demarcation between civilizations and primitive societies. There is an overwhelming majority of ordinary
people in the membership of even the most advanced and
progressive civilization; and the humanity of all these people
is virtually primitive humanity." *

In view of this disheartening picture of humanity it might
seem reasonable to suppose that the author would interpret
the course of history according to some hypothesis of diminishing returns; but in the present status of his vast undertaking
one looks in vain for such a conjecture. Nor can we ease the
pain of this picture by imagining it to be an isolated statement
that has overrun the author's unusally prudent and sober pre-
sentation; on the contrary, he has supported it by a quotation
from Henri Bergson which is no less disillusioning in respect
to human nature. "The truth is that, if Civilization has profoundly modified Man, it has done so by making his social
milieu into a kind of reservoir for accumulating habits and
skills which are poured into the individual by Society in each
successive generation. Scratch the surface and efface what we
receive from an education which never ceases, and we shall

* *Ibid.*, III, 242, 243.

rediscover something very like primitive humanity in the depths of our nature....Human nature is the same today as it always has been." *

Hence the spiritual problem of raising the cumbersome and inert mass of men to the heights attained by the privileged reduces itself to the "dubious expedient" of mimesis—to that form of social drill in which imitation takes the place of inspiration, and perfunctory gestures of moral routine that of spiritual illumination. The perfect way of inspiring the receptive soul, as Plato recorded, is to impart the divine fire from one soul to another "like light caught from a leaping flame"; but Toynbee grants that this is "an unpractical counsel of perfection." Indeed, he is at pains to show that even the alternative way of mimesis is at once dangerous and sterile—a "vehicle of mechanization in the medium of human nature." † Nor does he hesitate to dwell upon the obvious resemblance between the arbitrary and conditioned repetition of behavior patterns implicit in mimesis and the fixed repetition of movement inherent in the machine. ‡ At best mimesis is a two-edged sword: under its spell the automatism of the masses may infect its leaders, resulting in a denouement in which the blind shall lead the blind; and, in turn, under this dispensation, there is a loss of self-determination that can only result in ultimate disintegration and dissolution. Only in a static community, where the "cake of custom" remains unbroken, is the blade of mimesis safely sheathed: in a dynamic society it is a necessary but precarious expedient. "...This baring of the blade means the removal of a safeguard; and the necessity of using the tool of mimesis without the protection of a customary régime—a necessity which is the price of growth—condemns a growing civilization to live dangerously. More than that, the danger is perpetually imminent, since the condition which is

* Henri Bergson, *Les Deux Sources de la Morale et de la Religion*, pp. 133, 169. (Quoted by Toynbee, *A Study of History*, III, 243.)

† Toynbee, *A Study of History*, IV, 127.

‡ It is noteworthy, as Lewis Mumford has ably shown in his *Technics and Civilization*, that the regularity of ritual and regime in the monastic orders served as a precursor to the machine; and that clocks, registering and facilitating this order, were, significantly enough, among the earliest examples of mechanical instruments (compare page 77).

required for the maintenance of the Promethean *élan* of growth
is a condition of unstable equilibrium in which 'the cake of
custom' is never allowed to set hard before it is broken up
again. The *tour de force* of the exploit of Civilization lies in
this necessity of resorting to mimesis without a possibility of
taking precautions at any stage. In this hazardous pursuit of
the goal of human endeavours there can never be such a thing
as a provisional insurance against the perils which mimesis
entails. There can only be an ultimate and radical solution of
the problem through the complete elimination of mimesis in
a society which has transformed itself into a communion of
saints; and this consummation, which is nothing less than the
attainment of the goal, has never been even distantly approached by any civilization hitherto." *

With this final quotation from the pages of *A Study of History,* we must take leave of this great work, not without ac-
knowledging an indebtedness to the author for his spiritual
insight and vast scholarship. Yet, facing the problem that confronts us, the conclusion of the passage quoted above seems
to complete a circle of reasoning that leaves little room for
hope. If the salvation of man lies in the transformation of society into a community of saints, while, at the same time,
human nature is asserted to have remained unchanged and
presumably to be unchanging, and the device of mimesis by
which it is sought to remedy the gap of spiritual vacuity in
the masses of men is patently but a mechanical subterfuge of
dubious value and dangerous portent, then indeed it would
seem as though mankind must forever find itself thwarted in
the attainment of that higher destiny which only the few have
glimpsed. This conclusion, from which there seems to be no
escape, appears all the more conclusive if we return to a consideration of the individual in the society of the future; for
on this basis, as we have seen, it is clear that the very source
and fountainhead of spiritual enlightenment, in the emergence
of privileged souls, is certain to be closed by the drastic suppression of all deviations from the dominant norm. Moreover,
in this sovereignty of the masses we may likewise perceive a

* Toynbee, *A Study of History,* IV, 128.

gradual displacement of an inner by an outer approach to the values of life; and even the more intangible and inscrutable aspects of existence are certain to be approached from the point of view of scientific intelligence rather than religious feeling—not because they are necessarily antithetical in nature but because they represent an inversion of values in harmony with the dominant trends of man's development. If the path of the mystic is to be attained not by knowledge but by wisdom, and not by wisdom but by faith, the path of the scientist approaches the illimitable and the intangible through the gateway of what is primarily perceptible, defined, known. Religion offers us truth sheathed in mystery; science offers us mystery enveloped by truth. And if the masses of mankind are incapable of accepting the discipline involved in either path, they will nonetheless find themselves at home on the periphery of things rather than at the core of being. Thus, the schism of the soul may be but a signal of the parting of the way in which mankind will enter upon a plateau region of assured, if limited, values and bounded vistas.

VII

The world is in transition—which is but to say that it is moving toward a new principle of integration. In the interim it is torn by a conflict of past and future values—or drifting in the void of their mutual clash. If society once drew strength and sustenance from the inner sources of being through the revelations of saint and mystic, it seems destined to abandon this well of inspiration in focusing wholly upon the external manipulation of its affairs and the purely mundane solution of its problems. The rift is not recent: it was already mirrored in the Christian ethos according to which the free will of the individual endowed man with a choice between damnation and salvation; between the hell of an atomistic, earthbound existence, limited and finite, and the mystically illumined vision of the eternal within. But in accepting the major promise, man hoped also to avoid the minor cost: it was the tragedy of human nature that man sought the eternal for himself instead of in himself. "Exorbitantly heartened by the truth that God is in him, and by the false conclusion that his ego is immortal, the willful individual went the way—not of the Christian ideal but of his all-too-animal human nature. The fires of the Christian world had *energized* him, but its values could not *aim* him. European genius abandoned the perpendicular Gothic spire and the deep Divine Comedy to launch into horizontal adventures: to discover and control the horizontal periphery of life." *

But in that release science came of age, and the world of the machine was set in motion. The rift deepened, and behind the conflict of values a new mode of social cohesion emerged. While the individual will of man, released from the protecting panoply of the Divine Will, moved impetuously toward chaos, another principle asserted itself. A vast system of external control, nurtured by man's earthbound intelligence, implicit in the logic of his machine, and inherent in the very necessity of his social relations, emerged in ever clearer form until its widening influence has encompassed his world. Thus, aware of the logic and necessity of his outward compulsions, while still sensitive to the inward power of his inherited values, modern man finds himself torn asunder by conflicting tensions. In this dilemma he has sought escape from his predicament without sacrificing the belief in his own power, responsibility, and freedom in the face of the inevitable by seeking refuge in a countervailing sense of guilt and failure. But behind this desperate rear-guard action lies an ominous sense of fatality; a tragic awareness that perhaps the high promise of mankind is passing in a movement of overwhelming scope and finality.

For the problem of social integration will not long remain suspended in midair between a resolution that we have left behind and one that we fear to accept. It is certain to be resolved, sooner or later, under the impact of historic forces in which the individual will find himself galvanized and directed by an outward compulsion, in the very degree in which his inward response has failed him, toward a unity beyond himself. If Western society is moving away from, rather than toward,

* Waldo Frank, *Chart for Rough Water* (New York: Doubleday and Company, Inc., 1940), p. 118.

the ideal of the Christian synthesis attained in the Middle Ages, the general trend of history as reflected in the transition from the guidance of the instincts to that of intelligence must inherently favor this wholly extroverted mode of social integration. How far this transition has progressed is indicated by the extent to which man no longer feels called upon, by an act of inward freedom, to accept the necessity of a higher principle of unity. But in thus finding his own inward compliance an irrelevant gesture, he has alienated himself from that mystic communion in the "Whole" which endowed his humblest act with a sense of participation in a supramundane order. In this surrender man has renounced his inward freedom: he has abandoned, for better or for worse, his citizenship in the *Civitas Dei* for that of the secularized state or, at the farthest, that of the world community. And though doubtless he has brought to his new allegiance the emotional overtones that once sanctified an earlier obeisance, he is discovering to his comfort or humiliation—as the case may be—that his feelings and attitudes are meaningless gestures in the arbitrary finality of events.

That he may retrieve his lost position is not impossible: that society as a whole may attain an inward freedom to which at best it distantly aspired under a more propitious dispensation seems unlikely and improbable, however, in view of an undeniable drift in a contrary direction. The salvation of mankind is not to be achieved by mystic and saint alone; and the hope that man might control the course of events in harmony with spiritual values he has never yet attained is denied in the very momentum of history itself. But in saying this it does not follow that humanity is doomed to sink, irretrievably, into chaos and confusion. Man has survived in the past and is likely to survive in the future. Indeed, he gives every evidence of moving in a contrary direction toward increasing cohesion and unity on the basis of what appears to be an irreversible principle. But, in viewing the future condition of man on this reckoning, it would seem that we are menaced as much by the threat of survival in terms of an arbitrary, dehumanized collectivity as by the danger of collapse and disintegration in the structure of our values. The challenge to the soul of man is thus seen to be a threat both from within and without; but in fact these threats represent obverse aspects of a single encompassing movement that promises to engulf the soul under an ever more stringently deterministic scheme of things. If man is not threatened, his soul is; and therein lies the profound dilemma of our entry into a future different from our past.

The dilemma is heightened by the fact that we are aware, however subtly and unconsciously, that our entry into the future will not so much be conditioned by us as we are certain to be conditioned by it. Thus we are left standing awkwardly on the threshold of a new dispensation, reviewing our inner resources against the overwhelming drift and pull of outward trends, uneasy in the knowledge that our response to the challenge of the future is limited to our heritage from the past. If the consciousness and the will of man represent indeed an eddy, as it were, in the cold determinism of matter, then the challenge behind the looming impasse of the future resolves itself into a choice between the creation of a society of transfigured members held together in the higher communion of their spiritual kinship with the Whole, with the Cosmos, which is God—and a barren collectivity of dehumanized individuals seeking mere continuity of existence in the sluggish stream of evolutionary development. Either the spiritual force at our command is equal to this basic challenge, and man will attain unity in a society of potential persons, or the "ravening" atomistic individual of the world must seek survival in the arbitrary, mechanical collectivization of the herd. Such, it would seem, is the fateful choice before us.*

Fateful choice! Are not these the words that have ever accompanied the inspired admonitions of prophet and seer? Yet all their exhortations, from a time when Ikhnaton, Lao-tse, Isaiah, and Plato might already have spoken of a venerable past, failed to win man to the paths of wisdom. Are we to expect preachments deeper in their mystical sources, more divine in their authority, than those of Christ? If we failed to understand the dialogues of Socrates, the parables of Christ,

---

* This theme is eloquently and deeply argued in the works of Waldo Frank; see particularly *Chart for Rough Water*.

are we to be saved by the insight of latter-day prophets lost in the "undergrowth of being"? The tragedy of man is the tragedy of numb idealism, of his vague, perplexed, indeed all too humble aspirations. Only in the deep imagination—in the illumination—of saints and geniuses of the spirit has man beheld far-off visions of himself projected against an illimitable firmament; in the world of his own closed horizons his hopes and aspirations have driven him only toward mundane ends in a spirit of animated complacency. The testimony of history supports the suspicion that man seeks indeed escape from freedom! The high road of the mystic may lead to spiritual freedom; the low road of mankind points only toward a predestined fate. And thus, conceivably, though man may have within him the spark of divinity, he will stumble on, unillumined, in the plateau regions of existence.

The spirituality of man is rooted in the freedom of the will. The unique and infinite worth of the person rests upon this premise; and though in turn this doctrine represents a central pillar of the democratic dogma, since it expresses the equality of man in his incommensurable value, it is equally the kernel of a conflict in the modern world in the relation between the State and the Individual. Thus, it is interesting to note, during the nineteenth century virtually every free and noble-spirited writer from Tolstoy to Thoreau, from Kropotkin to Emerson, rose in defense of the Great Tradition and the integrity of the individual against the steady encroachments of the state. But today it is no longer the state alone that is in conflict with the implications of these doctrines: it is a wider system of things wherein the state itself, in its supreme and sovereign aspects, is being drawn into the orbit of larger, world-wide agglomerations. Nor will the totalitarian pattern that has crept upon the state fail to emerge in these larger spheres of international scope. In this ubiquitous system of things the welfare of the individual rather than the salvation of the person is affirmed; and even the welfare of the individual is necessarily defined in the concrete terms of the welfare and security of the average—that is to say, of society as a compact and indivisible unit. As the gravitational force of the mass increases, that of the individual decreases, relatively as well as actually, until a final condition of solidarity and conformity is attained. At this level the individual is no longer sheathed in a halo of unique and infinite worth: he has only such relative values as may be ascertained in the language of statistical averages—those basic averages and percentages upon which the emerging system of the future is inherently predicated. But in this mechanization of society and dehumanization of the individual we cannot fail to see the eclipse of the spiritual structure of man.

The historical analysis of this transition reveals the machine as a primary agency in the transformation of society. The hope that society might absorb the benefits of the machine while avoiding the evils of mechanization has thus far proved illusory; and the gloomy predictions of certain nineteenth-century philosophers concerning the inevitable impact of the machine upon our civilization have been answered, not by the course of events, but by the words of twentieth-century prophets who, attacking mechanization as the basic cause of our plight, assure us that under proper guidance and control the machine and its technology, directed toward balanced and humane purposes, will become the open-sesame to a new era for mankind. For they believe that the machine will in time be "tamed" to its proper function, and that "...the mass man, with his mass thinking and mass ethic, whose projection in the world of the crashing wheel was toward chaos, may tend to disappear." * But a deeper comprehension of the nature of the machine as an integral, and indeed perhaps inevitable, concomitant of the transition from the guidance of instinct to that of intelligence sustains the conviction, apparent in the cumulative drift of industrialized civilization, that the hope of retaining the machine while avoiding the consequent mechanization of society is wholly wishful and fallacious. For the logic of the machine, repeating always its fixed and predesigned patterns, is a mass logic; and collectivism, as Karl Marx perceived, is inherent in its laws and implicit in its operations. Thus man is called upon to pay a price for his adventure into the richer potentialities

* Garet Garrett, *A Time Is Born* (New York: Pantheon Books Inc., 1944), p. 234.

of the material realm by a corresponding externalization of his own nature.

The communal impulse in man, of course, long antedated the advent of the machine: indeed, it was the norm of primitive social life, being itself a kind of biologic mechanism whereby man triumphed in his collective strength over his adversaries and his environment. But that earlier collectivism, which arose out of a wholly innate and primal social impulse, made coherent and explicit through the instruments of symbol and language, differs, as we have seen, from its modern surrogate. For it arose out of the instincts, in unconscious or preconscious patterns of behavior, whereas the collectivism of today is born of the inherent but nonetheless deliberate acceptance of the dictates of intelligence in the conscious organization of society. If, in time, out of the rich soil of man's heritage, his traditions, his myths, and his beliefs, purified and etherialized, bore fruit in the high conception of a communal society of autonomous souls, united in their spiritual bondage to God; if man attained, however imperfectly, a form of religious communality in response to an innate need of divine guidance, he has long since abandoned that vision. This highest social version of the Christian ethic was at once the crowning expression of the primitive community and the nearest approach to the *Civitas Dei* Western man appears to have achieved; but it gave way after the anarchic interim of the "unleashed ego" and the "atomistic individualism" of modern society to a new collectivism, no longer of the spirit, but of the conscious mind—an organized collectivism in place of a collective organism. And in that contrast the hopes and ideals, the means and the ends, of two worlds are seen in final and decisive opposition.

If the communal life of early man appears to us an inherent phase in our primitive development under the guidance of the instincts, its counterpart in the highly organized collectivity of modern society seems no less inevitable under the guidance of our intelligence. And just as language, myth, and symbol were the agencies of co-ordination in the primitive, localized community, so the machine constitutes today the effective instrument of collective integration in the social structure not merely of the community but of mankind as a whole. As myth and symbol epitomize in poetic form distillates of feeling and emotion, so the machine, epitomizing the principle of intelligence, acts as a pure and primary crystal of organization—an external agency, unifying, co-ordinating, crystallizing the structure of human society. In this contrast of inner and outer modes and agencies of attaining social cohesion man will necessarily come upon new procedures, new concepts, new values, and new attitudes. For he will have come upon a new age.

And thus we may ask ourselves whether he will establish a new synthesis of values, awaiting only his own high courage and direction, in which the future will be seen in time as the fulfillment and enrichment of the heritage of the past; or is man emerging through a hitherto undisturbed surface into another dimension, into a new form of existence—indeed, into a new and perhaps final phase of human evolution? In these pages an attempt has been made to state that question not in the light of contemporary events, however inviting to speculation, but rather in terms of a basic morphology of man's twofold approach to the problems of life: the primal approach through instinct, and the secondary but ultimately dominant approach through intelligence. If the conclusions arrived at in the course of this argument appear to support unequivocally the notion that man is entering upon a new phase in his development, different in direction from his past, that is not to say that our own response to this vista of the future is likewise unequivocal. If our logic can pierce, ever so haltingly, into the future, our hearts cannot. It was the belief of the ancient Egyptians that the heart was the seat of thought; it will be the mark of the future that man will distinguish between thinking and feeling as he learned, long ago, to distinguish between his dream world and his waking world. The dissociation of feeling and thought will alter our sense of reality, opening up to us a new world, more rigid, impersonal, and arbitrary than that of the past: plainly, its values will be alien to our values, its vistas alien and unfamiliar to our vision. The character of this new dispensation will patently be in harmony with those factors and forces most deeply involved in bringing it about—and perhaps the least of these will be our own spiritual aspirations, our own inmost sentiments, our hopes and our fears.

By the same reasoning it may seem vain and futile to attempt to project ourselves into that future which will belong, in any event, not to us, but to our far-off descendants. Our faculties are certain to fail us in piercing that future, if only because our fantasies and visions are so often a response of the heart. Nor would the very terms of our language, rooted in the past, prove adequate where thought and imagination are balked. Nevertheless, it is clear that we may venture upon certain basic, if abstract, generalizations. Thus, noting the inherent, obligatory, and accelerating trend toward increased organization in every aspect of life—a process tending toward the final crystallization of society—we perceive that the world of the future will be characterized by a wholly new type of universal collectivism arising out of an inexorable principle of social integration. The impact of the machine in effecting this transformation of society is clear and undeniable. But to assess more fully the significance of such profound changes in the structural fabric of society, and the role of the machine in bringing them about, it became necessary to inquire into the abstract meaning of organization itself. And here the interpretation of organization as a modulus of the triumph of intelligence over instinct provided a clue, not only to the nature of the historic process but to the function of the machine in effecting a decisive change of direction in the further evolution of human society. For if the future is indeed subject to prediction, the past must already reveal—if not its incipient form—at least the evidence of an inexorable principle, a law of historic determinism, upon which its course might be predicated. Such a principle seemed clearly affirmed in the slow but inevitable dominance of intelligence over instinct; it remained necessary to establish on this basis the peculiar potency of the machine in precipitating and accelerating this inherent drift.

Through the vehicle of analogy we arrived at an interpretation of this phenomenon in accordance with a thesis first enunciated by Henry Adams; namely, that the stages in the course of human evolution may be comparable to changes of state in a purely material system as expressed by the Rule of Phase in thermodynamic theory. The transition from an earlier, instinctual stage to a later, universally organized condition of society under the dominance of intelligence seemed to suggest some such *change of phase;* and on this basis it became apparent that the machine—as a pure and archetypical form of organization itself—served as a primary crystal in effecting the structural transformation of society. If such an interpretation led to the conclusion that human society was moving inexorably toward a condition of total crystallization in its structural edifice, the trend of history, revealing mankind entering ever wider orbits of co-ordinated relationships, certainly seemed to support rather than to deny this implication. The analogies suggested by such an approach to the interpretation of the historic process seemed justified and strengthened, moreover, by the profound transformation in status of both the individual and society under the impact of the machine. For the depersonalized emergence of the individual as an atomic constituent of the social mass—defined in terms of averages and percentages—clearly suggested those mass aggregates amenable to thermodynamic interpretation on the basis of statistical mechanics.

Behind these generalizations dealing in wide perspective with a new phase in human evolution, we come upon intimations of more detailed aspects of the future. By and large the direction of man's psychic orientation, at least within the span of history, has moved from a more subjective, introverted position to an increasingly objective, extroverted one: doubtless his expanding command of the outer world weakened and narrowed the domain of his inner responses. The final depersonalization of the individual, implicit in the future condition of man, must complete this vast process of externalization to a degree perhaps difficult to conceive in terms of our own dichotomic natures. For the very source of inner values in the instinctive approach to life must gradually atrophy; and our sensibilities, drawing strength from the emotions, must inevitably become blunted and wither away. Meanwhile the patterns of behavior developed under the guidance of intelligence alone will spread and proliferate until the whole range of life will have become encompassed. But that is not to say that mankind will henceforth have done with all contrary tendencies: at critical moments in the course of events leading ultimately to a condition of social fixity, movements of opposition will arise, remotely analogous perhaps to those reactions called for in the physico-chemical domain by the principle of Le Chatelier.* But it is amply clear, in any event, that the drift toward increased externalization is in harmony, if not indeed synonymous, with the explicit depersonalization inherent in the dominant forces of the future. And without fear of carrying the logic of the argument to some *reductio ad absurdum,* we may perceive that the trend of events must ultimately approach a condition of stable equilibrium in which the individual will be a rigidly fixed component of the mass in an objective continuum of society and its environment.

The inevitability of these aspects of the future touches upon the nature of human freedom. For we may perceive that freedom, seen against a backdrop of inevitability, can hardly be a matter of choice in direction: at best it may remain a factor in the dimension of time. Thus the retardation traditionally exercised by the conservative—the conservator of values, forever betrayed by the reactionary—may express an intuitive sense of the fleeting character of our values and our world; a fear that human freedom, like the hourglass, has only its appointed run. Conceivably freedom is an illusion arising out of the infinite range of combinations in the patterns of instinct and intelligence available to the individual in his every action. If instinct alone functions as the activating agency there can be no freedom; in the functioning of intelligence alone there

* Significantly, Alfred J. Lotka warns us that the principle of Le Chatelier can only be applied to biologic phenomena on the basis of more or less remote analogies. A careful reading of Lotka, however, would seem to indicate that a wider principle than the one enunciated in the domain of thermodynamics by Le Chatelier may be implicit in biologic phenomena, but its formulation remains to be established. See Lotka's *Elements of Physical Biology,* pp. 281 ff. It is interesting to note that Lawrence J. Henderson in his book *Pareto's General Sociology* (Cambridge, Mass.: Harvard University Press, 1935, p. 47) relies upon the very interpretation of this principle by W. D. Bancroft which Lotka assailed as unjustified and inapplicable to social phenomena.

is likewise no freedom of action. Thus freedom may be a purely *historic* reality—unknown in the remote past and destined to evaporate in the remote future. Only in the interim of subtle and balanced reactions may we taste to the full the peculiarly human sensibility of freedom; and from this point of view we may understand why Lao-tse was concerned *not* to build a bridge across the stream separating his village from one so close the barking of the dogs could be heard! For this paradoxical wisdom embraces a profound thermodynamic principle: the principle, namely, of retarding the flow of entropy. The slowness, not the speed, of man may be his saving—temporarily.

The life span of man's evolution may thus conceivably be subject to his choice and his will; it is questionable to what extent he can affect its direction. Even his knowledge, which constitutes the fulcrum of his actions, is no longer his individually: it belongs in its massed volume and extent to the community as a whole. Thus the momentum of society becomes less and less contingent upon the pace or the direction of its component individuals; while, contrariwise, that of the individual will inevitably come to depend ever more stringently upon the dicta of society. The conclusion thus descends upon us that man's course is set in all but the dimension of time; and that even here the determining factors of his development will allow him no final escape. For the process of crystallization, which constitutes an inherent aspect of this all-embracing determinism, is a converging, cumulative, essentially irreversible process that approaches a condition of stable equilibrium as its limit. And the ultimate stabilization of human relationships toward which man is drifting implies a gradual reversal and slowing down of the tempo of his history: in place of an accelerating rhythm of change he will experience a gradual abatement and exclusion of all change and variation, until at length he will find himself in an ever more securely established milieu—in a period of unchanging continuity. He will have passed through the transitional, historic phase of his evolution, and attained at length a posthistoric stage.

In the course of his development he has been constrained from time to time to abandon his most cherished myths. Thus he has abandoned his animism; his Ptolemaic astronomy that assured his position in the center of the universe; his faith in a hereafter that endowed him with eternal life; his belief in the supreme and infinite worth of his person that assured him a position of isolate dignity in an otherwise meaningless and impersonal world; and even perhaps his faith in a God whose attributes, under the impact of man's rationalistic scrutiny, became ever more abstract until He vanished in the metaphysical concept of the Whole. The shedding of these inestimable illusions may be merely stages in his diminishing stature before he himself vanishes from the scene—lost in the icy fixity of his final state in a posthistoric age.

INDEX

INDEX

Adams, Henry, quoted, 110, 114, 115-16, 117-18; on formulation of science of history, 113, 119, 120, 121, 122, 123, 124, 136, 163, 170, 234-35; on irreversibility of evolution, 150; mentioned, 111, 128, 129, 164
Adams, James Truslow, 118, 122
Alexander, S., 162 n.
American Historical Association, 114
Analogy, nature of, 136; and second law of thermodynamics, 136-37
Appollonius of Perga, 129
Aquinas, Thomas, 204
Archaism, Toynbee on, 210
Archimedes, 129
Architecture, functionalism in, 101, 102; internationalism in, 102; and town planning, 102
Aristotle, 35, 109 n.
Art, in Egypt, 86, 87; abstractionism and originality in, 87

Bacon, Francis, 61
Bancroft, W. D., 236
Becker, Carl, quoted, 51, 56; mentioned, 113
Bellamy, Edward, 12, 98
Bergson, Henri, quoted, 32, 35, 103, 219, 223-24; on intellect, 104; on creative few vs. uncreative many, 218; on role of mystics, 221; mentioned, 222
Berle, A. A., Jr., quoted, 10
Bernal, J. D., 198
Bertalanffy, Ludwig von, on organization, 5; mentioned, 141 n.
Blum, Harold F., quoted, 151
Bodin, Jean, 69
Boas, Franz, quoted, 40; on development of man, 43
Boltzmann, Ludwig, 121, 139, 143
Book of Coming Forth by Day, The (The Book of the Dead), 76
Book of the Netherworld, The, 76
Borel, Félix, 147
Borel's monkeys, 147
Born, Max, 157 n.
Bradley, F. H., 221
Breasted, J. H., 86

Bridgman, P. W., quoted, 108, 156-57 n.; on analogy, 136; mentioned, 158, 159
Briffault, Robert, quoted, 43
Buckle, Henry T., 114
Bunyan, John, quoted, 214-15
Burnham, James, 11
Butler, Samuel, 77, 98, 188 n.
Bury, J. B., on progress, 63, 66; quoted, 65, 69, 138; mentioned, 74 n.

Capek, Karel, 12
Calvin, John, 204
Catholic Church, 17, 59, 99
Cattell, Jaques, 188 n.
Cayley, George, 173
Certainty, relation of to probability, 142
Change. See History, Progress
Chase, Richard V., quoted, 220 n.
Chase, Stuart, 11
China, 83, 92, 204
Choice, instinct and intelligence as instruments of, 165-67, 169
Christ, 204, 211, 229
Civilization, distinguished from culture, 83-84, 103; meaning of, 103; Spengler on, 81-82, 206 n.; Toynbee on, 208, 214, 222 ff.
Circumnavigation of the globe, 69
City of God, Toynbee on, 209 ff.; mentioned, 213, 216, 228
Clarke, J. R., 141 n.
Clausius, Rudolf, 145, 146
Clock, as symbol of world of mechanics, 77, 99, 224 n.
Collectivization, as end of organization, 13, 14 ff., 30; rise of, 111, 112-13, 138; of intelligence, 178; distinguished from communalism, 232; in knowledge, 237. See also Organization
Communalism, distinguished from collectivism, 232. See also Primitive society
Communication, as perimeter of the future, 72-73
Compton, A. H., 156
Comte, Auguste, 109

241